Santa Claus Don't Come to No Colored Girl's House

A NOVEL

Janice A. Vailes

Copyright:
ISBN: 1434879968

Disclaimer: This book is a work of fiction. Names, characters, places and incidents are products of the author's imagination or are used fictitiously. Any resemblance to actual events or locales or persons, living or dead, is entirely coincidental.

ACKNOWLEDGMENTS

First and foremost, my overwhelming thanks to the Devine Spirit, who blessed me with insights and inspirations to write this book. My, thanks to my mom Annie, my sister Threasa, my children; Phillip, Curtis and Wendii and a host of relatives who waited patiently for me to finish and publish this novel. Appreciative words of thanks to the various people who supported my efforts, and listened to my ideas. This is not a complete list, and I apologize to any who are left out: John Aubrey Fairman a one-of-kind personal friend and confidant, Sheila Joann Redding, my chief fighter for the cause, a special thanks to Authoress Jean Renee Johnson, who turns patience into new ideas, fun and excitement in the world of creativity in writing.

A special thanks for the wonderful friends and other special people in my life who added additional support, encouragement and blessings through out the creation of this book, and in the past, my wonderful father who constantly told me I could do anything.

I would like to acknowledge some of the wonderful men and women authors, whose writings inspired me to write my book. Authors; Maya Angelou, Tina McElroy Ansa, Sandra Brown, John Grisham, Terry McMillan, Toni Morrison, Tyler Perry, Delores Phillips, Danielle Steel, and Alice Walker.

Prologue

It is winter. It is cold, bone chilling cold. Old grandma is sitting on an old wooden crate with quite a few boards missing. No need to panic or worry I thought to myself. She will not fall or tip over. She is so small and thin it will hold her leathery brown, wrinkled old body as she gingerly leans forward…toward the small fireplace and throws a few more sticks, and some balled up old newspapers into the fireplace. The burning sticks and paper make crackling sounds, popping sounds, almost hypnotic to the ears.

Strange I thought standing here in this old room, remembering what it was like when I lived here. Nothing has changed. The house is still standing, old, weather beaten, damp and musty. The same cracks in the windows, and the same cracking floorboards. It was as if time had stood still embracing this old house with longevity and preservation. Humph! …probably waiting for one of us to return. I should stand here, in the middle of the room and yell at the top of my voice, no… speak quietly about my past sorrows, and disappointments and yes …how much I hated this town, this old ass house, and some of the people who were a part of our lives. Did I come here to forget or did I come here to remember.

Chapter 1

Tapasalle County, North Carolina… middle 1950's

For a lot of us and for a short while, home was in a small area of country land that sat back in a heavily wooded area in the northeastern part of North Carolina. It was called, "Southend" and it was in Tapasalle County. Nobody but colored people live there. Yes indeed, as far as the eye could see. A few old shanties left over from post slavery days served as their homes. The others merely disappeared from erosion, allowing the earth to retrieve its own.

You would never believe white people lived in Tapasalle County. That's because the county was divided in two sections, the colored section that was in the deep wooded and rural areas, called Southend and the white section that was nick-named the Pearly Gates. When you enter Tapasalle County, there is a sign that sat just off the highway that says Welcome to White Hills Gate, Tapasalle County, North Carolina. There is a tall wooden cross sitting a few feet away from the sign. It has tar and chicken feathers all over it. The cross has noticeable black burns in some areas. It is a clear message that says coloreds are not welcome here.

Majority of the people that live in the county are white and own businesses of their own and half of the county work for them. If you are colored or frequently referred to as Negro, you seldom saw a white person unless you walked or hitch hike the five or ten miles into their section to wash, iron, clean their houses for them, and of course if you were fortunate to take the greyhound bus out of the county. Growing up in Tapasalle, was a hard and miserable life for colored people especially because of the civil rights movement and white people making it very clear they wanted no part of us unless they said so. It seems as if everything we attempted to do to survive was hard, difficult, and yes, sometimes very dangerous for the Negroes. I was young, but I knew in my mind that it was not true that White and Negro people did not like each other. I figured that out as much, because Negros cleaned their homes, work their farmland, picked their tobacco, waited on their sick, and wipe their ass if it became necessary. White people had to like you to a certain degree if they let you get that close to their ass!

However, things did not get any better when my sister and I came to live with grandma in Tapasalle County. I remember the event, as if it was yesterday. My sister and I woke up to the sounds of a lot of loud yelling and hollering. I could hear my mama shouting, "Then you take em! I can't keep them any longer!" I could hear a man's voice and a woman's voice shout, "Come on let's go!" I heard the door close with an earth shaking bam! Minutes after the man and woman left, mama came in and told my sister and me to put on our coats and sweaters. Our coats were thin, and torn under the sleeves, and stretched from wearing too many sweaters underneath to keep warm. I grabbed the sweaters off the bed. A faint odor of mothballs slowly began to rise from the heap of sweaters. I suddenly remembered where they came from. One cold winter Sunday, I remember my sister, mama and I sitting by the back door of the church.

The old wood stove was not heating up the church, and I guess our shivering and complaining about how cold it was sitting on the benches bothered the two old women sitting in front of us. The strong odor of peppermint permeated from their mouths. They turned around…they looked at us, and they got up quietly and left the church. A little while later, they emerged with an armful of sweaters for my sister and me. The two old women laid them in my mama's lap. "Here, these are for you and the little girls," they whispered quietly through toothless grins. Mama told us to take off our thin raggedy coats and put the sweaters on underneath our coats. She wrapped the left over sweaters around our shoulders. They were much too big and smelled like mothballs. We never went back to the church again.

Mama threw those same old sweaters on the bed yelling "Hurry up! Put the sweaters on now! We got to leave here tonight. We can't stay here no more!" Mama spoke to us as if we had done something bad. She was crying and wiping her face with the back of her hand.

I was too young, and could not understand how we went from having money, plenty of food to eat, birthday cakes and clothes to wear to… almost nothing. Mama grabbed a blanket off the bed, opened the front door and pulled us along, out into the cold winter night. We left the warmth of the apartment and what memories we had there. It had snowed a few days earlier, and some of the snow had started to melt. We stepped into puddles of icy cold mud and water. The shoes we had on were too low to the ground and soaked up the icy cold snow that had turn to slush in some places. We did not have on any socks and no scarves on our heads or a hat. "Where are we going?" I asked mama. "I don't know Myrtle. Just don't ask any more questions!" It was a while before I noticed mama was not holding our hands. I grabbed my sister's free hand to keep it warm and placed the other hand under her sweaters.

We had walked for so long my sister began to cry. She was cold, wet, and hungry. I kept walking, not saying anything. Finally, we came to a small dark gray building with wooden benches sitting on both sides of a large wooden door. Mama walked up to the door and opened it. "Go on inside and sit down," mama said sadly. Holding my sister's hand, I led us to an old wooden bench. It was cold to the touch and rocked to one side as we sat down, so I held my sister in my lap.

A few people were standing by a rusty old pot bellied iron stove trying to warm their hands. I wanted to go over and stand by them. Mama jerked me by the arm and told us to sit back down and be still! The long walk and cold air made us very tired and sleepy. I remember, being awakened by an old white man standing over us. "Where's your mama? Little girl where you from?" he asked. He was shaking my arm. I was frightened and scared and I kept my arms around my sister. Suddenly the old white man snatched something off Sugar's sweater. It was a brown piece of paper with a hole in it.

The old white man walked over to a lantern hanging by the door, and looked at the small piece of brown paper. He quickly walked over to where we were still sitting, and in a softer voice told us to get up and come with him. I did not move. My sister did not move. She clung to me shaking and crying softly, asking over and over, "Where is mama?" I was scared and frightened. We did not know who this man was! Mama was nowhere to be found. However, I was old enough to realize we had been abandoned…left alone, and mama was not coming back. "Don't cry little girl. I am going to take you somewhere warm," he said. The old white man picked up my sister, grabbed my hand and dragged us out of the cold building. He lifted us up into his truck. I had never ridden in a truck or a car. I sat motionless. My sister had gone to sleep with her head in my lap. The truck made a lot of noise and it smelled bad. The back window was broken out and cold air blew into the truck.

The old white man finally stopped driving. He jumped out, and came over to the other side and opened the door. "Come on y'all get out! We are here now," he said. I nudged my sister awake and I jumped out of the truck and held out my hands to help my sister off the front seat of the truck. We stood in front of the old white man, waiting for his next move. As if he could read our minds, he walked toward an old house. My sister and I followed. The wooden steps were broken and one step was missing. I scratched my knee when I fell into the open space. Even though it was almost daybreak, it was still too dark to see where we were walking.

Knock! Knock! "Ms. Emma! Hey! Ms. Emma! It's ol' Willie! Open up! I've got two little colored girls I found at the bus station!" He yelled through the door. We heard a voice through the door and the tone was not at all friendly. "What time it is ol' Willie?" she asked. "Wait let me get a blanket!" She yelled through the door again. The door suddenly jerked open. My sister and I were standing in front of an old colored woman. She had dark skin the color of brown leather and a few tuffs of gray hair knotted in three plaits that stood up directly on top of her head. As she leaned closer to get a good look at my sister and me, I noticed her breath smelled like baby shit. "Oh my goodness ol' Willie! Where did you find them?" The old woman asked as she unwrapped the many sweaters that were around my sister's shoulders and me. "Who are they? Why they here?" She questioned him something awful. Her voice sounded like she was mad too! It was dark in the room, and I could not get a good look at her. I turned my head to avoid that awful smell coming from her mouth.

"They were curled up in the bus station in Southend wrapped up in this here old dirty blanket. A note was pinned on the young girl's sweater. You know Ms. Emma it's too cold out there. They could have frozen to death! The note said to bring them to you Ms. Emma." My sister and I stood there shock and numb from the cold. I was the oldest, eleven years old and "Sugar Pudding" was only five years old. As the old white man turned to leave, he leaned down and whispered to us, "Y'all little colored girls stay here with Ms. Emma." He turned and left quickly.

"Well, why you standing there? Come in and close the door behind you," the smelly old woman grumbled. She walked into another room and returned quickly with an arm full of old blankets, and some clothes. "You two can sleep right here on the floor. Don't get to close to the fire. You might get burned," mumbled the old woman as she left us in the cold room alone. My sister and I lay down on the pile of blankets and old clothes. They smelled bad, like an old wet dog. I glance up at the old woman. The light from the fire lit up her face. It wasn't a bad looking face. She had a few teeth missing from the sides of her mouth. She has dark brown eyes and the white of her eyes almost as yellow as the rest of her teeth. I had never been that close to an old person before. I thought, maybe she's blind.

We woke up a short time later. Something smelled good. I sat up quickly and shook my sister. She gave me a smile and clung to my arm. The old woman came into the room, and told us to come with her. We walked into a smaller room where an old table sat. It had three legs, and there were two old wooden crates holding one corner of the table up. "Here sit down! You look like you haven't eaten in while. Its oatmeal and some biscuits left over from yesterday. I don't have much food. But, I will share what I have and what I get with you. Y'all been to school? How old are you?"

This cranky ass old woman was firing questions at us, hardly giving us a chance to answer anything. "I haven't been to school much, and my sister is too young to go to school. She stays at home with our mama," I answered, trying very hard not to say too much or get to close to her mouth. "Humph! Well, you will have to go to school. You can't hang around here all day!" The old woman's voice sounded like she was mad at us. Our mama was mad with us. The old white man talked to us as if he was mad. Why is everybody mad at me, and my sister? What have we done that was so terrible? I wanted our mama to come and get us. I could not understand why she left me, and my sister in that old cold building.

I felt the old woman's eyes watching me, and my sister from across the table. The three plaits that were sticking up on top of her head looked like the horns of the devil. I wanted to get up and leave. As I attempted to get down off the rickety chair, the old woman suddenly spoke. "Y'all don't know who I am, so I will tell you." Crumbs from the biscuit she was eating fell from her mouth as she spoke creating tiny little mountains on the old table. "Everyone calls me Ms. Emma. You can call me grandma. I don't want no one asking questions about who you are. Y'all understand me? People will get in your business and then it ain't your business anymore! Peoples ask you anything don't say nothing. You can say you is visiting. Did you hear me!" she snapped. I mumbled "yes." I could not look at her. My sister shook her head up and down clinging to my arm. "You ain't got to hold onto your sister like that!" she yelled at Sugar. "I don't bite! Finish eating your food. I'll find some clothes for you to put on. We are going to walk over to Ms. Ruth's house and see if she has some things you can use."

While the old woman was looking for some clothes for my sister, and me, I started cleaning off the table where we had eaten. "Well, you may as well get use to it...cleaning that is, you is gonna be doing a lot of that soon enough!" She pointed her crooked finger at me as she walked out the room. I looked around the kitchen for the first time since we had arrived. The room was very small. It had two windows on one side of a wall. A wood stove sat near the back door. A large metal washtub with dents the size of boulders with dishes and rags piled in it, was sitting in a corner. A calendar with a smiling white baby with pink cheeks sitting in a white kitchen sink, holding a bar of white soap in her hand hung on the wall next to the kitchen table. The month on the calendar was April 1954. I walked over to the calendar on the wall to turn the pages to the month of November 1954. "Why is you changing them pages? Did I ask you to touch anything? Huh! Did I!" The old woman hollered at me across the room. I jumped! The old woman frightened me. "I stammered, "It is not April." The old woman yelled back, "I don't need reminding of what month it is! They are all the same, you hear!" I found myself answering her in a voice that did not sound real. "The months are not the same. I learned that in school. November has Thanksgiving and December has Christmas and today is November the third." The old woman just stood there staring at me. My sister was sitting where she had been all morning, in a chair with her legs dangling over the edge of the seat. Too scared to move, but watching me ever so closely with those large brown eyes. I walked over to my sister and picked her up. "Put that girl down!" The old woman hollered. "She can walk. Now, both of you come over here and see if any of these clothes fit you."

We had been living with 'grandma' for a week before she started calling my sister and me by our real names. To tell the truth, we were afraid of her. She didn't talk to us, she hollered. I made the mistake of calling the old woman, Ms. Emma, instead of grandma, and she threw a piece of kindling wood at me! It missed my leg, but scared me all the same. Hell, we didn't know her. This old woman was a stranger to us. It came as a shock to both of us suddenly placed in a strange place, in a broken down house to stay with a strange old woman that has a bad smell. It never occurred to me when she started calling my sister and me by our real names. I guess she heard me call my sister by her name, 'Sugar Pudding' and of course, my sister called me Myrtle. I didn't like my name. The kids in the school I used to go to called me Myrtle the turtle. I remember asking mama to change it. Of course, she said no, the reason being she liked it. I didn't like my middle name either it's Ilene.

However, grandma was right about one thing, everybody called her Ms. Emma. Hardly a day went by where someone did not stop by to visit her or just call out to her. "Morning Ms. Emma! How you Ms. Emma!" This morning I over heard grandma telling a woman who introduced herself as Ms. Ruth, that we were found in an old bus station by ol' Willie and he brought us to her house. "How you going to take care of two young girls Ms. Emma?" asked Ms. Ruth. She held a cigarette between two brightly polished red fingernails. As she inhaled long and hard on her cigarette, she made squeaking noises with her lips.

"Are you going to take in everybody they bring to your door? The last person lived with you, stole all your washing money and some of your clothes," she commented in a nasty tone of voice, and at the same time pulling a small brown glass bottle from between two very large brown breasts, she slowly began sipping from it. "Yes I know Ms. Ruth…but what can they steal from me now? I don't have much. I've got to take in more laundry or clean more houses for them white folks in Tapasalle County so we can keep food on the table. I ain't that young no more," grandma replied sadly. She reached over and grabbed the bottle from Ms. Ruth's hands before she put it back between her breast, and grandma poured a little of the brown liquid in the cracked cup she was drinking out of.

"Well, a new family just moved in Tapasalle. I'm told they is a nice white family and got one little girl name Nancy Rose. You better do something today before one of them other women goes down there," Ms. Ruth warned as she placed the bottle between her breasts and adjusted her left breast to hide the top of the bottle. "Thanks Ms. Ruth, I can go tomorrow if you watch the girls till I get back. I may have to walk all the way, because Ol' Willie's truck is broke again. And, even if it was working, I don't have no dollar to give him for taking me in town," complained grandma as she shook her nappy plaited head of gray hair from side to side. She stood up and pulled her wrinkled old dress from the between the cheeks of her behind. Where she had been sitting, perspiration or pee had formed a very large wet spot on the back of her dress.

Later that afternoon, grandma, my sister and I walked Ms. Ruth home. Ms. Ruth opened the door to her house and told us to stand by the door. "Just stand there! I don't want you tracking mud and snow on my floors. I just swept them yesterday!" The tone of her voice told Sugar Pudding and me she was mad too! Grandma stood with us waiting patiently until Ms. Ruth returned.

Ms. Ruth's house was clean. There was a little yellow rug lying on the floor with flowers painted on it. There were some thin curtains hanging at the windows; so thin, you could see right through them. She had a lacy looking sheet spread over the back of the couch that sat next to the wall as you came through the front door. A black potbellied stove sat in the middle of the room. Every now and then, a small puff of smoke would rise from the top of the stove. Old pictures hung on the walls. One picture I found strange, was a colored woman lying in a white long box, with a black hat on her head, and holding a church fan in her folded hands. There was an old faded blue curtain attached to a long rope that divided the small area in the room where we were standing.

Suddenly, someone snatched the curtain back. A man appeared. He was lying on a small cot. Pieces of dirty cotton were sticking out of a large hole in the mattress. Several blankets covered the cot, but not that great big hole! The man sat up on the edge of the cot, yawned a coupled of times and started scratching himself. Sticking his hand in the front opening of his pants, he rearranged his 'private parts' with no regard that children; namely girls, is standing in the room. He had a small face and a mustache over his top lip. He lay back down and stared at us for a minute.

"Afternoon Mr. Leon, how are you?" grandma asked. The room suddenly began to smell funny. A bad smell, like something had died. Mr. Leon asked who we were. Before, grandma could answer, and fortunately, for grandma, Ms. Ruth entered the room with two large bags. Hearing the man's question, Ms. Ruth spoke quickly. "Mr. Leon this here is Ms. Emma's grandchildren, the tall one is Myrtle and the other one's name is Sugar Pudding! I have no idea why her mama named her that! Maybe she was drunk or something," said Ms. Ruth laughing as she sat the two bags in front of grandma. Mr. Leon looked from one of us to the other, shook his head and laughed too! Grandma just stood there and said nothing. "Here are some clothes and some shoes Ms. Emma. Maybe some of the things will fit the girls. Keep what you want. You can give the rest away if you like, or use them for cleaning rags," she said as she waved her hands in the air as if she was dismissing us. "Thanks a lot Ms. Ruth, this is a big help! I'll see you tomorrow and good afternoon Mr. Leon," she yelled back and picked up the bags. She threw one over her shoulder, and carefully dragged the other one across the road in the snow, making every attempt not to walk too close to the mud.

    The sun was not shinning and there was plenty of ice on the ground. Sugar Pudding and I are cold and shivering. We had on two sweaters and an old blanket that grandma had torn in half and threw around our shoulders. Our shoes were the only things we had on our feet. We did not have any socks or stockings. Our clothes and what few things we owned, were left behind the night mama took us to that building. After what seemed like hours of walking, we finally arrived back to grandma's house.

    As we got closer, I noticed a white man, dressed in brown overalls with a yellow jacket and brown cap on his head standing on the porch. His arms were folded across his chest and he had what look like a package in his hand. Grandma walked quickly and carefully up the rickety wooden steps. Just barely missing the space where a step was missing. "Afternoon sir! Who...who you looking for?" asked grandma in a shaky-kinda-voice. "Your name Ms, Emma?" the white man asked. "Yes, I'm Ms. Emma! What's wrong?" "Oh, nothing wrong Ms. Emma. I got this here package for you. You got to sign for it! Can you write?" he asked abruptly. "Well, I don't write that good. Can my granddaughter sign for it?" grandma asked eyeing the white man suspiciously. "Well, I guess there ain't no harm in her signing. Have her write your name the same as it is on the package, you hear!" He sounded inpatient like this was the last place he wanted to be. He kept looking around, as if someone was after him. Grandma notice too... he was acting a little nervous. "Myrtle, sign my name on the paper, okay!" I carefully wrote 'Ms. Emma Jackson,' exactly what I saw on the package. The man handed grandma the package. I attempted to give him back the pencil. "That's all right girly, you keep it," he said coldly. He was so busy staring back at me as he walked down the steps. He almost stepped into the hole where the step was missing.

Chapter 2

Just being neighborly...

"Ms. Ruth, you are a bitch! A sneaky bitch!" "Why you calling me names Mr. Leon?" Ms. Ruth hollered back. "It ain't like you is a saint or you is better than me!" "Then why you let Ms. Emma think you don't know about them girls?" Mr. Leon asked blowing into his hot cup of coffee. "I promised ol' Willie I would not say anything when he dropped off his laundry this morning," answered Ms. Ruth. "You don't think she ever gonna find out, do you?" "You can look at them girls and see they is not all colored like us is! Why them girls' skin is real light and they sound funny when they talk," said Mr. Leon, as he roughly sat the hot cup of coffee down on the table.

"I wouldn't worry so much if I was you Mr. Leon. What good it gonna do if Ms. Emma knows they is her nieces? You know Mr. Leon, Ms. Emma told me the youngest one had a wrinkled up piece of paper pinned on her sweater. Ms. Emma never showed me the paper. I guess ol' Willie read the paper and took the girls to Ms. Emma that same night. Don't you say anything to ol' Willie...Mr. Leon he has enough problems as it is. I overheard Mr. Reynolds talking to his wife last week. You know when ol' Willie's grandmother died she ain't leave him nothing! Not a damn cent! You know them people always had money Mr. Leon! Something awful must have happened for that old white lady not to leave him nothing!"

"Well, I'll help Ms. Emma as much as I can. The girls don't have much. I can collect some clothes from some of the houses I clean and go through the clothes that the church collects on Sundays. They haven't been to school since they got here. I told Ms. Emma she can't keep them home too much longer cause peoples will talk. They may think something is wrong with them girls. Bad enough the school is going to ask questions Ms. Emma can't even answer. You know Ms. Emma can't read and she can barely write her name. I will ask the oldest girl…I think her name is Myrtle, what school she went to when she was with her mama," Ms. Ruth rambled on. Mr. Leon watched as she reached inside the front of her dress and reached down between her large breasts and pulled out a crumbled pack of cigarettes, lit one and inhaled deeply.

"It's strange Mr. Leon that their mama would leave them with nothing and don't tell them where she is going." As she exhaled the smoke from her mouth, it formed small circles rising above her head creating tiny little white clouds. "Yeah, Ms. Ruth, I know it's strange, but don't you go getting in Ms. Emma's business, be careful what you say. You been running your damn mouth for the last fifteen minutes! You gonna mess up and talk too much in front of the wrong person! Look Ms. Ruth, Ol' Willie done told you too much of his business. We got to be careful of white folks. I don't trust them. Is ol' Willie taking you into town tomorrow?" he asked pouring himself another cup of coffee. "No, I will have to walk, cause his truck is still not working," she answered flatly.

Chapter 3
Settling in....

There was too much excitement and activity going on this morning I thought to myself. Grandma is up early. I thought I heard someone knocking at the door, or was I still dreaming. It felt warmer in this old house. Grandma had cleaned out the smallest room next to the living room and kitchen for Sugar Pudding and me. It was not too bad. It had a large bed in the center of the room.

The windows were boarded up so that the only light came through was between the cracks in the wood. An old black dresser sat in one of the corners of the room. It had a drawer missing, and there were three other drawers with old clothes packed in them. Some of the clothes were old and smelly, and needed washing and ironing. The loud calling of my name brought me back to the present! "Myrtle! You and your sister come here! Hurry up! I ain't got all day! Y'all is going to school today! I got a ride with ol' Willie! Find some clothes and put them on, ya hear!"

I shook my sister. She was still sleeping. I worried about her. She was so quiet, and hardly talked anymore since our mama left us. Grandma doesn't say much to us unless she wants us to eat or help her clean up. She avoids us as much as possible. Sugar Pudding and I are on our own much of the time. I take care of Sugar and I bathe her and comb her hair. Lucky for us our hair is easy to comb. I found some old shoestrings and tied one around Sugar Pudding's hair. I did the same to my own. I open the drawer to the old dresser and found some clothes for us. There were some socks balled up and a little too big for our small feet; so I showed Sugar how to fold the top of them under her feet so they would fit in her shoes.

Sugar Pudding and I walked into the small kitchen. Grandma was standing over the wood stove. I guess we looked all right. Grandma did not say anything about the clothes we had on or the way our hair was combed. I remember when mama combed our hair, she always told us how pretty we looked and that we smelled good enough to eat. I remember how mama would grab Sugar Pudding by the arm and pretend to eat her little arm off! Sugar would squeal and giggle with laughter, trying to get away from mama. The memories hurt badly. I put them aside and tried to find a mirror.

The only mirror grandma had in the house was taken from the door of an old abandoned milk truck that sat in the back yard. Someone had removed the doors and leaned it up against an old outhouse. A bottle tree leaned over on the other side like it was just waiting for a strong wind to knock it all the way over to the ground. Well, I couldn't see how I looked because Grandma had propped the mirror up with two small pieces of wood and it sat in the corner of the room where she slept. Even though we have been here for about two weeks, I did not feel comfortable walking around the house, let alone venturing into her room.

We sat down to eat the oatmeal and cornbread she had fixed for our breakfast. Silence. I could hear grandma's raspy breathing and the soft chewing of Sugar Pudding eating her cornbread. "Hurry up and eat! Ol' Willie will be here soon. He gonna take us to the school over in Southend. It ain't too far, but it's too cold out there for me walk this morning. If you all stay today, you can walk back with some of your school friends, okay!" "Myrtle! You answer all the questions. I can't read, but I will tell you what to say to them people," she said. "Okay grandma, I answered quickly." We finished our breakfast and went back to our room. We were sitting on the bed when grandma came in the room. She threw some coats at us and a few headscarves made of rough material. We hurriedly went through the coats, found two that fit us and put them on. Thank God, there are buttons on the coats! I helped Sugar

Pudding with her coat, and scarf and told her to put her hands in her pockets to keep them warm. "But I can't hold your hand Myrtle," she complained. "That's okay Sugar Pudding, just walk close to me, okay!"

We heard this noise in the front of the house. It was ol' Willie and his truck! Sugar Pudding and I started to walk to the side of the truck to get in. Grandma suddenly stopped us. She waved her hand at me and yelled, "Y'all ride in the back of the truck!" Ol' Willie lifted us onto the back and threw a smelly blanket back there for us to sit on.

We finally arrive to the school. I had never seen a school with red doors before. I was really feeling uncomfortable. Sugar Pudding felt it too! She looked at me with those large brown eyes. I could see tears forming as she held my hand a little tighter. I whispered, "Don't worry, everything will be all right!" Sugar Pudding smiled faintly and shook her head up and down slowly breathing in and out.

Ol' Willie interrupted our quiet moment, and yelled, "We are here! Come on, I got to get back to work!" Sugar Pudding and I, was lifted out of the back of the truck, and grandma told us to come with her. Ol' Willie got back into his truck and drove off.

The school is a small brownish red brick building with trees on both sides of the road leading up to the front entrance. Some children around our ages were playing outside of the building. There was a playground with broken swings and a sliding board with no slide attached. Some of the kids paused to stare at us, and others paid us no attention. Grandma was walking up ahead. It really looked like she was trying not to walk with us. A small white and brown dog rushed up to greet us, barking, and jumping and running around in circles. I was afraid of animals, but Sugar Pudding reach out and patted the dog. He licked her hand and ran off to play with some of the other kids.

It seemed like minutes before we reached the door of the school. We walked up the road, and some of the children ran on ahead of us, and opened the door. There were two teachers calling to the children to settle down and come in. My sister and I followed grandma. Some children greeted us with a "Hi" and others said, morning! Some just stared. Not smiling, or talking, just staring at us. It would be a few days before my sister and I would realize why, we were being stared at.

Grandma stopped the first person she saw, a tall dark skinned woman with chalk all over her black dress. The woman spoke to us in a friendly voice. "Good Morning! My name is Ms. Peters. Are you lost?" she asked. "No, we ain't lost Ms. Peters. These here girls is my grandchildren and they is staying with me, and they needs to go to school," grandma quickly explained. "Oh, I see you want to enroll them today! That's fine! Please, walk down the hallway three doors down, and when you get to the third door, knock and have a seat. Some one will be with you shortly."

Ms. Peters smiled at us and walked away. Grandma walked up to the door. She gave it one hard knock and sat down in the chair by the door. About five minutes later, a short bald-headed colored man opened the door. He stared at us for a minute and asks us to come into the room. Grandma walked in first and stood there. I guess she was waiting for the man to say something. It was so quiet in the room you could hear an ant piss on cotton. Finally, grandma spoke. "These are my grandchildren and they need to go to school." "Oh, yes they do," he answered giving us a long stare. He had a very large mouth and it looked as if he had a hundred teeth. "Well first things first! What are their names?" he asked. Grandma looked confused, so I quickly answered. "My name is Myrtle Jackson and this is my little sister Sugar Pudding. I guess her last name is Jackson too. I have seen my name in writing. I have not seen hers. But we are sisters," I answered quickly.

The bald-headed man asked if we had any other family. Huh, I was thinking, we were just as ignorant about our family history, as the day our mama abandoned us. There is no father, and I knew very little about my sister and me. I was not going to tell the bald-headed man my sister and I was abandoned by our mama, so I answered nicely, "No, just our grandma." I looked over to where she was sitting, looking for some sign in her facial expression that I was doing all right answering the bald-headed man's questions. "Have you been to school this year?" he asked. "Yes, I went to school for a while in Southend County. I was in the fifth grade, and my sister's never been to school." I was not finished with my answer. The bald-headed man interrupted, and ask how old we were. I told him I was eleven going on twelve and my sister was five. I should have said six years old for my sister, but I did not think to lie. The bald-headed man shook his head and said, "Sugar Pudding is too young to go to school, but you could enroll today." He looked at me and gave me a smile that was scary. The lips turned up as if he was smiling; all you could see was his bottom teeth. I realized he was funny looking and ugly.

Grandma was leaning forward, straining her ears to hear and trying to understand what the bald-headed man was saying. She started to shuffle her feet and move about uncomfortably in her chair; all the while trying desperately to find the words to talk to this man. "How-old-is-you-got-to-be-to-go-to-school?" she asked the bald-headed man. "Well, Sugar Pudding... and he rolled his eyes toward the ceiling while questioning grandma. "Is that her real name?" Again, I answered quickly, "Yes that's my sister's real name!" I spoke up with a little anger in my voice. "I see. I am sorry Myrtle. I meant no harm. Seldom do we get a child at this school named after a dessert. It's different to say the least." He tried to explain by adding, "Sugar Pudding is a fine name for a sweet little girl," and reached over and patted Sugar Pudding's knee.

To answer grandma's first question, the bald-headed man continued, "To start school, you have to be at least six years old. When is Sugar Pudding's birthday?" he asked. Okay, I was not prepared, for this question and I had to think about this. I didn't remember Sugar Pudding having a birthday party and I don't remember when Sugar Pudding was born. I was thinking, she was just there, a part of my family. I answered, "I think her birthday is in… I paused suddenly remembering the calendar in grandma's kitchen, and the day we arrived was November 3. I had changed the calendar from April to November. November and December are my favorite months of the year, I thought to myself. I answered, "Sugar's birthday is in December….uh…December 25th," I answered happily. Grandma smiled. That's the first time she ever smiled at me, and I smiled back at her. "Well, now let's see, if she is five now, and her birthday is in December, we may be able to enroll her in school too," the bald-headed man smiled and patted Sugar Pudding on her knee.

He handed Grandma some papers, and told her to sit outside of the office and fill them out. We walked out the door to a small table with two chairs sitting under it. Grandma pulled out one chair and sat down and I reached for the other. Realizing Sugar Pudding did not have a chair; I pulled her over to my side and sat her on my lap. "Myrtle you fill out the papers, because I don't see none too good," grandma said. I took the papers from her hand. I could read, and was a good speller in the last school I attended.

I looked at the two sheets of papers, and filled out the first line asking, "What is your name?" I printed Myrtle Jackson. When I got to the address part, I asked grandma what was our address. She thought for a moment and answered, "1923 Hollowcreek Road, Tapasalle North

Carolina." Well, I am stumped! I could not spell "Tapasalle." Anyway, I skipped that one and went on to the next question. When were you born? I printed April 14, 1943. The next question asked, "What school did you last attend?" I remembered the school, but I could not remember the name. I felt bad. "Grandma, I can't remember the name of the school I used to go to. All I remember is "Apple" something!" "It was Appleton County Elementary school Myrtle. Just write that, okay," she answered impatiently. I finished the first paper and started on the second one. I filled in Sugar Pudding's name and when I got to her date of birth, I printed December 25, 1948. I felt so good about Sugar Pudding's birthday because she would get two presents.

Some of the other questions were about grandma. I was a little afraid to ask her age. I just did not want her to holler at me. I braced myself and asked, "Grandma what is your name?" She answered, 'Emma Jackson' and looked away. "Your name is the same as mine and Sugar Pudding's," I said. I wrote 'Emma Jackson' and filled in the address and the last question was grandma's birthday. "When is your birthday grandma?" I asked quickly. "My birthday is in April, Myrtle. I was born April 14, 1896," she answered solemnly. Suddenly, I remembered the calendar on the wall when we first arrived there. The calendar was on the month of April when I turned the pages to November.

I knocked on the door of the bald-headed man's office and handed him the papers. "Wait let me read over them first. You can have a seat until I am through," he closed the door. We sat outside of the door for an half an hour. The door finally opened, and the bald-headed man asked if we had a telephone. Grandma answered, "No, but Ms. Ruth will take calls for me," she answered reaching into her bag and pulling out a piece of white paper with numbers written on it, and handed it to the bald-headed man. He wrote something on one of the papers, and handed the piece of paper back to grandma. "Wait here, Ms. Emma. I will have Ms. Peters show Myrtle and Sugar Pudding where their classrooms are, and then we can talk."

Grandma looked at us for what I believe was the first time. She really did not say anything. She watched us leave with the tall woman who helped us find the bald-headed man. The first classroom was Ms. Foster. "This is where Sugar Pudding will be," said Ms. Peters. I quickly glance down at Sugar. I did not know how to tell her she had to walk in and have a seat with the rest of the girls and boys. I suddenly felt like crying. I did not want to leave her. Sugar Pudding did not make it any easier, holding onto my hand and gripping it ever so tightly.

Ms. Peters stooped down to Sugar Pudding's height, and gently explained this was her classroom, and she would meet some nice boys and girls to play with. Sugar Pudding looked up at me. I could see tears beginning. I had to stop them somehow. If she started to cry, then I would cry too! "Sugar Pudding, I will come get you when it is time to go home, okay. You will be just fine. I love you." I bent down and kissed her on the forehead. She gave me a hug and grabbed Ms. Peter's hand. They walked in the room together. I stood behind Ms. Peters and listened as she introduced Sugar Pudding to the class. My sister was seated in the first row, right in front of the teacher. As Ms. Peters turned to leave, I over heard Ms. Foster say, "Boys and girls, this is your new classmate Sugar Pudding Jackson. Please welcome her." I heard the mumbling of voices, clapping and laughter as we left.

Ms. Peters and I walked up to the next floor. My classroom was on the second floor, room number one, right next door to the girl's bathroom. I was ushered into the classroom, and introduced to the teacher and to my surprise the bald-headed man's name was Mr. Jenkins. "Ms. Peters, please watch the class until I am finished in my office. Glad to have you in my class Myrtle," he said as he shook my hand. I stood there frozen. I looked around the room. I felt all alone. I could not understand why I felt every eye was staring at me.

Ms. Peters sat me in the second row next to a large girl with very large glasses on her face. She said Hi, and I said Hi too! A few minutes later, Mr. Jenkins returned, and introduced me to the class. "This is Myrtle Jackson; please welcome her to our classroom."

The first day for me wasn't too bad. I had a lot of catching up to do. I was handed two books; a reading book and a small black and white notebook with lines on the paper, some used pencils and three sheets of very large line paper. Some of the boys and girls had boxes of crayons. Mr. Jenkins explained we had to share our crayons with the other kids, and preceded to hand me a brand new box. Later that morning, he called me up to his desk, and spoke quietly, "Your grandma had left word with me to pair you up with another student who lives close by you, so you and your sister would have someone to walk to school with. Her name is Anna and she sits right next to you," he said pointing to Anna. I returned to my desk. Anna glanced up at me, but she didn't say anything. I gave her a smile and sat down.

I finished most of my class work before the ringing of the bells announced lunchtime. Most of the kids pulled bags and assorted wrappings from their desk. It was a combination of food odors surrounding me. I was hungry, but the odors were making me sick to my stomach. One of the boys, who stared at me when I first entered the classroom, walked over to my desk and offered me part of his sandwich. I said, "No thank you." He looked puzzled and rubbed a dried up bugger off the tip of his nose on to the sleeve of his sweater, and asked if I was going to eat. I simply explained to him I did not bring any lunch today. I opened a book and started to read. The hum of their voices, chewing sounds and giggling did not disturb me. I pretended to be somewhere else, anywhere except this classroom.

Suddenly, I heard my name called. I Looked up and saw Mr. Jenkins walking toward me. He had a small little brown bag in his hand, and he sat it down in front of me. "Here Myrtle, I know you had not expected to stay all day, you know, your first day back to school! It's chicken. I hope you like chicken," he smiled at me and sat the bag on my desk. His smile was more like a dog snarling, lips turned up, showing only the bottom and sides of his teeth. I was thinking, Mr. Jenkins strange and ugly smile, will take some getting use too I guess, as well as the strangely uncomfortable feeling that comes over me, when he is near; as if a dark shadow was standing beside me.

The questions, "What did you bring today?" "Can I have some?" "Give me a piece!" and the noisy opening and closing of lunch bags and boxes--suddenly stopped and all eyes were on me. I heard one of the kids mutter angrily and loudly, "Mr. Jenkins ain't ever gave any of us a sandwich!" Without warning, a girl ran up to my desk as I was opening up the bag and snatched it from my hand! I jumped up from my seat and snatched it back! "Didn't your mama ever tell you it is not nice to take things from people?" The girl just stood there still staring. I felt uncomfortable and did not want to say anything else to this girl. I had never been in a fight. I would not know how to protect myself if she hit me. Finally, she left my desk and went back to her seat. I sat the bag with the chicken sandwich in it, on the floor under my chair.

The day went by fast. I glanced at the black rimmed clock on the wall. It is two-forty-five, and Mr. Jenkins was reminding us of our homework assignments, and passing out extra paper to do the homework. As he reached over to hand me, some writing paper, that same girl who had snatched my lunch earlier, forcibly pushed me aside with her body and said rudely, "That's my paper!" She snatched it before I could get my hands on it. Mr. Jenkins scolded her for being rude and told her to go back to the rear of the room until the rest of the class was dismissed.

The girl I sat next to named Anna; suddenly walked over to my desk and whispered, "Come on let's go and get your sister." With all the commotion going on in the classroom, I forgot about Sugar Pudding.

"Mr. Jenkins asked me to walk with you and your little sister when school is dismissed. You live in Ms. Emma's house?" she asked. "Yes, that's right. Ms. Emma is my grandma. You know my grandma?" "I really don't know her, but I have seen her before," she said softly pushing her glasses up on her nose. We walked together to Ms. Foster's room and there was Sugar Pudding sitting with her back to me. Ms. Foster smiled and motioned with her finger for us to come in. "Sugar Pudding, your sister is here. You can finish coloring that picture tomorrow, okay." Sugar Pudding jumped up when she saw me, and ran over to show me the picture she was coloring. It was a brown turkey! "Oh! What a pretty turkey!" I said. "It's not a pretty turkey; it's a thanksgiving turkey," she giggled.

I raise the paper in the air and went on and on about the pretty thanksgiving turkey! Ms. Foster said Sugar Pudding colors nicely and asked if she had any crayons at home. I told her no. As I gathered Sugar Pudding's coat and scarf and helped her with her things, Ms. Foster gave me a box of crayons. "Here take these home and help Sugar print her name." "Thank you Ms. Peters. I will help Sugar Pudding as much as I can." "Myrtle, don't forget, there is no school on the twenty-six and twenty-seventh of this week!" Ms. Foster called out to us as we were leaving, "It is a holiday; we will see you next Monday!" Oh! Suddenly I remembered Thanksgiving is this week, and how could I forget that.

I really did not know what to expect when I went to get Sugar Pudding. The only time I could remember my sister and I being apart was when she got sick and stayed in a hospital for a long time. I was relieved and happy for one brief moment; Sugar's first day at school was just fine.

Anna, Sugar Pudding and I walked out the door of the school. As I looked toward the gate, there was that mean old girl who had snatched my papers. I kept walking pretending not to see her. I held Sugar Pudding's hand tightly, and Anna walked to the other side of Sugar Pudding and grab her other hand. Avoiding the girl from my classroom was not going to work. She walked up to Anna. That nasty girl was so close to Anna's face their noses almost touched! The nasty girl angrily asked Anna, "Why you walking with this white girl, and her white sister?" Anna reached up to push her glasses up on her nose, and the nasty girl smacked her hand down! Before I could do or say anything, Anna quickly knocked the girl to the ground! "Stay outa my face Bitch!" Anna yelled at the nasty girl.

To look at Anna you would not believe she had any fight or argument in her. Evidently, yelling and calling the nasty girl a 'bitch' was enough to chase her off for the moment. However, the words "white girls" were still ringing in my ears! What did she mean calling me and my sister white? Anna was calling my name. "Myrtle, Myrtle! Come on let's go. If we stand here any longer, she may start something else. She's doesn't like white people," Anna explained. "White people!" Where's the white people Anna? I am not white and neither is my sister!" I yelled at Anna. "Well, you look white and you don't sound like us! Look, I don't care if you are white Myrtle. I like you because you are the only one in class who has ever spoken to me," she sounded very sad. Anna pushed the oversized glasses back up on her nose. I felt bad. I should not have yelled at Anna.

Later, as we were walking home, Anna told me how the kids tease her because of her thick glasses, the color of her skin and her thick dark brown hair. Anna said, "I am not as light as you, but the kids still pick on me. I always ate alone until you came into the classroom, Myrtle. None of the other kids made friends with me or even bothered to talk to me," She said very softly. "I didn't mean to yell at you Anna. I just haven't had much time to think about how I look to other people," I explained. "Now I understand why the kids stared at Sugar Pudding and me. Can we still be friends?" I asked. Anna linked her arm through mine, smiled and pushed her glasses back up on her nose again.

We walked the rest of the way home in silence. Anna turned down another street, waved and yelled, "I will see you tomorrow morning, okay!" Sugar Pudding and I continued to walk toward grandma's house. Grandma was standing on the porch when we arrived.

"Well, what you got in your bag?" She asked as she reached for my bag. Grandma was very nosey! Hardly giving us a chance to tell her about my first day at the new school, and Sugar Pudding's first day ever! "It's some writing paper for my home work and a box of crayons for Sugar Pudding. I have to help Sugar Pudding print her name," I answered, happy to talk about our first day in a new school. Without any warning, grandma snapped, "You can do that later! I picked up some washing today. You and Sugar Pudding can help me with that. I have to take it back Wednesday morning!"

Grandma was acting kind of strange. She was okay when we left for school this morning. I told Sugar Pudding to go to our room and take off her coat and scarf. I laid my things down on one of the rickety old kitchen chairs. I really wanted to go in the small room with Sugar and start my homework. I knew I had to help grandma or risk being hollered at again. I finally got up enough courage and asked, "What do you want me to do grandma?" "Just fold the sheets piled on the table," she answered without raising her head from the tablecloth she was ironing.

Later that evening, I folded all the sheets and bed spreads. It looked like she had been washing all morning. It was after eleven 'o' clock that night before I finished folding the wash. I made a small space at the end of the kitchen table to do my homework. After I finished, I went in to check on Sugar Pudding. She had gone to sleep, clutching the picture of the thanksgiving turkey she had colored earlier, in her hand. She was probably too tired and too hungry to stay awake.

I went back to the kitchen to get a glass of water, and grandma was sitting at the table folding some very small green towels. "Grandma, can I ask you something?" "Yes, what you want to know Myrtle?" she asked dryly. The sound of her voice told me I had made a mistake trying to talk to her. But, I continued anyway. "Did you know thanksgiving is this Thursday?" Silence. Then finally, she spoke. "Yes I know when it's thanksgiving. Why you think I'm a doing all this washing for? We gonna have a chicken and maybe some greens and biscuits. The church gives out baskets on Wednesday morning, and I asked ol' Willie to take me to the church early. If I'm not late, I'll get a basket," she answered tiredly.

I did not bother grandma anymore that night. I wanted to tell her about the nasty girl and how Anna, took up for us. I decided to leave it alone. I did not think I would have any more problems with the nasty girl thanks to Anna. However, I found out the next day, her name is Macy Allen and she is the bully in the classroom. She has a reputation for kicking some kid's ass everyday, and Aaron, the 'bugger eater' edging her on.

For the first few days of school, it was embarrassing especially during lunchtime. Grandma fixed us very little food to take for lunch. One morning she packed some cold lumpy oatmeal in an old green colored mason jar with pieces of day old cornbread, and told Sugar Pudding and me to eat together because she did not have another jar. I threw the jar and everything else in the trash. I found out later Ms. Foster shared her lunch with Sugar Pudding and Mr. Jenkins always brought extra sandwiches incase I did not bring lunch.

    I can't remember the morning grandma started packing our lunch "the right way," however, it happened shortly after Sugar Pudding brought home a bag with part of a sandwich wrapped in a pretty blue paper napkin. I guess it dawned on grandma someone cared enough to feed us in school. We did not worry about lunch after that. Sugar Pudding and I had other things to worry about. Will our mama ever come back for us? What happened to her, and why are we living with the old woman who is not our family, in an old house that is falling apart, and most of all…where is our daddy? As long as I can remember, mama and I lived alone until she brought Sugar Pudding home and announced, "This is your baby sister!" I do not remember saying the words 'daddy, papa or father.'

    For a while, men would come to visit my mama. We learned to call them Uncle Billy, Uncle Charles or 'Uncle' whatever name they had. After a while, they stopped coming to the house. It was just mama, Sugar Pudding and I. We seldom had enough money and just enough food for the three of us.

    I remember things started getting bad a few years ago. Mama got sick one day and we had to stay with a woman who said she was a friend of mama's. We stayed for along time and I did not go to school. The woman's name was Lily. I called her Ms. Lily. Sugar Pudding didn't call her much of anything. Ms. Lily lived in a house with her Uncle Ted who was crazy. All he did was talk to himself all day, picked his nose and rubbed the buggers on anyone that came past him. Every now and then he would pee on himself and Ms. Lily would cuss at him," You crazy old bastard! Piss again hear! You will sit in the shit until tomorrow!" The house smelled like pee and shit all the time. I was afraid to go to sleep, even though Sugar Pudding and I slept together.

However, there was a boy who appeared to be about twelve or thirteen, who lived in the house too. He was what they called 'simple minded' and wore diapers tied around his neck because he could not keep his spit in his mouth. He sat in a corner all day playing with small wooden blocks with letters of the alphabet painted on them. Sometimes he would holler, or he would just rock back and forth sitting in puddles of spit and pee. He scared Sugar Pudding and me, so we played in our room or on the back porch.

Ms. Lily did not cook for us. An old colored woman named Ms. Evelyn would come to the house every morning about six o'clock, cook enough food for us to eat and leave in the afternoon. She never said much to Sugar Pudding and me, but sometimes she made us cookies and brought them to us either in our room or on the back porch. She was nice to us and sometimes gave us a hug or a gentle pat on our shoulders.

Ms. Lily had all kinds of people visiting her. They never stayed long. Sometimes they would drop off an old man or old woman, and Ms. Lily would take them to another part of the house. A few days later, some people would come and get them. I seldom saw the old man or old woman walking or moving around. Later I found out, Ms. Lily would keep or watch them for money. However, Ms. Lily had one regular visitor, a woman who dressed like a man. She was fat and brown-skinned with a few scratches on her face, wore men's pants, shirts and old leather brown work boots, always covered in dry mud. Her hair was cut very close to her head like a man and she always wore a baseball cap with dirty grease spots all over it.

One morning Ms. Lily and this woman were sitting in the kitchen, smoking and drinking. A cloud of smoke was hovering over their heads. If you did not know any better, you would have thought the house was on fire. They were talking very loud and suddenly, Ms. Lily was asking the woman to keep her voice down, "would you please stop the yelling! I have kids in the house!" The woman continued to yell and holler at Ms. Lily to shut up before she slaps the shit out of her! I heard something like a chair fall to the floor, and glass breaking. Sugar and I were sitting on the bench on the back porch. Even though the window was open, we were afraid to look. The loud noise and hollering frightened Sugar Pudding and she quickly crawled under the wooden bench that we were sitting on. I was lying flat down on the bench. There was a window above my head and the bench where we were sitting was directly under it. I whispered to Sugar Pudding to be quiet.

  I rose up a little to look through the window to see what was going on. The fat 'man-woman,' that is what Sugar Pudding called her, picked up her glass and threw the liquor in Ms. Lily's face! Ms. Lily yelled; "get the hell out of my house! I don't want you to come back here again! Get the hell out! You fat ass black bitch!" Ms. Lily was trying to get to the screen door. The fat man-woman snatched Ms. Lily's dress from the back, ripping it off her shoulders. Ms. Lily tripped and fell on the floor. The fat man-woman kneeled down, pulled Ms. Lily up by the torn part of her dress and slapped her upside the face. "You want me to get out! You want me to get out! You ain't saying that shit when I was fucking your ass Bitch! You wouldn't have this house if it wasn't for me! I sent these here peoples to you! You get paid bitch for doing nothing!" Ms. Lily was still lying on the floor. She did not move. The fat man-woman kicked her in the back, spit on her and left.

  Sugar Pudding and I sat on the porch a long time. It was dark before we had gathered up enough courage to go back inside. We stayed with Ms. Lily until late fall. Mama came to get us and took us back home. Mama was still sick and could barely take care of us. I did most of the cleaning and looking after Sugar Pudding. Sometimes one of our 'uncles' would stop by with food or give mama some money. As the weather began to change so did mama. She was tired all the time, and yelled at us a lot, like she was mad at us! She was mad the night the people came to the house…the night we left our home.

Chapter 4

Holiday disappointments ...

Grandma was standing on the porch when we arrived from school. Her gloveless old hands tightly held the scarf closely around her neck, trying to keep out the cold November wind. "Put your things down, but don't take off your coats," she said as we walked up the steps. Ol' Willie's truck would not start this morning," she explained, that is why she was waiting for us to get home from school, so we could walk the few miles to Greater Old Zion Baptist Church.

It was a long, cold and disappointing walk for all of us. When we arrived at the church, the caretaker, Mr. Riley told us a few baskets were left with some potatoes; corn and collars, but there were no more chickens left. He helped us put the rest of the food into two baskets and we carried them back home. Thanksgiving came and went.

Anna met us Monday morning with a different look. She still had on those big glasses, but her hair is comb differently. It really looked nice. She had a ponytail like Sugar Pudding and me. Only, she did not have a dirty shoelace around her ponytail...she had a pretty, yellow ribbon tied around her hair. "I like your ribbon Anna. Did your mama buy it for you?" "Yes, I have some more at home. I will cut you and Sugar Pudding a piece and bring it tomorrow okay," said Anna. "Sure that's okay! I can hardly wait until tomorrow!" We walked the rest of the way talking about the color of ribbons we liked.

Mr. Jenkins was not at his desk this morning. I was happy to see Ms. Peters sitting at his desk. "Good Morning class, Mr. Jenkins is running a little late. He will be here soon! Now, take out your spelling notes. Mr. Jenkins said you have a spelling test this morning. Myrtle, please pass out some paper, and we can get started," she said cheerfully. I got up from my desk and started over to the table where Mr. Jenkins kept the line paper. I reached for a few sheets and began to place a sheet on each desk. Unfortunately, I had to start from the back row and that is where Macy sat. As I made my way to her desk, she stuck out her foot to trip me. She missed! A few kids laughed, and others just stared. Ms. Peters asked them to be quiet.

I backed out of Macy's way, away from her feet, until I had reached the next row. I finished passing out the paper and went back to my desk, thankful that I sat up front and not in the back next to that hateful girl. Just as Ms. Peters began to call out the first word for the spelling test, Mr. Jenkins walked in. "Good Morning Everyone! Thank you Ms. Peters! Now, if everyone is ready I will say the first word for the spelling test." We had twenty words, and I knew I had spelled each one correctly. Mr. Jenkins asked Anna to collect all the papers. When Anna got to Macy's desk, she refused to give her paper to her. Anna kept walking and collected the other kids' papers without incident.

We were reading silently, when another teacher came into the room and asked Mr. Jenkins if she could speak with him. Mr. Jenkins stepped into the hallway, and slightly pulled the door behind him. I glanced around the room and caught Macy walking very fast, back to her seat. The next thing I felt was a hand and some cold water running down the side of my face. I opened my eyes and there was Ms. Peters and Mr. Jenkins. "What happened? Why am I laying here?" I tried to get off the floor. Ms. Peters helped me sit up. My mouth felt dry and my head hurt something awful. I looked up again, and saw Mr. Jenkins standing over me. "You were hit from behind. I am so sorry Myrtle. Macy threw a rock from my collection and it struck you in the back of your head! Ms. Peters will take you to the nearest hospital. I will let your grandma know what happened," he said softly trying to comfort me as he reached down and patted my knee. I jumped at his touch. His hands were clammy and scratchy. Everyone was looking down at me. I felt pain and my head begin to spin. I, could barely make out Ms. Peters face, my vision was blurry.

Ms. Peters put her arm around my waist and helped me get to her car. It was light blue and had a cross of Jesus hanging from the rear view mirror. I remember the cross sparkling, and I passed out. When I came to, I was lying in a narrow bed and a white sheet folded across my chest. I looked around the room. A large light was hanging directly over my face. Over in a corner, stood a large table with bottles full of liquid lined up in a row, scissors and rolls of white tape lying on a silver tray. I remembered riding in Ms. Peter's car, but I do not remember much of anything else. My head still hurt and my mouth was very dry. I heard voices outside of the room. Suddenly grandma ran in the room. I could make out bits and pieces of what she was saying, "I came to get Myrtle," and Ol' Willie drove her here in his truck. "For once the truck is working," grandma complained irritably.

I did not have to stay in the hospital. The doctor was nice and told me not to move around for a day or two, and that I had a nasty bump on my head, but I would be all right. He turned to ol' Willie, "If she has any problems bring her back to the emergency room." The doctor patted my hand and left the room. The nurse came in. "As soon as I wipe the dried blood from her face and hair, she can go home."

Ol' Willie stood by the door watching the nurse, and grandma was sitting out in hall by the door. After the nurse had finish, ol' Willie picked me up off the table and carried me to the truck. As he carried me in the house, grandma asked me if I was I feeling all right. I told her I was fine. She carefully pulled back my hair to see the small bandage on the back of my head. She was very quiet the rest of the evening until I went to sleep. I do not know if I was dreaming, nonetheless, I thought I felt grandma's hand pat my head very softly.

The next few days, I did very little, but lay around the house. Anna took Sugar Pudding to school and brought her back home. When I returned that following week, Mr. Jenkins told me that Macy was sent home for two weeks for throwing that rock. Well, that did not sit too well with her mama. After the incident, grandma had a visitor about two days after I had gone back to school. Macy's mama was standing on the porch when grandma came home, after cleaning and washing for the new white people that had moved in the Richardson's house.

Macy's mama was a tall muscular woman. She had a white rag tied around her head, and part of it hung down her back. She walked right up to grandma and before grandma could say anything, Macy's mama's voice became high and hysterical with anger. She yelled at grandma, "Your granddaughter got my child Macy sent home from school for two weeks! Why your light-skinned gal thinks she can get away with murder and no one does anything about it! I want you to call that Mr. Jenkins and tell him you want my Macy back in school, and that it was your granddaughter's fault she was sent home!" She was flinging her arms about as if she was going to hit grandma.

Grandma stepped back. She never took her eyes off Macy's mama as she sat her bags on the floor of the porch. Grandma eased her old body down carefully, and sat down on one of the wobbly wooden crates. I stepped back behind the screen door, just incase grandma decided to throw something. I did not want to get in her way.

Without getting up from her crate, grandma looked up at the very tall woman, anger flashed across her face and she exhaled slowly, "The color of my granddaughter's skin ain't got a damn thing to do with your daughter being sent home. Your mean-ass girl has been picking on Myrtle since she started going to that school! You need to teach your girl not to be so damn mean and hateful!" Grandma's eyes narrowed as she continued to stare straight up at Macy's mama's face. Grandma wiped her brow with her hand. "Now, I am very tired and don't feel like talking to you! I want you to git the hell off my porch and if you so much as come anywhere near my house and if, your mean-ass-hateful child ever hit Myrtle again, I will git the county sheriff on y'all quicker than a pole cat can lick his ass!" Grandma waved her hand at her! Well, this took Macy's mama by surprise!

    Colored people were scared of the sheriff and the police in Tapasalle County. Everyone knew that if you called, the police wouldn't do anything if you were colored. All the wind had been knocked out of Macy's mama. She wasn't so big and bad after all. When Macy returned to school sometime later, we did not have any more problems with her.

Chapter 5

Nature and strangers bearing gifts...

It was December. Christmas time. I love to see the decorations on the houses. When we lived with our mama, she would take us into town for a walk, and show us the few decorated store windows in Southend.

During one of all our walks, we ran into a man begging for food. Mama reached inside of her coat and gave the man a quarter. The old man pulled the two brass colored Christmas candles out from under his arm and gave them to her. Mama took the candles and when we returned home, she placed them in the window. Unfortunately, we had no way to plug them in. The plugs had been removed, but they looked pretty all the same. We may have been the only colored family in Southend that had Christmas decorations. We did not have a decorated tree; however, the candles were still a part of the holiday.

Money was scarce in our house. Most of it was spent on food, and clothes if there was enough left. Christmas was like any other day in our house. I remember not opening the door...afraid my friends may ask to see what I got for Christmas. I couldn't tell them I did not get anything. I would just wish for the day to hurry and pass, and then everything would be back to normal.

Grandma didn't talk much about the holidays. She was very quiet and stayed in the front room most of the time sitting in front of the fireplace. She left only when she had to go into town to clean and wash for the white people. We had not seen much of ol' Willie since my incident with Macy.

As if we needed more problems, my 'monthly visitor' started. I knew a little about it because I had heard some of the girls in my class talking about how they hated it because it made their stomach hurt. That morning when it happened I told grandma. She just stared at me. Finally, shaking her head and causing the three plaits on top of her head to shake, she warned, "I don't want you messing with no boys, you here! You mess with them and you will get pregnant! We don't need no more mouths to feed in this house. You gonna have to help me with the washing and cleaning so I can make more money. You got to have things to keep yourself from messing your clothes. I don't have much money, but if you help me do the Tompkins and Reynolds cleaning and washing, I'll see that you have what you need." "Okay, grandma, I can do that!" I answered relieved I did not have to tear up some old towels or sheets to put in my underwear.

That morning I did not go to school. Grandma told Anna I was not feeling well, and thanked her for coming to get Sugar Pudding. Grandma took the Tompkins their clean wash and return later that evening with a purple box of sanitary napkins. I read the information on the back of the box, about how to use them, and put the box in my drawer. The next day I went to school as usual. I did not tell Anna I had started my 'monthly visitor,' as grandma called it. I really did not know what to tell her. So I kept it to myself.

It was a bitter, cold morning, and not all the clothes I had on kept me warm. I was so glad to get in the classroom. We kept our coats on much of the day. Mr. Jenkins did all he could to keep the room warm. He closed all the windows and pulled the shades down. The windows that had cracks were stuffed with old rags and newspaper. Junk and other kinds of stuff were removed off the radiators so we could feel the heat. Most of us got sick anyway with colds and pneumonia. For about a month, we had no more than eight kids in our classroom.

One morning it was so cold, we did not do any class work. Mr. Jenkins told us to sit close together to keep warm. Anna and I were sitting together when Aaron, one of the boys in the back of the classroom walked over and asked if he could sit next to Anna and me. I didn't like Aaron the first time I met him in the classroom. He was a troublemaker and encouraged Macy a lot of times to pick on other kids in the room, especially the girls, and I was her main target. Aaron was not much to look at and something was wrong with one side of his face. He had very large lips and his top lip turned up in the corner of his mouth exposing his gum and almost touching his nose, and exposing teeth that were too large for his mouth. Hell! He was one ugly ass boy!

I told him to sit next to some of the boys, only the girls were sitting close together to keep warm. I had just barely finished my sentence, when Mr. Jenkins told Aaron to go back to his seat. "Why can't the boys sit next to the girls Mr. Jenkins?" asked Aaron, his tongue darted in and out of the gap where his upper lip should have been. Mr. Jenkins told Aaron to be quiet and to continue reading. Around noon, the room began to warm up a little and we went back to our classroom activities.

When school let out that day, Mr. Jenkins asked me to wait a few minutes he wanted to talk to me. I wondered what he wanted. My homework was turned in. I am never late for school, and I don't bother anyone. Mr. Jenkins came over to my desk after the other kids had left. He pulled up a chair and sat down next to me. I could smell tobacco smoke and onions on his breath. "I have something for you Myrtle. I know you have a birthday coming up soon, and you are such a good student, I brought you a little something." He reached in his pocket and gave me a little box wrapped in yellow paper.

"Thank you Mr. Jenkins!" I was so excited. I had not been given a gift in such a long time. My hands shook nervously as I tried to remove the paper from the box. I finally opened the box and to my surprise, there was a little bracelet with a heart dangling from it. It was the prettiest thing I had seen in a long time. I was so busy admiring the pretty bracelet, it had not occurred to me that Mr. Jenkins had got up from the chair he was sitting in, until I felt his hot breath on my neck as he whispered, "Go ahead Myrtle, try it on." He placed his hand on my shoulder, and I suddenly felt a strange coldness in the room. I jumped up suddenly. I felt I had to get out of there. "Thank you Mr. Jenkins for the bracelet. I have to leave now and pick up Sugar Pudding." I was half way out the door, when Mr. Jenkins called out, "You are welcome Myrtle, but look… don't tell anyone who gave it to you. That's a secret between you and me!" He put his finger to his lips, and winked his eye. I started down the hallway, to the steps. The hall was quiet, so very quiet.

    I ran down stairs to get Sugar Pudding. I stopped at Ms. Foster's door and put the bracelet in my pocket. I didn't want anyone to see it. As I opened the door, Ms. Foster called my name. "Myrtle, it's about time you got here! Sugar Pudding's been ready for a while." I looked around the room. "Where's Anna?" I asked looking around the classroom. "Anna?" she repeated looking at me. "Why Myrtle, Anna did not come to pick up your sister. I decided to wait until you came down from class. Try not to be late tomorrow, okay." "Okay, Ms. Foster. Come on Sugar Pudding let's go!" I grabbed her hand and we walked down the hall and out the door. I looked up and down the road, but I did not see Anna. I wonder why she left us. That was not like Anna to leave us, because we usually walk together I thought to myself.

    That evening after we ate, I hurriedly finished the dishes and folded the clothes grandma had left in the clothesbasket. Sugar Pudding went through her usually activity of printing her alphabets and numbers and jumping up and down after she had printed each letter to get my approval. Grandma was washing the last bag of clothes she picked up this morning. I helped Sugar Pudding get to bed early that evening. Grandma had a radio that she sometime listened to when it was working. All you could really hear was static and a few voices. It was virtually impossible to hear what they were singing or saying. That old radio irritated me. I did not like the sounds that came from it so I went into the room where Sugar Pudding and I slept. I leaned over and listened to Sugar Pudding's breathing. Yes, she was sleep.

I got my coat and took the bracelet out of the little box. I looked at it and rubbed it over and over again, feeling the smooth chain in the palm of my hand. The heart had a little purple flower painted on it. I put the bracelet back in the box. I looked around the small room trying to find some place to hide it. Suddenly, I saw a corner of the room that had part of the floorboard loose. I pulled up the loose board, dropped the box on the dark dirt, and put the board back. I went to bed. The bracelet was in a safe place.

Earlier that next morning, grandma told me she had to go into town. The new people she worked for were having a few houseguest and they wanted grandma to clean the house and have everything ready when they arrived. She had to be there by six-thirty in the morning. We lived too far from the bus stop, that why ol' Willie would give you a ride if you gave him a dollar for gas.

After that colored woman was arrested, for not giving her seat to a white man, grandma did not like riding the bus anymore. She was afraid the same thing would happen to her. So she walked, hitched a ride with other white folks who recognized her or paid ol' Willie. Grandma was more afraid to ride in a car or the back of a truck with the other coloreds. She had heard stories from her friends that the white police would make them pull over to the side of the road for nothing and check their bags.

As if that was not bad enough, the police would make them dump everything in the car or truck on the ground. Sometimes that included the freshly washed and ironed laundry that they threw in the dirt. Ms. Ella told grandma one morning when they were walking into town, the police stopped her and wanted to know what was in her bags. She opened the bags and watched as the white policeman peed all over the sheets and table cloths she had just washed and ironed for the Reynolds daughter's wedding that was to be held the next day.

Chapter 6

Anna's disappearing act...

I had been up since five-thirty and made some breakfast for Sugar Pudding and me. I found some clothes for us to wear to school, that were not 'too' wrinkled. I could not use the iron. Grandma said I might mess around and burn myself, and besides that's the only iron she owned and she needed it for doing the ironing for the white people she cleaned and washed for. I woke up Sugar Pudding, combed her hair and we got ready to leave for school. Grandma had to leave early that morning and told me to lock the bottom lock and close the screen door.

Sugar Pudding and I had walked a little while before we realized we had not ran into Anna. We finally met up with some other kids and walked the rest of the way with them.

I walked into the classroom, and there was Anna sitting there. I walked over to her. "What happened to you this morning? Did you get up late?" "Nothing happened this morning. You and your sister know the way by now. You don't need me walking with you. Besides I was just doing you a favor," she said sadly. Anna sat hunched over in her chair, her body slightly turned away from me, as if she did not want me to look at her. "Is anything wrong Anna? Are you feeling okay?" I asked. Anna never answered me. Lunchtime came. Anna and I usually pulled our chairs together, ate our lunch, and talked about school, her dog or anything we felt like talking about. However, today she got up, sat over in a corner, alone, and finished her lunch, away from everyone. I noticed Mr. Jenkins was watching Anna. He gave her a warning look. Pointing his finger toward Anna, he asked her, "Why are you sitting in that corner?" He ordered her to move back to her regular seat, which was next to me. Anna moved back to her seat.

She would not talk to me the rest of the day. I was hurt and disappointed. I had done nothing to her, and could not figure out why she was not friends with me anymore.

Anna wouldn't talk and that went on for a few days. I was worried and I missed talking to my friend. The next day I waited for her after school. I was tying Sugar Pudding scarf around her head when Anna walked past us. "Hey Anna, wait a minute!" I yelled. I ran up to her and grabbed her by the hand. "What is wrong with you Anna? Are you mad with me?" She turned around and looked me in the face. She was crying softly. She wiped the tears from her face with the back of her coat sleeve. "I can't tell you," she said sadly. We walked together in silence and we parted as usual a few blocks before we reached grandma's house.

Chapter 7
The development…

"Mr. Reynolds did you take that package to Ms. Emma Jackson? We should have heard from her since then. It's been over three months! Shit! The holidays are gone!" ol' Willie said sharply.

"Yes, Sir ol' Willie, I took the package out there like you told me. One of them little half-white colored girls signed for the package," he answered dryly. "We will just give her a little more time. She needs to get someone to read the papers to her. It's very important that she answers them as soon as possible," said ol' Willie. "What if she don't answer the summons? She only got thirty more days left!" said Mr. Reynolds, his voice edged with tension.

"Well, we just gonna have to take my grandmother's houses and the land around it. Hell, Ms. Emma don't know them two houses belongs to them half-white colored girls. Look, she don't even know who they are. I didn't tell her anything. Anyway, I got a lawyer looking into the case. We are still trying to find the girls' mama. When the mama took off last winter, we lost track of her. She just left a note saying take them to Ms. Emma's house. I had no choice but to take them there. Shit, what am I gonna do with two half-white little colored girls. I could have turned them over to the county, but I couldn't do that because they are Clemmons kids, and he would kill me! We are brothers, and we suppose to look out for one another! Clemmons is due out in two months. He will have finished his time in the Upper County Pinewood prison. He's expecting to come back to one of them houses, and they don't belong to us no more!"

"Look, just talking about this shit upsets me! Mr. Reynolds, did you check the houses today? Ain't no squatters in them, is there?" asked ol' Willie. "No they are locked up. Mr. Harvey checks on them every now and then.

I give him ten dollars a week to keep the place clean so won't nobody be snooping around. I told him make it look like someone is living in them. Every now and then, he takes one of his nigger women to help clean the place and he goes in, and turns on the lights at night and goes back and turns them off in the morning. Sometimes I let him sleep in the houses. That's okay ain't it ol' Willie?" asked Mr. Reynolds looking at ol' Willie from the corner of his eye. "Yea, I don't suppose it can hurt anything. Is the furniture still in there?" ol' Willie asked. "There were a few beds, some tables and chairs the last time I checked. Yeah ol' Willie they still in there," answered Mr. Reynolds with a touch of impatience.

"Well, I got to take Ms. Emma in town tomorrow, to the Tompkins house," yawned ol' Willie. "Why you got to take her in town, can't she take the bus like them other coloreds do?" Mr. Reynolds asked, chewing on a wad of tobacco, and the brown juice was running down the side of his mouth. He looked frantically around the room for a can to spit in. "Well for one thing, since you ask... Ms. Emma's afraid to ride the bus and she says it's too far for her to walk with the laundry bags and all. So I charge her a dollar for gas, and when I can't take her, I tell her the truck ain't working. On those days when I don't take her; them girls walk with her and help carry the bags," explained ol' Willie.

"That older girl sure is pretty! Neither one look like they is kin to Ms. Emma," Mr. Reynolds gave a sneaky little laugh. "You keep your damn mouth shut Mr. Reynolds! You ain't supposed to know that! Them kids belong to Ms. Emma's younger niece Rachel Jackson! She is Ms. Emma's sister's child! Hell, I know Ms. Emma don't know they is kin to her!" snapped ol' Willie. "Ms. Ruth may know ol' Willie, because Mr. Leon served a few years in prison with Ms. Ruth's brother Malcolm Macklin before he died from food poisoning. Ms. Emma's sister Ilene and him were real close," said Mr. Reynolds. "I don't care who knows who! We is in big trouble when Clemmons finds out the state can take the two houses because we were left out of grandmothers' will and we have no proof of ownership.

Ever since our grandmother died, the houses have just sat there! Clemmons lived in the smaller one until he went to prison a few years ago. When Clemmons went to jail for six years, involuntary manslaughter, that left me to take care of the houses. The will was read a few days later after the funeral. I never made it to the reading of the will, and neither did Clemmons. He was still serving time.

We both thought grandmother had left the houses and land to us. Grandmother's lawyer contacted me and told me the bad news over the phone. I got sick Mr. Reynolds, just plain old sick. Mr. Baylor told me he would give me and Clemmons time to find Rachel and any other heirs to the will. I did not say anything to nobody because Rachel and the girls were living in another county and Clemmons was serving time for other added charges of theft and first-degree assault. Hell, I didn't know Rachael would abandon them little colored girls. I thought they all were gone for good," ol' Willie explained impatiently.

"What happened to Rachel's mama, you know Ms. Emma's sister?" asked Mr. Reynolds. "Well, we don't quite know. They found Ms. Ilene sick, outa her mind one morning. She was talking to herself. Some people believe the man she was living with poisoned her because she was found, in his bed, with all this white foam around her mouth and coming from her nose. She stayed in the hospital a while as the story goes. Shit! I don't know if she's dead or alive! We ain't heard nothing from her in years. I didn't know Rachel was still here until I accidentally found them little girls at the bus station. You know sometimes I wonder what if I had not gone to work that morning, would they have been turned over to the county, or taken to Ms. Emma's house like the last two people who were abandon there.

Well ain't no sense in going over that again, I tried to keep the houses in the family, but that old trouble-making grandmother left the houses and land to Rachel Jackson and the girls to get back at Clemmons for sleeping with a colored girl! You see, Mr. Reynolds if we tell them lawyers there ain't no living relatives, the houses and land is ours to keep!" Willie explained with a little excitement in his voice.

"How you gonna prove there ain't no living relatives?" Mr. Reynolds asked, with his head cocked to the side and arching his left eyebrow. "Well, I got a plan. Ms. Emma don't know all the truth, she think she is just taking care of some half white little girls that were left in an old bus station. We are gonna let her think that, and we gonna get her to sign those court papers that says she ain't no kin to them girls. I had a friend of mine write them papers up like they were just doing a little investigation about the girls living with her, and all she got to do is write how the girls got there, that's all. Once she sends them papers back. I get a copy and file for ownership of the two houses."

"Ol' Willie this plan of yours might not work if the girls' mama shows up anytime soon. We don't know if this here Rachel Jackson knows about the will. Ol' Willie, why did them colored girls' mama leave Southend so suddenly? What more you know about them girls being left in a bus station in the deep cold of winter?" Mr. Reynolds gave him a suspicious look.

"Look Mr. Reynolds, you can ask all the questions you want to ask. I only know what the note said," answered ol' Willie in an irritated tone of voice. "You still got the note?" Asked Mr. Reynolds with that left eyebrow still arched. "Yeah, I still got the note, but all it said was take the girls to Ms. Emma's house!" ol' Willie responded angrily. "Don't question me Mr. Reynolds! If I knew more,

I would tell you! Just don't do any more talking about this to nobody! Not even my brother Clemmons! You understand! You and I are the only ones who know who those houses belong to!" ol' Willie yelled at Mr. Reynolds.

"Hell, ain't no one gonna live in them, because the state wants to build that new highway and they is interested in buying all the land and the houses! The houses are worth over $350,000 apiece and that is not including the land around them! You see now…Mr. Reynolds why it is important for you to keep your damn mouth shut! Them colored girls is too young to live in them houses by themselves, and Ms. Emma's been sick off and on. Shit she ain't gonna live forever. You know if anything happens to the old colored woman while she still got them girls, I'll see to it that they find good homes, maybe working for some of them white people over in Stafford County." "You think you got all this work out, Ol' Willie, but you is forgetting about Ms. Ruth," warned Mr. Reynolds.

"Yeah, you just keep a close eye on Mr. Harvey. Watch who he's talking to. I'll take care of everything else," cautioned ol' Willie. When ol' Willie heard Mr. Reynolds truck pull off, he pulled the crumbled old note out of his pocket and read it again:

"These are my girls and I love them dearly, take good care of them for me. Whoever finds them, please take them to an old lady named Ms. Emma Jackson in Tapasalle County. Rachel Jackson."

Old Willie folded the wrinkled note and placed it back in his wallet.

Chapter 8

A much-needed vacation…

There was something different about Anna over the last few days. When Mr. Jenkins called on her, she suddenly became very clumsy, dropping her pencil, accidentally knocking over her books and fidgeting with her glasses…all the while never looking directly at him. We still sat together and ate our lunch but she did very little talking. It was the same walking home in the afternoon. However, I was determined to find out why she was so sad. I'll just wait a few more days and I will ask her again.

The weather was trying to get a little warmer. It was the end of March and grandma was still washing and ironing for the Tompkins. I had never met them. Grandma always picked up and carried their laundry back while I was in school. Nonetheless, as fate would have it, I finally had the chance to meet their daughter Nancy Rose. Grandma answered a knock on her door very early one Saturday morning. I got up when I heard the banging. I walked into the front room just as grandma was opening the door. There was this tall white man with sandy colored hair, wearing a black coat with a white scarf around his neck. A girl with two long ponytails tied with pink ribbons peeked from behind him, smiled and waved to me.

"Oh my goodness! Mr. Tompkins why you here this early in the morning? Did I forget to bring something back?" Grandma was fidgeting with the buttons on her raggedy old robe and her voice sounded a little nervous. "Why no Ms. Emma," he answered nicely. We need you come to the house this morning. Senator Lyles Baker and his family are stopping over on their way to Marshallville and the missus does not think the house is clean enough. Can you get dressed and come with Nancy Rose and me?"

"Why I would be happy to come," grandma answered. "Who are the girls?" he asked. Sugar Pudding and I were standing there staring at the white girl. "Oh, these is my granddaughters, Myrtle and this little one is Sugar Pudding." Grandma gave a weak smile as she looked over at us. "Myrtle and Sugar Pudding, this here is Ms. Nancy Rose, Mr. Tompkins daughter." We both said good morning and started back to our room. Suddenly, Mr. Tompkins said, "Ms. Emma, you can bring them along too!" "Is it all right for them to come?" asked grandma not quite believing her ears. "Why of course, they maybe some help to you or they can play with Nancy Rose."

He smiled nicely at Sugar and me. Mr. Tompkins told grandma they would wait in the car. We quickly put on some clothes and as we got ready to leave, grandma warned us about how to act in the white man's house. "Don't say nothing unless some one says something to you, understand! Don't beg for nothing! Wait until it is offered and say, 'No thank you mam' when it is! Come on let's go! Get in the back seat and be quiet! Don't act like you never been in no car!" I had no idea what she meant. How is Sugar Pudding and I suppose to act? I have been in a car before and Sugar Pudding and I have both ridden in a truck. My first thought was, don't they all ride the same?

Grandma locked up the house, picked up her bag and we carefully walked down the broken steps to Mr. Tompkins's car. It was beautiful! Black and shinny with large seats made of black leather. The ride only took about thirty minutes, but we passed some pretty houses and other pretty cars like Mr. Tompkins. He turned on the radio. The music sounded so nice. There was no static or humming noise like grandma's radio. Nancy Rose sat up front with her father talking a mile a minute about what she wanted to do as soon as she got home. Grandma sat there not saying a word, but she has had this strange look on her face ever since we left this morning. One time I thought I saw a smile.

We finally arrived at the Tompkins house. It was a very large white and green house with a gravel road, which led to the front door. Before we could get out, Nancy Rose jumped out of the car and ran toward the front door. "Mommy! Mommy! I've got some girls to play with!" Grandma told me to grab Sugar Pudding's hand and follow her. It was too late! Sugar Pudding had walked through the front door running behind Nancy Rose! Mrs. Tompkins came out, waved at us and told us to come in, but grandma walked around to another side of the house. At first, I couldn't figure this out! Why did grandma walk all the way around that big house to go in? I thought to myself, the front door is closer. Sugar Pudding and I found ourselves standing in this beautiful room with plants and flowers all over the place. The floors were dark brown and shining like glass. I thought it must have taken Ms. Tompkins all morning to clean this floor.

Pictures of white people, old, young, some with very long dresses, standing next to horses or holding small dogs, decorated the pale yellow colored walls. Some of the pictures included children that look like Sugar and I. The furniture in the living room is white with green flowers. There are curtains hung at the windows with lots and lots of ruffles, so thin you could see directly through them. There is a black piano sitting in a corner with a candleholder sitting on top of it. The piano looked just like the one I once saw in a magazine.

As I reached for Sugar Pudding's hand, she quickly walked over to the piano and stared at it. She walked over to Ms. Tompkins tugged her dress and asked her to make some music. Mrs. Tompkins looked surprised, but she took Sugar Pudding by the hand, and they walked over to the bench and sat down.

Nancy Rose sat next to her mama and turned the pages on the book that sat over the piano keys. I stood by the bench waiting for Mrs. Tompkins to play the piano. I watched intently as her fingers seem to fly quickly from one key to another. The piano did not sound like the piano the old women played in church. Ms. Tompkins played two songs for us and tried to get Nancy Rose to sing. She put her hands up to her face, hid behind her mama and started giggling. When Ms. Tompkins finished playing, she asked Nancy Rose to take us up stairs. We followed Nancy Rose up several floors. Each floor just as pretty as the one we had passed. We finally came to a large room painted light pink and white. There were large dolls sitting all over the floor and a pink elephant sat in a huge white rocking chair. There were two beds with identical bedspreads and pillows. Pictures of flowers and more old white people decorated the light pink walls. The room was very pretty. I would have loved to have a room like this.

Sugar Pudding and I were standing in the middle of the room. I guess we looked somewhat strange. Nancy Rose walked over to us and said, "Come over here and sit with me. I very seldom have anyone to play with. I am so happy my daddy brought you here. Can you stay a long time?" she asked tugging on her long ponytails. "What do you mean by a long time Nancy Rose? Sugar Pudding and I have to leave when our grandma finishes her cleaning." "This house is not dirty. Mama likes it clean because of me. I stay sick a lot," she said sadly. "I am twelve years old. I had a birthday party last year. I hope mama and daddy plan a party for me this year. I want you and your sister to come," she said with enthusiasm.

Nancy Rose walked over to a large white dresser with a large oval mirror attached to it. She opened and closed several drawers quickly. She was looking for something and mumbling to herself, 'where did I put them.' "What are you looking for Nancy Rose?" I asked because I was curious. At that moment, Mrs. Tompkins walked in the room. "Nancy Rose what on earth are you looking for?" "My ribbons mommy, where did you put them? I want to give Myrtle and Sugar Pudding some ribbons to tie on their hair. It's alright mommy, I have plenty of them!"

She was a feisty little girl. She placed her hands on her hips, and moved her head in such a manner, her two ponytails moved back and forth, as she talked. Mrs. Tompkins walked over to where Sugar Pudding and I were sitting and reached up over us and pulled down a large red hatbox off the top of the dresser. She opened the box and to my surprise, it was full of ribbons in different kinds of colors. "I'll have these ready for you when you are ready to leave." She said, grabbing a large handful of the pretty ribbons out of the box. Nancy Rose's mama paused a moment, thinking perhaps one handful was not enough, took out some more of the ribbons and placed the hatbox back on top of Nancy Rose's dresser. I quickly said 'thank you' to Mrs. Tompkins, but told her, grandma would get mad at us if we take the ribbons. "Don't worry about Ms. Emma; I'll talk to her myself. You girls enjoy yourselves. If you get hungry tell Nancy Rose," she smiled at us as she left the room, leaving a faint smell of roses.

I felt so good. I had not felt like this in a long time. I wanted the feeling to stay with me for the rest of my life, even though I knew it would end soon. We ate, talked and played a card game Nancy Rose taught us. When it was time to leave, I felt sad leaving that beautiful big house. Mrs. Tompkins handed grandma a large box and two large brown paper bags with handles as we were getting in the car. "Thank you kindly, Mrs. Tompkins for the things," said grandma. I looked at grandma's face. She looked like she was ready to cry. Her lips trembled as she tried to finish her good-byes especially to Nancy Rose.

Later when we got back to grandma's house, she explained Nancy Rose was leaving to go into a hospital in up state New York for a while. "Nancy Rose is very sick and her mama and daddy are taking her there so she can get better. Oh! There are some things in the box and bags for you and your sister. Mrs. Tompkins gave them to you. She said to tell you, 'they are pretty things for pretty girls.' Grandma put the box and bag in the room where we slept. She was very quiet the rest of the night. Sugar Pudding was too tired to look in the box and bags with me. She fell asleep as soon as we sat on the bed. I carefully opened the box, not knowing what to expect. There was soft white paper lying on top of the clothes. As I moved the paper, what I saw surprised me! There were dresses, sweaters, and slips, socks trimmed with pink and white lace. Ribbons of every color in the rainbow and two small yellow pillows trimmed in white lace and embroidered with the words, "Sweet angels lay their heads on high" lay at the bottom of the bag, on top of a pink-checkered blanket. I was crying and did not know why, but I continued to empty the bags with the handles. Inside of another bag were several pairs of shoes made of shiny black leather and two other bags, which I found out later, were school bags Nancy Rose used to carry her books. I laid down on the clothes and the bags and fell asleep.

    For a while, Sugar Pudding and I were dressed like most of the kids that we went to school with. The clothes Mrs. Tompkins gave us were prettier then anything grandma gave us. I talked to sugar almost everyday, asking her to please be careful, and do not get her dresses dirty. Grandma made us wear the dresses over two or three times, before she would wash them again. Even though the dresses were nice, we often wore them wrinkled as well.

    I shared a few of my ribbons with Anna. These days nothing seemed to cheer her up. Grandma still went to work for the Tompkins and the Reynolds. Every once and awhile someone would give her a piece of furniture or some curtains. The house didn't look too bad, but it was still cold and ugly. Maybe if someone moved the old rusty milk truck, busted up car tires and junk out of the back and front yard, it wouldn't look so awful. There was also, what was left of an old 'out house' as grandma called it, sitting in the back yard, and the roof had fell in one summer during a bad storm. She said the county came through one year to install some plumbing, which is when the bathroom was built in the back of the old house by the county. But, the toilet never did work right. Somehow, the county workers could not get the water running in the bathtub, sink or toilet. Grandma said she was so tired of dumping the slop bucket every morning and every night. She was afraid something…an animal or snake would attack her going into that old out house and dumping the bucket at night.

Every once and a while, beggars begging for something to eat or a drink of water would try to fix the water as payment, just trying to be of help. However, grandma complained they did not know what they were doing. She explained ol' Willie told her if she cleaned for the Reynolds; he would fix up the toilet so she could use it.

Stories about the Reynolds were all over Tapasalle County. The Reynolds did not like colored people, and everyone that worked for them left after a few months. Grandma went to work for the Reynolds and so far, she has worked there the longest. The toilet still sits in the back of the house as a fixture, and grandma and I take turns dumping the slop bucket in the evening. We beat the ground and bushes with sticks and holler out, just incase a fox or a snake is hiding in the old out house.

Late one evening grandma was standing on the porch looking up in the sky. She mumbled something about it looks like we gonna get some rain. Suddenly we saw two bright headlights pull up in front of the house. I recognized the car as Mr. Tompkins. He quickly got out and ran up to the porch just barely missing the hole where a step was missing. Out of breath he said, "Evening Ms. Emma, girls!

Ms. Emma I got sort of an emergency. Mrs. Tompkins is not feeling well and want you to come to the house and help out for a while. Jenna, our maid is back, but she can't cook, clean house, and look after Mrs. Tompkins too," he explained, never stopping to catch his breath.

"Mr. Tompkins I'm so sorry for your wife, but I have no way of getting to your house every morning," grandma said sadly. "No, Ms. Emma you don't understand. Mrs. Tompkins wants you to stay for awhile, a few weeks at the most!" He pleaded, holding his hands out in front of him. "Who gonna look after my girls?" Mr. Tompkins. "They can come too, Ms. Emma. We have extra rooms! Please, go get what you all need and I will wait in the car." Grandma didn't have to ask Sugar Pudding and me to get our things. We were excited and ready to go with the nice white man. We packed quickly, and grandma checked the locks on the doors. Sugar and I got into the large black car, we leaned back to smell the leather upholstery. Grandma sat up in the front seat with Mr. Tompkins staring out the car window.

The drive was nice, but Sugar and I did not see the pretty houses this time, because it was dark, and all we could see were other headlights and nothing but black darkness. When we arrived at Mr. Tompkins house, a colored woman met us at the door and introduced herself as Jenna. She took Sugar and I upstairs and put us in a room on the second floor. Grandma stayed downstairs. The room is beautifully decorated, with white wallpaper, with tiny little yellow flowers painted on it, and yellow curtains at the windows. The furniture is white with yellow lace scarves on each dresser. The mirrors were so tall; I could see my body from head to toe. Standing bottles of perfume and two sets of combs and brushes for the hair lay on the dresser. A rocking chair sat next to one of the windows, in it sat a very big doll with a red dress and yellow yarn for hair.

It seems like all the walls had pictures of white people mostly of old women with umbrellas, and long dresses. Sugar Pudding couldn't believe her eyes. She walked around and touched everything ever so gently as if it would break or better yet…disappear. When she had finished looking around the room, she walked over and grabbed me by the arm. I looked at her face and those big brown eyes were getting ready to tear. I know everything was a little strange to her. We have move around so much, but never in such a beautiful house as the Tompkins.

I sat down on the bed next to Sugar Pudding, and gave her a hug and told her not to worry. "We will have fun playing with Nancy Rose's toys, reading her books and playing with her dolls. Maybe…just maybe…her mama will play the piano for us," I said, trying to make her feel more comfortable. She gave me that smile, and I knew she would be okay.

Grandma stayed down stairs in a room next to Mrs. Tompkins. Evidently, her room was just as nice as ours was because she had been in the room for an hour and when she came out… and for the first time since we came to live with grandma, she had fixed her hair differently. She did not have much to work with, but she managed to brush it back. Grandma was wearing brand new brown combs, one on each side of her head, holding her hair in place. She looked very nice in her gray and white uniform. Grandma said the white shoes hurt her feet, but she wore them anyway. Jenna, told grandma she had to wear the shoes during the day. I heard Jenna tell grandma the next day, "Mrs. Tompkins took ill, worrying about poor Nancy Rose. The doctors put Mrs. Tompkins on some medication and all she does is sleep."

Sugar and I did not miss a day from school. Mr. Tompkins took us every morning and Jenna picked us up in the Tompkins station wagon. For a while, Sugar and I enjoyed the attention we received from Jenna. Ever now and then, I would catch bits and pieces of her conversation with Mr. Tompkins. Mostly, it was about the color of our skin, or why are we living so poorly, and last but not the least, where is their mama? Mrs. Tompkins began to feel better and she did play the piano for us. We stayed for one month...that is when Nancy Rose came home. For the Tompkins, everything was back to normal, but for Sugar Pudding and me, it is back to the old house and silence.

Chapter 9

Trouble makes its move…

It was early May; Sugar Pudding is printing her name nicely and still coloring her pictures. We never celebrated Sugar Pudding's birthday and mine was in April. Even though we were staying at the Tompkins all of April, I never said anything about my birthday or grandma's birthday.

I had turned twelve years old. I was developing quite fast, and my breasts were trying hard to catch up. I was wearing bras grandma had got for me, hand me downs. Some were too big and others were too small, but I made do with what I had. Sometimes in class, I notice Mr. Jenkins staring at me. He made me feel very uncomfortable. I avoided him as much as possible. I missed Anna in class, and felt guilty because I hardly thought about her while we were living at the Tompkins's house. I knew she had missed quiet a few weeks from school, and she was behind in her schoolwork. Anna was smart and got mostly all A's. However, she could not pass to the next grade unless she caught up with the rest of us.

I really didn't want to bother Mr. Jenkins, but later that afternoon when school let out, I walked up to his desk and asked if he would give me some schoolwork for Anna. "That's very sweet of you Myrtle," he said in a rush. "I will drop some work off to her on my way home this afternoon," he answered. I watched as he quickly stuffed school papers into what looked like a small suitcase, and he started for the door. "Mr. Jenkins," I called quickly running up to him. "Where does Anna live? I would like to visit her." "I am…I'm not sure," he stuttered and looked away. "I will have to check in the office." Somehow, I knew he was lying. I forgot about it until it was time to go home. I picked up Sugar Pudding and started walking out the front entrance of the school. I was half way out of the yard when Aaron the ugly boy stopped me. "Can I walk with you and your sister?" He asked. "No Aaron, we are going over to see Anna," I said quickly. "Well you are going the wrong way," he said pointed down the street. "Okay, if I let you walk with us as far as Anna's house, will you leave us alone?" "I was just trying to be friends' wit ya," he said picking at his nose and rubbing the buggers on his shirt.

    We walked as if we were going to my house, however, Aaron turned down a dirt and gravel road. As we continued to walk, we came upon this gray house sitting behind a large fence made of wooden poles and chicken wire. An old rusty wire gate was attached to it and a dog was running around in the yard dragging what looked like an old rag in his mouth. Ever so often, he would shake it, drop it to the ground and pick it up again. When he saw us at the gate, he stopped playing with the towel and started barking at us. I didn't like the way he was barking, so I told Aaron, "Lets go! Let's go now!" I grabbed Sugar's hand. Before we could get a head start running, a boy, a little older and taller then me, and wearing glasses, came running up to the fence.

    "Wait a minute! Are you looking for Anna?" He yelled. "Yes, I'm Myrtle and this is my sister Sugar…" He interrupted me, and he finished it. "It's 'Pudding,' yeah, I know," he laughed. "Anna told me about the only two white girls going to Appleton County Elementary school," he said smiling. "We are not white, I said angrily. I am tired of people saying we are white!" "Hey! I ain't meant no harm. Did you come to see Anna?" "Yes, is she home?" I asked the boy. "Yes, she home, but she won't talk to no one, not even me, and I'm her brother. My name is Jonathan. Who's the boy in the back of you," he asked frowning up his face and pointing to Aaron. "Oh, that's Aaron, he's in our classroom. He showed me the way here. I didn't know where Anna Lived. I asked Mr. Jenkins our teacher, but he said he had to check in the office." "Is Anna sick Jonathan?" Sugar Pudding asked. "No, I don't think so, but our mama is going to take her to the doctor tomorrow. All of us are going except our father. He works in the mines, so we see him about once a month." "Would you tell Anna we came by? We have to go now. It's getting late, and sugar Pudding and I have a long ways to walk." "I know where you live. Wait let me get my keys and lock the door. I'll walk you part the way there, okay!" Jonathan yelled, "Get back!" at the dog as he opened the gate. Jonathan was very nice, and didn't ask too many questions. He did not look like Anna. He was sort of cute, especially when he took off his glasses. He talked about the high school he went to, and he talked about wanting to join the Air Force when he finishes school and fly planes. He walked and talked to Sugar and I as if he had known us for a long time. "Thanks for coming to see Anna," he said sadly. "I hope the doctor can help her. I will tell her you came by." Jonathan wave bye to us, and started walking slowly back down the road, the way we had came.

When we got home, we found grandma in the kitchen with her head lying across her arms. I knew something was wrong right away, most of the freshly iron tablecloths were all scattered about the floor. I was frightened. I had never seen her like this. I shook her arm, no response. Grandma was too heavy for me, and Sugar Pudding to move. We left her where she was sitting, and ran out the house to go get Ms. Ruth. I remembered where Ms. Ruth lived, but it was getting dark and I had never walked the road at night.

Half walking and running, we finally got there. I ran up to the door and knocked as hard as I could. "Ms. Ruth! Ms. Ruth! It's Myrtle and Sugar Pudding!" Mr. Leon answered the door, scratching and fumbling with the front of his clothes. "What y'all doing here, this time of night?" He sounded like he was mad! "Grandma is sick, we can't wake her up! Where's Ms. Ruth?" "She ain't here yet, she working at Mr. Raye's. Come on in, let me get on some clothes, and we will go back to see what wrong with Ms. Emma." Sugar and I watched Mr. Leon as he walked quickly back to the kitchen. Ms. Ruth had a telephone and Sugar and I could hear Mr. Leon dialing the telephone, and finally hearing him telling someone to hurry up and get here quick! Sugar Pudding and I stood by the front door and waited for Mr. Leon to get some clothes on.

A few minutes later, we heard a familiar sound, ol' Willie's truck. He came running in the house looking all around and calling out, "Where's Mr. Leon?" "We are waiting for him to get his clothes on," I answered a little afraid of ol' Willie. "Y'all go get in the truck, in the back you here! Wait there!" He hollered. It seemed like fifteen or twenty minutes before they came out. Mr. Leon smelled like he had been drinking and ol' Willie was wiping sweat from his forehead. When we pulled up in the yard, ol' Willie jumped out first. We left the door unlock, so he ran in, calling grandma. "Ms. Emma, Ms. Emma!" there was no answer. Ol' Willie ran over to the table where grandma was sitting, her head still laying across her arms. "Come on Mr. Leon help me get her in the truck," ol' Willie called out to Mr. Leon. Grandma did not look too good. I thought she had died. We got back in the truck and ol' Willie took her to a Hospital. As we walked through the hospital door, everyone stopped and looked at us! Ol' Willie spoke first. "Ms. Emma is not well, and she needs to see a doctor." An old gray haired white nurse told ol' Willie to lay her on the table in the next room, and told Sugar Pudding and I to have a seat in the hall. I remember when Macy hit me in the head with that rock and Ms. Peters brought me to a hospital. The hospital had a terrible smell and made my eyes water.

It was daybreak, before we found out what had happened to grandma. Ol' Willie and Mr. Leon had gone back to the truck to take a nap when the doctor came out. He asked who was with Ms. Emma. I told him we were her granddaughters, Myrtle and Sugar Pudding. The doctor smiled and asked, "Where's the man who brought you here honey?" "Oh, he's in the truck, "I answered. The doctor sent someone to get ol' Willie, and he came back in smelling like stale cigarette smoke and liquor. "Yes sir doctor," he stepped forward pulling up his pants up by the waist, "What's wrong with Ms. Emma?" "From what we could tell, she had a fainting spell sir. She said she felt sleepy and laid her head down to take a nap. I gave her some medicine for the spells, but she needs a few days rest, okay," the doctor answered cheerfully. "Yeah, okay." Ol' Willie sounded disappointed that grandma was going to be all right.

    The next few days we stayed home from school taking care of grandma. She did not seem to be getting any better. Ms. Ruth and Mr. Leon took her back to the hospital. We sat out in the hall like last time. Finally the doctor came out and said grandma had to stay awhile, she was very sick. Ms. Ruth looked like she had been crying and Mr. Leon just stood there. Ms. Ruth walked over to where Sugar Pudding and I were sitting, her large body standing over us like a dark shadow, her hands on her hips, and balancing a cigarette between her large lips said, "You girls will have to stay with Mr. Leon and me. You can't stay in the house by yourselves and I can't come over everyday to check on you. I have a small room in the back, you two can share it until Ms. Emma gets better, understand?" Just like that! Sugar and me were moving in with strangers again.

    We were always packing or unpacking, living with people we hardly knew, and never really staying anywhere for a long time. I packed as much as I could get in our book bags and shoved everything else into whatever bag I could find. I went into grandma's room to get the old car mirror off her dresser. Her dresser drawers were open and it looked like she was looking for something before she got sick. Clothes were all over the dresser, and some were on the floor. I picked up the clothes from off the floor and started putting them back in the drawers. One drawer was stuck, so I pulled it out to see why it would not slide in, and there was this large brown envelope sticking in the back of the drawer. I reached for the envelope and read the front of it. Why this is the same package, I signed for more than a year ago. I took the envelope and put it inside my bag. I closed grandma's door to her bedroom and went in the front room. Ms. Ruth and Mr. Leon helped us put our things in the back of ol' Willie's truck.

I really did not like Ms. Ruth or Mr. Leon, but we had no choice but to go with them. I was really scared and worried. How would Sugar and I make it?

Sugar and I stood on the steps of Ms. Ruth's house, waiting for her to tell us when to come in. Mr. Leon saw us standing there. "Why are y'all standing there in the cold? Anything wrong?" he asked. I answered, "No, but the last time we came here Ms. Ruth did not want us to come in the front room. She said she did not want her floors dirty." "No, now it ain't gonna be like that! Come on in girls. This here is my house too. Don't be afraid to walk in here, understand now!" he said holding the screen door open for us to walk in. "If it's all right Mr. Leon, we don't want anyone mad at us," I said. "Well, we ain't mad with you; sit down until Ms. Ruth gets the room ready." Mr. Leon smile at Sugar and I and pointed to the couches. We walked over and sat down on the one closer to the door. Sugar Pudding was sitting under me like a second set of clothing. Those big brown eyes looking cautiously around and ready to fill to the brim with tears.

We sat for what seem like hours. Sugar Pudding went to sleep with her head in my lap. I leaned my head back and just as I closed my eyes, I heard this loud gravely voice, "Aw, Hell No! Y'all girls get your prissy little half–

white asses up and help clean this place up!" That was Ms. Ruth! We jumped up off the couch, but before we could move another inch, Mr. Leon came in the room, and asked what was all the hollering about! "Why you yelling at them girls? Go on back and clean that room so they will have somewhere to sleep and stay outa your way!" I wasn't sure if he was helping us or making things worse. The look that old woman gave me and Sugar was enough to melt snow and start a fire, and that let us know, we are going to have some rough times staying here.

For a while, we did not have a problem with Ms. Ruth as long as Mr. Leon was around. It took awhile for us to settle in. Mr. Leon taught us another way to walk to school. We had missed a few days, but we managed to catch up before school closed for the summer. We stayed out of Ms. Ruth's way like Mr. Leon said. We helped around the house, mostly dusting and mopping the floors that stayed dirty all the time. Ms. Ruth did everything else including washing our clothes.

One day shortly after school had let out, we walked outside to go to Ms. Ruth's and there she was standing in front of an old black car waiting for us, grinning from ear to ear. My first thought was grandma was coming home; she had been gone for three weeks. I realized right then and there…we were much better off with grandma. Ms. Ruth ran over to us…pulling us close to her waist, her large breast poking us in the face. She pulled a hairbrush out of her bag and began brushing our hair. "Why are you brushing our hair Ms. Ruth?" "Just be still. Y'all going with me and I will do the talking! Don't y'all say nothing you hear!" she warned.

From the look on her face and she was acting very nervous, I knew this was something very bad or something I was not going to like. Sugar Pudding clung to my arm. Ms. Ruth walked us to the dusty old black car and opened the door for us to get in the back seat. We did what we were told. She slammed the door shut and climbed into the front seat of the car. Ms. Ruth sat up front with this strange man talking about Sugar and I staying with her and she was our closest relative, and our grandma is in the hospital, and she did not know when she would be home. The strange man just drove and listened to her. He never opened his mouth, just kept his eyes on the road.

We finally came to this gray building with a sign that read, Tapsalle County Court House, with very long steps that led up to the front entrance. We walked in, and a slightly bald-headed white man dressed in a wrinkled brown suit that looked too small for him, asked if he could help us. Ms. Ruth squeezed her large lips together and gritted through her teeth, "Remember don't say nothing, I will do the talking!" she turned around and looked the white man straight in the face, "Why yes, yes you can help me. I am Ms. Ruth Macklin and I am here to see someone about getting custody of my two nieces," she answered trying to sound important. "Walk down the hall to Court room 1D and tell the clerk the same thing you told me, understand?" He sort-of gave Ms. Ruth a strange look, turned and walked back the other way.

Ms. Ruth walked down the hall and turned into the courtroom. She looked around until she saw the clerk. Dragging Sugar and me by the arms, she walked over to him and told him why she was there. After a few minutes, we heard her name called. "Ms. Ruth Macklin, please stand. You are here today to file for custody of Myrtle Jackson and Sugar Pudding Jackson is that correct?" asked the court judge. "Yes Sir, that's correct," she answered cutting her eyes at me. "Ms. Ruth Macklin, how long have the two girls been living in your home?" he asked staring at Sugar and me. "They have been in my home for three months sir, since their grandma got sick," she answered nicely." Why that lying hateful ass woman, I thought to myself! What is going on here? I held onto Sugar Pudding's hand, and listened to the lies Ms. Ruth was telling the judge.

"Do you receive any money for their support?" the judge continued. "No Sir," she answered. "How much would you say you have contributed to their keep?" "At least $75.00 dollars Sir," she answered chewing awkwardly on her bottom lip. "As of today I can award you temporary custody of the girls for sixty days. In the mean time you must verify that their grandma is hospitalized and can no longer take care of them, that you are the next of kin, and of course a letter from three people including the grandmother stating they were abandoned by their biological mama," the judge said.

"Mr. Sheldon, the court clerk must witnessed and sighed the letters. That's the gentleman standing over there," he said pointing to the tall thin white man standing over by the door. "Upon you producing those papers, the court can see fit to award you full custodial care for as long as the grandma remains incapacitated. If and only upon the grandmother passing, the custodial care will be changed to permanent custody. In the mean time, you will receive $25.00 a month for the girls. If at anytime the grandmother's health improves and she returns to her home, the custodial care award will cease and desist immediately. The courts will maintain and monitor the grandmother's condition as well. Ms. Macklin, do you have any questions?" he looked at her over the rim of his glasses.

"Yes sir, I have one question. What if the grandmother cannot read or write?" "That's easy enough; you must get a letter from the doctor stating the same, or have the grandmother state this fact in your presence and that of a witness." From the look on Ms. Ruth face, she did not like the answer the judge gave her. "If there is nothing else, Ms. Macklin you may leave." "Thank you sir," she said as the judge handed her the papers, and she placed them in her purse.

We got back in the car and we went back to Ms. Ruth's house. Ms. Ruth did not look at Sugar Pudding or me. She was very quiet. I was quiet. I refused to talk to the lying bitch! Why, she is no kin to us. Why did she tell that man all those lies? Before we got out of the car, she warned me, and Sugar Pudding not to tell anyone where we had been today.

Chapter 10
The awakening ...

"How long you think Ms. Emma's going to be in that hospital ol' Willie?" asked Mr. Leon. "Awww, I don't know Mr. Leon, maybe another month or two. The doctors said She's doing fine right now," answered ol' Willie. "I'm glad to hear she is okay. The girls went to see her twice. They could only stay a few minutes because they is under age. The nurse took Ms. Emma down for a walk and she saw the girls in the sitting room," commented Mr. Leon.

"You know ol' Willie; we can keep the girls as long as we have to! Hell, they ain't no trouble. You hardly knows they is in the house. Tell that to Ms. Emma, the next time you see her okay. I don't want her worrying about the girls. Hell, school be out soon and they can be a lot of help to Ms. Ruth down at the club. I know they is kinda young, but they can help wipe off the tables and wash the dishes.

Ms. Ruth sort of, runs the club now that old Mr. Raye is out with a stroke," said Mr. Leon as he watched ol' Willie dump his cigarette ashes on the freshly swept floor. "I really don't think that is a good idea Mr. Leon, you know them girls working in that place, around a lot of men and women drinking, smoking, and doing things they ought not to be around and seeing...Mr. Leon," ol' Willie commented, still dumping his cigarette ashes on the floor. "Ol' Willie... Mr. Leon paused for a second. "Well I don't think the girls can come to any harm, but they can stay at the house with me until Ms. Ruth comes home," he agreed with ol' Willie. "Evening ol' Willie, Mr. Leon!" Ms. Ruth called from the doorway. "I'll fix something for us to eat as soon as I get settled. Girls go on in your room. I want to talk to ol' Willie and Mr. Leon, and "Little pitchers got big ears!" "Ol' Willie you seen Ms. Emma?" "Yes, I was just telling Mr. Leon here, she doing fine, but don't know when she'll be coming home.

How are the girls acting without their grandma?" asked ol' Willie. "Oh, they don't be no trouble; they can stay as long as they have to. I was thinking earlier today, they can help me around the house and sometimes in Mr. John Raye's club, down in Leesville." She was trying to sound as if everything is all right. "I don't think it's a good thing Ms. Ruth. The girls are too young to be around a lot of drinking and smoking. Ain't that right, ol' Willie?" Mr. Leon looked over at ol' Willie and winked his eye. "I'll keep an eye on them!" Ms. Ruth snapped at Mr. Leon, flashing her eyes sharply at him, letting him know she don't appreciate him siding with ol' Willie. "No, Mr. Leon is right Ms. Ruth, the girls shouldn't be there."

Angry that ol' Willie had sided with Mr. Leon; she left the room in a hurry. "I'll talk to you later Mr. Leon. Take care of them girls!" ol' Willie called out as he walked out the door and down the steps.

Ms. Ruth waited until after dinner and everyone had gone to bed. She stared at the large white envelope with all those papers in it. She read the one she signed stating she is the girl's next of kin. "I've got to figure out away to get Ms. Emma's signature without telling her what these papers is for, she thought to herself. I can use that extra money the county will give me. Ms. Ruth was deep in thought, when she heard her name called. "Ms. Ruth!" "What you want Myrtle, I thought you was sleep," she said rather agitated. "Can I ask you a question Ms. Ruth?" "Yes, what is it, she yelled through her door?" "Will you be picking up Sugar Pudding and me again…tomorrow?" "No, walk home with your friends, I'll be at work," she yelled back in a nasty tone of voice. Myrtle was glad because she did not like Ms. Ruth and she wanted to stop by Anna's after school. Maybe this time, she thought she might even see Anna.

The next morning Sugar Pudding and Myrtle was ready when Mr. Leon called them to get ready for school. "Good Morning Mr. Leon, I didn't wait for Ms. Ruth to fix our breakfast. I gave Sugar Pudding a bowl of corn flakes and milk, and made two sandwiches for our lunch." Mr. Leon looked in our bags and dropped an apple in each one. Mr. Leon wasn't too bad after all. He keeps us out of Ms. Ruth's way and he doesn't mind walking us part of the way to school some mornings, and sometimes he packs us a nice lunch. Well, at least we can eat everyday and the food is good.

I grabbed Sugar Pudding by the hand and walked as fast as our legs would carry us to the school. I did not want to be late, and hoped that I might run into Anna. I walked in the classroom. Anna was not there. I really didn't expect to see Anna after her brother told me last week, she was sick and would not talk to anyone. However, it would have been nice to see her sitting at her desk next to me. Well, she will talk to me this afternoon. I will make her talk to me and tell me what's wrong.

The day went by very slowly. Mr. Jenkins gave us a lot of work to do. He was running in and out of the classroom with Ms. Peters. They acted as if something was wrong. Mr. Jenkins kept wiping drops of perspiration from his forehead and Ms. Peters was dropping everything in her arms on the floor. They bumped into one another trying to pick up the many papers and folders that had fallen to the floor. Mr. Jenkins left that morning very early and Ms. Peters taught the class.

We didn't have any homework and before I left, I asked Ms. Peters for some schoolwork for Anna. Ms. Peters looked at me strangely when I said Anna's name. She hurriedly gave me some papers and placed them in a brown folder. "Myrtle please say hello for me. I miss Anna. Sometimes she would help with the first graders during recess. Oh, give her this too. It's a book of poems, I thought she might like, and I have one for you too! Run along now, it's getting late." Ms. Peters turned away quickly. When I looked at her face, she had tears in her eyes. Maybe someone died in her family or she had received some very bad news.

I picked up Sugar Pudding and we started out to Anna's house. As I got closer to her house, I started to feel a little a chill. I held onto Sugar's hand and walked up to the gate. Jonathan was standing on the porch, and waved at me to come in. "Where is that mean old dog, Jonathan? How's Anna? Can I see her today?" "Yeah, but you got to make it quick! My mama is not here right now and I am not supposed to let anyone in, okay. Go inside, walk up the nearest steps and turn right. The dog had puppies and is in the shed out back." "Thanks Jonathan! Can Sugar Pudding stay down here with you?" "Sure, it's fine. I'll show Sugar Pudding the new puppies!"

I ran up the steps as fast as I could. I wanted to see Anna. I miss her a lot. She is the only friend I have. I walked up to the door and knock softly. When I did not hear 'come in,' I pushed the door open slowly. There was Anna standing by the window. "Hi Anna, can I come in?" Anna turned around and looked at me. Her eyes are swollen; almost shut and her hair was very nappy, and had not been washed and combed in days. I walked over to the dresser and reached for her brush and comb. There was a small chair beside the window. I asked Anna to sit down in the chair so I could comb her hair. Surprisingly she did. Silence. I tried to brush her hair and make a ponytail. It took awhile because she had so many knots and tangles. "Am I hurting your head Anna?" I asked. She did not answer, just silence in the room.

"Anna please, talk to me. Why are you so quiet? What did I do?" I turned and looked her straight in the face. "If I tell you something, you got to promise me you won't tell, even if I die," Anna said weakly. "I promise Anna, but you aren't going to die." "You remember the afternoon, Mr. Jenkins asked you stay a few minutes after school?" she asked. "Why yes...I guess I remember Anna. Anna, did something happen to you while you were waiting for me? Did the other kids bother you? I know it was Macy. That mean old nasty girl…wasn't it?" "No, the kids didn't bother me Myrtle. It did not happen that day, it happened the day before." "Before? What happened Anna?" I asked getting somewhat anxious and curious as to what she has to tell me. "I was helping Ms. Peters stack some books in the supply closet in the basement of the school. I thought Ms Peters was still in the basement across the hall in the book room. I was waiting for her to bring more books to put on the shelf. I heard footsteps and sounds I thought belong to her." Anna became quiet again, swallowing real hard, like something was stuck in her throat. Her eyes were closed and tears were running down her cheeks. She was shaking her head from side to side. Her fingers were balled up in a tight fist. I was getting very scared. I did not want her to hit me! I didn't know what to do. I stopped brushing her hair and laid the brush down.

I asked myself, what in the world was she trying to tell me. "Anna, it's all right," I said, as I patted her hair in place. "You don't have to talk about it if it makes you feel bad." "No, she answered slowly, I'm all right. I got to tell you Myrtle, you are the only friend I have. I can't ever go back to that school again," she said in a frightened voice. "Who was in the basement Anna? Anna were you locked in the basement? Did Ms. Peters leave you by yourself?" I asked, anxious to know what in the world had happened to her to make her so sad. What is the reason she could not return to school. Nothing but silence…

After a long pause, Anna spoke barely beyond a whisper. "I heard the door close, and when I looked around it was Mr. Jenkins." Her voice dropped so low, I could hardly hear her. "Mr. Jenkins," I repeated. Silence. "He came over to me and asked what I was doing in the basement. I told him I was helping Ms. Peters stack some books. Myrtle he came over to me, and grab my hand, he pulled me down on his lap. I was scared and told him I had to leave, I had to go home. He told me to be quiet and just sit still. He put his hands under my dress and started rubbing the inside of my legs. Myrtle he started pulling my underwear down and I was struggling to make him stop. I started crying and he put his hand over my mouth and told me if I did not make any noise, he would by me a bracelet. He pulled my underwear all the way down to my ankles and when I wouldn't stop struggling and crying he took off his tie and tied it around my mouth…" I could not take my eyes off Anna. She was crying and breathing heavy. "Myrtle he told me this was our little secret and I had better not tell anyone not even you Myrtle. She paused again, and began rocking back and forth in the chair. Her head was hanging down. Anna wouldn't look at me as she described what Mr. Jenkins did to her.

This was very hard for her. I found myself crying for her and how badly she must have felt. She cupped her hands to her face spoke into them… "Myrtle he unzipped his pants and pulled out his …silence… and made me touch it and hold it in my hand. He smelled bad and he had sweat all over his face. He parted my legs and stuck his hands up in me. I started to get sick to my stomach. Mr. Jenkins pushed me down on that cold cement floor and got on top of me. Myrtle he tried to stick his thing in me. I tried to crawl from under him…trying to back away from him…I must have passed out… because the next thing I knew he was standing over me. His pants were wet and blood was on my legs and the floor. I crawled to a corner of the basement to get away from him. He threw some paper towels at me and told me to clean myself up and get the hell out of there. He said he would kill me Myrtle if I told anyone." I watched Anna rock back and forth, holding her face in her hands. I was crying with Anna. I felt so sorry for her.

We sit together in silence for what seemed like a long time. I didn't want to think about what she had told me. I just remembered when Mr. Jenkins asked me to stay after school one afternoon and that's when he gave me that bracelet. This awful thing could have happened to me…I was frightened and afraid to go back to school. I was so caught up in what Anna told me, I forgot Jonathan said I could only stay a few minutes. I don't care; I can't leave Anna like this. "Did you tell your mama Anna?" "No, when I got home she thought I had started my period. The next day she told me I had to go to school because she had a doctor's appointment and there was no one to stay home with me." "So, that is why you did not want to sit next to me and talk to me, I asked?" "Myrtle that same afternoon, you remember Mr. Jenkins asked you to stay for a few minutes. I was afraid he was going to do the same thing to you, so I slipped into the next room and watched him from a crack in the window. I saw him give you the little box with the bracelet in it. I was scared he was going to do to you what he did to me. I ran out of the room and went home. When you came to school the next day, I knew you were all right. I couldn't come back and sit in that room. He hated me and I hated him for what he did to me," she said and started crying all over again.

"When are you going to tell your mama Anna? You can't keep this from her and your daddy." I said quietly, afraid someone may over hear us talking. "Mama already knows Myrtle," she said in a whisper. "She found out when she took me the doctors. I couldn't eat and was not sleeping at night. The doctors after examining me, told mama I had been raped and asked her if she knew who did it. Mama started crying and told the doctor she is afraid to tell daddy because he will kill Mr. Jenkins, and she did not want my daddy to go to jail. This morning, two white police officers with guns came here today looking for my daddy, and mama told them he was away in the mines. They took my mama with them. She has been gone a long time Myrtle. I am glad I told you, but you got to be careful Myrtle. Mr. Jenkins is a bad man. You better go now; I don't want mama to catch you here. She don't want any body coming to the house," she said as she wiped her face with the corner of the bedspread. "Myrtle… am I still your friend?" she asked trying not to cry. "Yes, Anna, you are still my friend, my only friend."

I left the house before Anna's mama came back. I did not know what to think or do. I know I had to stay away from Mr. Jenkins. If he comes anywhere near me, I'll tell Mr. Leon or ol' Willie.

When we got home Ms. Ruth had rearrange the furniture, fix dinner and had baked a cake. It had been awhile since Sugar Pudding and I had a piece of cake. The mean old bitch was smiling when we walked in the kitchen. "Hi girls, y'all had a good day? Look some people is coming to the house later this evening. They want to see how we live and they may want to talk to you and Sugar Pudding. If they ask you who Mr. Leon is, you tell them he is your uncle, you here. Don't call me Ms. Ruth! Call me 'Aunt Ruth' and Mr. Leon, 'Uncle Leon.' We is a family," she said through clench jaws and anger in her eyes.

I knew better than to ask why. I did not want this mean old lying woman to yell at Sugar Pudding and me. I answered; "Yes Aunt Ruth" and I told Sugar Pudding to say the same thing. She did and we went to our room to listen to the radio. At least we could hear some nice music.

Later that evening two white men came to Ms. Ruth's house. We could hear voices and an occasional cough could be heard. I have no idea how long they stayed because Aunt Ruth never called us to come out the room. Sugar and I went to sleep.

Chapter 11

The beginning of the end...

When I arrived to school the following morning, Ms. Peters was sitting at Mr. Jenkins desk. She told us he would not be back and that she will teach the class until school closes for summer vacation. I was relieved Mr. Jenkins was gone and never coming back. I hope they put him in jail for the rest of his life. Anna will never be all right again. I lost my one and only friend.

Summer came. Sugar Pudding is printing her name, writing sentences and counting numbers, and still coloring her pictures. We did not celebrate Sugar Pudding's birthday and mine was in April like grandma's. It came and went. I was Twelve years old and going to the sixth grade and Sugar Pudding was in the first grade.

We had been living with Aunt Ruth and Uncle Leon for three months. Ever so often, we would hear some good news about grandma, but never any news about when she was coming home. Uncle Leon was still keeping us out of the way of Aunt Ruth. He also avoided her as much as possible.

Chapter 12
Going home...

"Okay, Mr. Clemmons Hayden, you are free to go," said the warden. "Look, don't let us catch you in here again! Who's picking you up this morning?" "My brother Willie, he should be here shortly. I can't wait to get out of this hellhole! I got a lot of work to do to my houses and I may even do some farming. You know my granny passed while I was in here. I know she left the land to me and my brother Willie cause we is all the kin she's got. You are so right Warden; you won't see me back in here ever again. I think I'm going to turn over a new leaf. I am going to be a changed person! Yes sir, you wait and see! No, by God! you won't see me ever again!" he ranted on. "Hey!" The warden called above Clemmons ranting and loud talking, "There's your brother! Gate one opening up!" the warden announced. "See ya!" he yelled as Clemmons walked out the large gate.

"Man, am I glad to see you," said Clemmons hugging his brother and slapping him on his back. Tell me everything! What happened since I been gone? You were keeping the houses up?" he asked playfully poking Willie in the stomach. "Yeah, Clemmons, we will talk about when we get home. Calm down now! We got to talk about something very important." "I don't really like the sound of your voice Willie," Clemmons said. All the excitement of seeing his brother had changed the tone of his voice. "We'll talk when we get home, okay," answered Willie.

"I see you still got this same old tired ass truck," Clemmons said changing the subject. "Hell I been gone damn near six years or more. Why didn't you buy a new one?" he asked. "Buy a new one with what? It takes money to buy a new truck Clemmons," Willie answered slightly agitated by Clemmons ranting on. "Yeah, well I got an idea to farm some of the land granny left us. What you think about that Willie?" Willie almost missed his turn and suddenly made a sharp right turn that brought the old truck to a sudden stop! "Watch it man, you trying to get us killed," Clemmons laughed nervously. "Okay, we are here," announced Willie. "Here? Where? What do you mean we are here? Come on Willie, stop playing around! This here is your house," said Clemmons the smile suddenly leaving his lips. "Take me to granny's house!" he ordered. "I have to talk to you first Clemmons… it's about the houses and the land! Come on in and sit down, you gonna need a drink," Willie said very seriously. "Willie, what happened? Just tell me what happened! It can't be all that bad," Clemmons said as he paced around in Willie's little kitchen. "Well, I am afraid it is bad, but we maybe able to do something about it. You see Clemmons, granny as you called her, did not leave the houses or the land to you or me," he said quickly wiping his forehead and the back of his neck with his handkerchief. "Go on Willie! What are you saying? There ain't nobody else she can leave them too! We are her only kin!" he yelled at Willie.

"I know Clemmons," Willie replied slowly. "But she did leave the land to some kin, some kin you and I had forgot about Clemmons," Willie continued reaching for two small glasses from the kitchen cabinet. "What the hell are you talking about Willie? You are confusing me! What kin are you talking about?" Clemmons questioned vehemently, waving his hands and arms in the air frantically! "Calm down Clemmons, I will tell you. Granny left the two houses and the land, to Rachel's two little girls, Myrtle and Sugar Pudding and named Rachel as the power of attorney." Silence, over powering silence surrounded them in the small kitchen. "What the fuck! Man, you are lying! A colored woman got my houses and my land!" he yelled. He stood up and threw the chair he was sitting in across the small room. "Why Willie? She hated Rachel! I don't understand! Granny paid Rachel to keep her mouth shut! What the hell happened while I was gone?"

"There's more Clemmons," Willie said nervously. "Rachel abandoned the two girls about two years ago. I found them sleep in that old colored bus station in Southend, a few miles from Tapsalle County. They had a note pinned to their clothes saying to take them to Ms. Emma's house. I took them to Ms. Emma's house," ol' Willie explained hanging his head down and stretching his arms across the table. His hand clinched in a fist. "Willie they were living in Southend when I went to Jail. I didn't write or nothing. I didn't want anything to do with them. How could I explain to my friends, I had kids by a nigger woman? We was ducking and hiding. I knew it didn't make sense. I told her after she got pregnant the second time…we were through. I would send her some money when I got some, but that's all! I was sending her a few hundred dollars monthly until I was arrested for deer hunting and involuntary manslaughter! Granny stop sending the money to Rachel because of what I did Willie!"

Clemmons was crying uncontrollably. "I didn't shoot our mother! Granny said she would get me a good lawyer if I promised not to see or speak about Rachel and the kids as long as she lived! I did what she asked Willie! Where is Rachel now?" asked Clemmons pacing the small kitchen floor. "We …I have not been able to find her Clemmons, we lost track of her." "Who's is goddamit 'we'?" asked Clemmons tossing off another drink. "Oh, I had a detective trying to find her after the will was read. However, no luck! I ran out of money Clemmons. I had a friend of mine in the courthouse look into some things for me. She said if we could not find Rachel, or if no one appears as the next of legal kin and says that the two girls are not related to you or me, we maybe able to go to court and petition the will," he tried to explain. "Well what is the problem Willie?" asked Clemmons. His jaws were clenched tightly, and his eyes slightly narrowed.

"Ms. Emma is Rachel's Aunt. Ms. Emma's sister Ilene is Rachel's mama, and they are still living. No one knows where Ilene is. Ms. Emma is in a nursing home, and Rachel is no where to be found!" Willie explained in a flashing display of outrage. "So we need proof that the two girls are not related to me? Is that what you are saying Willie?" Clemmons arms were flaying about as if he was about to take flight. "Well, yes in a way Clemmons! You see Ms. Emma don't know the girls is her nieces. She thinks I brought them to her because they needed a home, someplace safe to stay. She don't know all that was in the note. I never told her who wrote the note. Besides, she can't read anyway," said Willie, his voice sounding tired and exhausted. "Okay, we have a problem Willie! All we have to do is get Ms. Emma to say the girls are not any kin to her, she was just helping them out because they did not have no where to stay, and she don't know who their mama is." "It's not that easy Clemmons. I told you Ms. Emma can't write. You will need some one to witness everything she says," Willie explained all the while watching Clemmons expression on his face.

"I know we got to do something because we is running out of time. I sent some papers I had drawn up by a friend of mine in the courthouse. All the papers say is how the two girls were found and that in order to protect the girls and make sure they are well taken care of she has to confirm the girls are no kin to her. The county will send her a check each month to help with the girls expenses. She was served the papers about year and half ago. The oldest girl Myrtle signed for them. Here, I got the receipt from Mr. Reynolds," he said waving it in Clemmons' face. "Well, what are you waiting for Willie? What happened to the papers?" Clemmons asked impatiently. "Ms. Emma took sick; the papers I guess are still in the house," answered

Willie. "We got to get them papers now! I'll go to the house tonight and look over that whole damn place until I find them damn papers, and I will get someone to sign them and take them to the court house tomorrow morning!" said Clemmons gulping down another drink. "You can't do that Clemmons! That's breaking and entering! Ain't you tired of going to prison," warned Willie. "We can get the oldest girl to find the papers. It wouldn't look so bad. Right now, they are staying with Ms. Ruth over at her place in Tapasalle County. Let's move kinda slow, all right... We got a little time to get the papers. We don't want anyone to get suspicious, now do we," Willie smiled weakly at Clemmons.

Chapter 13

Getting the message straight...

"Myrtle! Sugar Pudding, come here a minute. Look, I've got to go in town to handle some business. Do what Uncle Leon says and don't dirty up the place while I'm gone. I'll be back in time to go to work tonight! Myrtle you are going to the club with me. I need you to help put the tablecloths on the tables before the customers come in. You hear me!" she yelled. "Aunt Ruth, Uncle Leon said I was too young to go in that place, and I don't want to go around no men drinking and smoking. I'll stay here with Uncle Leon and Sugar Pudding." "Who the hell do you think you are talking to?" She suddenly turned her large body around like a small tornado. Up went her hand to slap me, and down came another hand just as powerful and grabbed hers. It was Uncle Leon.

"There ain't gonna be no hitting. You ain't go lay a hand on these girls! Myrtle is right the club is nowhere for her to be! Now, where ever you is going, go on, leave the girls be!" he said and walked out of the room. Whew! Save by Uncle Leon again. I left out of the room as fast as my legs would carry me. Even though I knew, deep down, this was not over.

I went into our room and read a story to Sugar Pudding and she went to sleep. Ever since she saw the puppies over at Anna's, she wanted me to read anything to her that talked about puppies.

I stayed in my room all night until the next morning. I was a little afraid to go into the kitchen, but I went anyway. I was very hungry this morning, because I did not eat dinner last night. Uncle Leon was in the kitchen frying bacon when we walked in. "Mornin, I am glad y'all got up early. I have to go to the hardware store and get some nails. Y'all want to come with me. We got to walk a little ways though," he said while patting Sugar Pudding's head. "Can I get a picture of a puppy?" Sugar Pudding asked Uncle Leon. "A picture of a puppy? Where am I gonna find a picture of a puppy?" She shrugged her shoulders and laughed. I like to see Sugar laugh. She seldom did. There was just not too much to laugh about.

We had finished eating and were on our way out the door, when Aunt Ruth came running up the porch steps. "Where y'all going this early in the morning?" "We going to find a picture of a puppy Ms. Ruth," answered Sugar Pudding. "What did you call me!" she yelled at Sugar Pudding. "I said what did you call me?" She looked and sounded very angry. I spoke up, "Oh, she meant Aunt Ruth. She just forgot that's all," I tried to explain. Before I, or Uncle Leon could say or do anything, Aunt Ruth smacked Sugar across the mouth. The ring on her finger drew blood from Sugar's bottom lip. Before I knew it, I had jump the bitch and was beating the hell out of her! "You don't put your hands on my sister! You mean old Bitch!" I knew I was in trouble now! I called Ms. Ruth a "bitch," a word Anna had called Macy, when Macy was picking on her.

Thanks to Anna's bad word, I was really in trouble. I felt a big hand grab me by the waist and the other hand had Sugar Pudding. I was crying and my eyes were blurry. However, I saw Uncle Leon pick up my sister, and had us half way down the street, before I realize what had happened. He stopped for a minute and wiped Sugar Pudding's lip with his handkerchief and then he wiped my face. I was still crying and Sugar Pudding was just standing there looking at me. Uncle Leon said, "Now we gonna be all right! Let's keep walking." We finally reach the hardware store. I was feeling a little bit better…but it took me a few moments to figure out why all these people were staring at us? I looked at Sugar Pudding's lip. It was swollen, but not bleeding. Oh! I remember it's the color of our skin and long curly hair. I guess we looked like two little white girls walking with this tall dark skinned man. Uncle Leon paid for the nails and treated us to icy pops. We were walking down the street with red colored icy pops and a tall black skinned man. The stares were forgotten in our haste to drink the delicious tasting drink before it got warm.

We could have taken the bus, but Uncle Leon said no we could walk. Uncle Leon met a lot people he knew as we walked back to the house. He invited a man named Mr. Harvey to stop by sometimes.

I really did not want the walk to end. I hated that woman and that house. "Uncle Leon can Sugar and I just go to our room and stay?" "Yes, that will be okay. I need to talk to Ms. Ruth when we get inside. I'll bring you something to eat a little later okay." Uncle Leon walked us in the house and saw that we got to our room without any problems.

Later that afternoon, we could hear Aunt Ruth and Uncle Leon arguing. She was calling him all kinds of no good, bastards and sons-of-bitches for taking up for us. I heard her say to Mr. Leon, "those half-white colored girls think they is better then us!" He told her, "you are wrong Ms. Ruth and Ms. Emma would be sick at heart if she heard how you were treating them." Later that evening I heard the door slam, and shortly thereafter Mr. Leon knocked on our door and told us she was gone for the night. Sugar Pudding was tired and went to sleep.

I was sitting there hoping that grandma would get better and come get us. I was straitening up the room, and going through some things that I had not unpacked after we moved in with Ms. Ruth. I found a writing pad and decided to write grandma a letter. I wrote about where we went today and the picture of the puppy Uncle Leon found for Sugar Pudding. I did not tell her Aunt Ruth smacked Sugar Pudding in the mouth and made her lip bleed. I folded the letter and placed it in the book bag Nancy Rose's mama gave me. I remembered no sense in mailing it because grandma could not read. I lifted the bag to put it back in the closet when the strap came loose and the papers including the package I took from grandma's dresser fell out on the floor. I had forgotten about the package. With nothing else to do, I opened it. It was addressed to Emma Jackson from Tapsalle County Court House.

"Dear Ms. Jackson, It has come to our attention that you are taking care of two colored girls that were abandoned in the Southend bus station on November 1, 1955. The court needs to know how the girls came to live with you and whether or not you are or are not related to them. If you are not related you can file for social services, temporary custody and receive a supplement to help you financially. If you are related, explain how you are related to the children.

Please read the attached forms. Fill out the information and sign them. You can mail them or bring them back to the courthouse. If you need help with the forms, please come to the court house on Mondays and Thursdays between the hours of 9:00AM and 3:00PM."

I read the letter over again and looked at the forms. They were asking the same information that was on the school forms I filled out for grandma. Some how I knew these papers were important. I wanted Uncle Leon to see the papers. I came out of the room hoping that aunt Ruth was still at Mr. Raye's club. Uncle Leon was in the front room listening to the radio. I walked in slowly and whispered his name, "Uncle Leon, Uncle Leon." "Come in Myrtle, it's all right," he said half asleep. "Uncle Leon I have some papers to show you," I said. He jumped up off the couch and walked over to me. "Let me see what you have here." I handed him the papers and I stood back while he read them. The look on his face told me, he was getting very angry. As I started to leave the room, he said "Myrtle, don't leave, come here. Look, don't tell anyone about these papers. I will take care of them. Don't worry everything will be all right."

Somehow, I knew I had done the right thing. I answered, "Okay I won't tell anyone. Uncle Leon, I have something else to tell you. Aunt Ruth said not to tell you, but I have to tell you in order to save me and Sugar Pudding." "What do you mean to save you and Sugar Pudding?" he asked reaching out to touch my shoulder. "Aunt Ruth took us to that court house and signed some papers to take us." Before I could finish he asked, "When was this Myrtle?" "About a month ago," I answered. "She told us not to tell you. She also told us to say Aunt Ruth and Uncle Leon, when those white men came here to talk to her about us. I don't want to live with her. We want to go back to grandma," I begged. "I know Myrtle, but your grandma's still not well enough to come home. Don't worry; I won't let nothing happen to you and your sister." "Are we in trouble Uncle Leon?" "No, you are not in any trouble. I will take care of this, don't worry." I went back to my room, finished putting our things away and went in the kitchen to get something to eat. Uncle Leon had made some sandwiches for us and covered them with a dishtowel. I took them back to the room and woke up Sugar Pudding so she could eat. Her bottom lip had gone down, and she looked fine. I kissed her on the cheek and gave her a great big hug. We ate and went to sleep.

Chapter 14
A Piece of cake...

"You are here rather early, the nurse said to Ms. Ruth. Ms. Emma Jackson is still asleep. May I ask why you are here before visiting hours?" asked the short and frumpy white nurse with one pair of glasses on her face and another pair hanging from around her neck. "I have some papers for her to sign. They are kind of important," answered Ms. Ruth switching her weight from one foot to the other. The nurse pulled her glasses down and looked at Ms. Ruth. "You can see Ms. Jackson after 1:00 PM. I suggest you go home and come back later," she said dryly as she walked away from Ms. Ruth. The nurse stepped behind her counter and continued what she doing before Ms. Ruth walked in.

Ms. Ruth pretended to leave and doubled back when she saw the hall and counter was clear of the nurse. Ms. Ruth took the piece of paper out of her coat pocket and read the room number, 212B second floor east. Well, she thought I'll just have to walk up the steps. I can't take a chance being seen on an elevator. "Lady where are you going!" It was the same nurse, who had told her to go home. "I told you I had to see Ms. Jackson. What I have to do won't take no longer than five minutes nurse!" she snapped. The old white nurse was angry. "If you don't leave the premises immediately, I will call the police," she said waving Ms. Ruth toward the door. "Okay I'll leave, there's no need to call them!" Ms. Ruth left in a hurry.

"Good morning, Mr. Willie, this is Nurse Rita Hinton calling from the state nursing home. Yes, I'm fine and you sir? No, Ms. Jackson is fine. She had a visitor, a Ms. Ruth Macklin. You know her sir? Yes, I told her she had to leave. Visiting hours are not until 1:00 PM sir. Sir, you asked us to call if there were any changes in Ms. Jackson's condition... well there is sir. She seemed to be doing much better, and went for a walk with one of the colored caretakers this morning. She's napping at this moment. Yes sir I will, Have a nice morning sir." She smiled to herself as she hung up the receiver.

Chapter 15

The devil in motion...

Ol' Willie woke up Clemmons. "Come on get up. I got to go see Ms. Ruth. She went to the state nursing home early this morning to see Ms. Emma. I got to find out why. You check on the houses okay. I'll see you when I get back." "You sure you don't want me to come with you?" Clemmons asked. "Hell No! For what Clemmons, seeing your face now will cause some more problems. I don't think anyone aught to know you're back in town. From what the nurse said this morning, it don't look like Ms. Emma is gonna die anytime soon! Them damn lawyers and tax people ain't gonna wait too much longer. They need an answer soon, that highway ain't gonna wait for no one," he said disgustedly. "Okay, Willie, I'll just wait until you get back...by the way, you sure no one else knows about them girls being mine? What about the people they is staying with?" questioned Clemmons. "Well, I'm not sure, but I think Ms. Ruth knows about the girls, but she don't know where the mama is. What puzzles me is why she ain't told Ms. Emma! I know Ilene and her sister Ms. Emma ain't never got along. Ilene left home before she had Rachel. Ms. Emma ain't ever seen her since. Now, twenty some years later, these girls, her nieces, pop up on her doorstep. I'm pretty sure Ms. Emma don't know nothing about you seeing Ilene's daughter Rachel, But I can't be so sure what Ms. Ruth knows," said old Willie scratching the back of his head.

"Now, that Mr. Leon is another story! At one time Ms. Ruth was running a boarding house. Mr. Leon got out of prison found a job working on the Reynolds farm. He didn't get along too well with Mr. Reynolds and he quit. He does piece work sometimes. He's a good carpenter. He has been staying at Ms. Ruth's house ever since. I guess he earns his keep fixing up the house. It sure looks better than it did a few years ago," he gave a little laugh. "So what you is really saying, we got to get rid of Ms. Emma, Ms. Ruth and find Rachael to make sure she's not coming back to Tapasalle County and before she find out about them houses," said Clemmons. "Where do we go from here, Brother Willie?" Clemmons asked angrily! "We will figure out something, I got to go," Willie said hurrying down the steps to his truck.

Chapter 16
The bonding…

"Uncle Leon are we going anywhere today?" asked Sugar Pudding stuffing her mouth with a biscuit and crumbs falling out of her mouth all over the table. Uncle Leon gave her a towel to wipe her mouth. "You gotta eat better than that Sugar Pudding," he said kindly. "Take your time; don't gobble your food, okay." "I want to finish before um…um, uh, uh… Aunt Ru…thu…thu… gets back," she stammered. Mmm…thought Myrtle, she almost forgot again. Aunt Ruth had scared Sugar Pudding so bad, when she slapped her, she stutters now from being nervous. "Don't worry about Aunt Ruth she left early this morning, but we are going into town. I have to pick up a few things and y'all coming with me. Now go on get dressed. I want to get out of here before she gets back," he said quickly.

Ms. Ruth was extremely angry. She was deep in thought and talking to herself. My whole day is messed up! How am I gonna get back to that home today she wondered. I have to get those papers signed. Shit! I could do them myself. Who gonna know. Ms. Emma can't read anyway. Besides, I gotta open Mr. Raye's club tonight. I got so much cleaning to do in the club from the weekend mess! Damn that Mr. Leon! How he gonna tell me who I take in that club, she mumbled loudly as she stuck her key in the front door. "Hey! Where is everybody? Damn it's quiet in here!" she said as she walked through the house. No one was there. Everybody was gone including the girls. They must be with Mr. Leon she thought. Well, I'll get my things together and go to the club early so I can clean up that mess!

As she put her hand on the doorknob to open the door, she was startled by ol' Willie. "Mornin ol' Willie, you scared me half to death! Why you here so early? Dropping off some cleaning?" she asked nervously and looking around for his laundry bag. "No, Ms. Ruth I just came to talk to you. Where you hurrying off to so early in the morning?" he asked flicking his cigarette ashes on her floor. "Excuse me ol' Willie, let me get you an ashtray for your cigarette." She walked over to the window and took one off the window ledge. "Here use this," she said handing him the glass ashtray. He took it from her hands, squashed out the cigarette and handed her back the ashtray. Ms. Ruth stood there holding the ashtray in her hand, waiting nervously for him to leave. "I am running late ol' Willie what did you want to talk to me about?"

She tried to sound cheerful and not be so damn nervous. However, her gut feeling told her, this is not a regular visit. She sensed some anger in the tone of his voice. "When the last time you seen Ms. Emma?" he ask. "Why that's strange of you to ask me that," she said trying to laugh and act like everything is okay. "I tried to see her this morning but I guess I got the visiting times mixed up. The nurse there told me I had to leave the premises and to come back at 1:00PM. I didn't get to see her at all," she finished quickly. "I have so much work to do today, I don't think I will have time to go back up there," she was rambling on and on.

Ol' Willie noticed she was kind of jumpy or up to something. "Where's Mr. Leon this morning, and how them girls doing?" "They left early this morning ol' Willie, and they doing fine, just fine! Mr. Leon has taking quite a liking for the girls, and they like him too," she answered still eyeing him cautiously. "You done had these girls for how long, Ms. Ruth? Would you say over a month or two?" he asked watching the expression on her face. "Yes sir, it been maybe close to a month and a half, why you asking," asked Ms. Ruth, pretending to straighten the little yellow rug on the floor with the toe of her shoe. "Well you know Ms. Emma is doing much better I hear, she's even walking. She might be home soon Ms. Ruth," he said nonchalantly. He saw the surprise look on her face.

Surprised by the news, he watched as she knocked over the ashtray she had place back on the ledge of the window. Now it was broke in many pieces. As she stooped to pick up the pieces, ol' Willie said, "I guess I better stop by Ms. Emma's house and check on things before she is ready to come home. Ms. Ruth, do you ever think them little girls mother will ever come back to Tapasalle County?" he asked looking straight at her. "I don't know ol' Willie, you know some peoples abandon their kids because they don't want them or they can't take care of them anymore. Who knows, maybe she ran out of money or got sick, and left the poor things to who ever would come along. I guess they is lucky it was you that found them and bring them to Ms. Emma's house," she answered feeling a little more calm and in control than she had been a few moments ago. Why don't the hell he leave, she thought to herself. "Well, I got to go Ms. Ruth….he paused… the next time you feel like going up to see Ms. Emma, let me know, I'll take you in my truck." He walked toward the door, turned the knob and left.

Ms. Ruth just stood there for a while. She thought for a moment, he knows I was there, but I didn't tell anyone where I was going! Her fingers shaking badly, she fumbled nervously down the front of her blouse, trying to find the sweat, soaked, crumbled and often wrinkled pack of cigarettes she faithfully carried between her large breasts. The cigarettes were wet from the moisture between her breasts. Ol' Willie had upset her so bad she broke out in a nervous sweat. Her hands still trembling, she secured the limp cigarette between the corner of her large lips, and quickly gathered up her bags and left for the club.

Chapter 17
The visitor…

"Good afternoon Nurse, I'm Mr. Leon Thomas and I come here to visit Ms. Emma Jackson. Could you tell me which room she in?" he asked nicely. "She is in room 212B, second floor east Mr. Thomas, but the girls will have to stay here. They can't go on the ward. They will be all right! You can leave them with me. I'll take good care of them." She smiled at Sugar and me. The nurse went behind the counter and came back with a round tin can full of cookies, and gave Sugar Pudding and I three a piece and a paper cup of water.

He got off the elevator and walked down the long corridor looking and turning his head left and right for room 212B. He found the room. He pushed the door open and quietly walked in. "Ms. Emma you wake? This Mr. Leon." "Why yes, Mr. Leon I'm woke. How you Mr. Leon?" she asked as she quickly sat up and turned her body toward Mr. Leon. "How's Myrtle and Sugar Pudding?" She asked pulling the sheet up over her legs. "They is fine Ms. Emma. They is down stairs, you know the nurse won't let them come up to see you, she says they is too young." "I know Mr. Leon the last time I saw them the caretaker took me down in a wheel chair. They may do it again if I ask them," she said. "Well… Ms. Emma wait a minute before you do that, I have to talk to you about something very important, okay," his voice was cracking and he knew he sounded nervous. "I don't know how to tell you this, but just to come right on out and say it." He nervously wiped his face and the back of his neck with his handkerchief. "Tell me what you got to tell me Mr. Leon," said Ms. Emma in an anxious tone of voice. "Ms. Ruth is trying to take Myrtle and Sugar Pudding away from you," he said slowly wiping the sweat from his brow. "Why she gonna do that? I thought she was my friend Mr. Leon!" Ms. Emma suddenly stood up straight raising her arms in the air and slowly shaking her head from side to side. "I think it's to get the money the state is gonna give her if she gets them girls in court. Look Ms. Emma, them papers you got a while back is trying to give you the same thing. Here look, Ms. Emma," he said anxiously as he pulled the large envelop from under his shirt. Mr. Leon was shaking the familiar envelope in front of her face. "Myrtle gave me the papers because she said they were important, and she was right," he explained to Ms. Emma. "What do I do now Mr. Leon? The doctors said I can go home maybe in a few weeks. I'm walking much better now."

Ms. Emma was looking through the papers. "Look Ms. Emma don't sign any papers Ms. Ruth brings to you, you understand, and don't talk to no one about the girls. You tell anyone that asked you about them girls, that you is their kin okay." Mr. Leon was relieved Ms. Emma understood. "I will Mr. Leon and thank you for telling me. What do I do with the papers you got there?" she asked in a worried voice. "I'll hold on to them. One paper that's very important, you got to sign. It says you have to sign if you the next of kin," said Mr. Leon. "You know I can't write that well, Mr. Leon, if you help me I'll sign them now!" He took the letter out of the envelope and handed it to her "You gotta sign your whole name, *Emma Jackson*." Can you write it if I help you hold the pen Ms. Emma?" He was nervous and scared. He wanted to get this over with as quick as possible before anyone comes in the room. "Yes I can," Ms. Emma said as Mr. Leon placed the pen in her hand. Ms. Emma slowly, with shaking steps, sat back down on the edge of the bed. She reached for the Bible that was lying on the white metal dresser. Mr. Leon placed the letter on the Bible and helped Ms. Emma guide the pen. She managed to scrawl her name crookedly on the dotted lines, and he filled in the date. It was over. Mr. Leon put the letter back in the envelope and placed it back inside of his shirt.

"Now, Ms. Ruth can't take the girls from you, Ms. Emma. You get some rest, and I will come back to see you soon." He patted her hand gently and left the room just as quietly as he came in.

Sugar Pudding saw Uncle Leon walking toward us. She ran up to him. Uncle Leon "How is grandma? Is she still sick? When can we see her?" "Whoa, wait a minute Sugar Pudding," Uncle Leon laughed as he picked her up. "Your grandma is doing just fine, and you and Myrtle will see her soon, okay."

We walked back to the sitting room for visitors to get the cookies and water the nurse gave us. Uncle Leon brushed the crumbs off Sugar Pudding's dress. "Those are two very pretty girls, Mr. Thomas," the nurse said. "Thank you, and thank you for watching them. They is my nieces," and he grabbed their hands and walked out into the bright sunshine. Mr. Leon smiled to himself, looked up toward the sky and said a little prayer, something he had not done in a very long time.

On the way back home, Uncle Leon stopped at the same hardware store we went to the last time we came into town. However, he didn't buy any nails. He bought us another icy pop as he called them. Today I wished he were really my uncle. We walked to the same bus stop with the bench in front of it. We sat down and prepared to wait the two hours for the bus. Uncle Leon said he wanted to get home early. He had something to do. I didn't like riding the bus. We were often squeezed in the back with the other colored people. We had to listen to the many hurtful questions and comments about our skin, our hair. Most often, we heard, "what are two young white girls doing with a colored man?" As time passed, Sugar Pudding and I began to ignore the white and colored people on the bus, and tried to think of pleasant things to make the trip go by faster.

Finally the bus came. As we stepped up on the bus, the white bus driver told me and Sugar to ride up front, and Uncle Leon to ride in the back. Uncle Leon said, "it's okay girls, go on sit down. I can see you from the back. I'll let you know when it is time to get off." We sat down and watched Uncle Leon walk back to the back of the bus.

We saw Uncle Leon talking to another colored man. I had seen him before. I remember Uncle Leon telling us they used to work together on a farm a long time ago. We got off the bus about a half a mile from the house. That is as far as any of the buses would take you. The roads were not finished, and we had to walk or hitch a ride the rest of the way home. Uncle Leon told Sugar Pudding and I he didn't want to hitch a ride today, because he was walking with Mr. Harvey a friend he met on the bus and Mr. Harvey was walking the same way we were going. Mr. Harvey was happy to see Uncle Leon again. He kept shaking Uncle Leon's hand, patting him on his back and asking him where he had been. Uncle Leon told him he lived in Tapasalle County in Ms. Ruth's boarding house. He had been living there since he left his job working for Mr. Reynolds.

"Yeah, those were some bad days for us Mr. Leon," Mr. Harvey said with a little laugh. "That Mr. Reynolds don't like colored people. I can only work part-time. He had some help, but the colored lady named Ms. Emma who worked for him, got sick." Mr. Harvey rambled on. "Mr. Harvey you know Ms. Emma?" asked Uncle Leon excitedly! "Yeah, she's not too friendly, didn't talk much but she kept the houses clean and got along with Mr. Reynolds." "What kind of work you do for Mr. Reynolds," asked Uncle Leon? "Oh, I just run a few trips into town for supplies and watch two houses that belong to a friend of his; you know the funny thing is that... Mr. Reynolds wants me to pretend that somebody is living in both of them houses. He told me he was doing a friend a favor watching the houses. I think he called his friend, ol' Willie or something like that. Told me not tell anyone that peoples don't live in them houses, cause somebody may break into them and steal everything that ain't nailed down," he laughed. Uncle Leon had a strange look on his face the whole time he was listening to Mr. Harvey. They shook hands again and Mr. Harvey told Uncle Leon to come on down to Mr. Raye's club and they parted ways at Coleman's street and we walked the rest of the way in silence.

As always after one of our trips into town, Sugar Pudding is tired and wants to take a nap. I went with her and laid down too, only to be woken up by loud yelling, cursing and name-calling. I didn't have to guess who. Aunt Ruth had returned and for what I could hear, was calling Mr. Leon a sneaky old bastard and a number of no-good-sons-of-a-bitches! I heard my name mentioned and something about the club. Uncle Leon told her she was not taking us anywhere! What is happening out there? I tried to listen through the door. I couldn't hear too well, so I sneaked out the room very quietly and stood to the side of the wall that separated the front room from the hallway.

"You can't take them anywhere! Ms. Ruth, them kids don't belong to you woman!" argued Mr. Leon. "I will take them away before I let you have them! You ain't got much say so anyway, cause Ms. Emma is coming home soon!" he yelled back at her. "You believe that shit ol' Willie is talking…Ms. Emma ain't coming home!" she yelled at him. She picked up a brick that was used as the doorstop and threw it at Uncle Leon. She missed him, but that made her even madder. "You best be leaving this house Mr. Leon, you can't stay here no more! I want you out by the weekend!" she yelled at him. Uncle Leon said, "I will be here until Ms. Emma comes home. Then I will leave!" He left her standing in the middle of the front room with her mouth wide open and eyes about to pop right out of her head! I slipped quietly back to our room.

If Aunt Ruth throws out Uncle Leon, Sugar Pudding and I are in big trouble. I really did not know where we could go. I thought about it until my head starting hurting. I had never had a headache before. I laid down and finally went to sleep. Suddenly Uncle Leon was standing by the bed, waking me up!

"What's wrong Uncle Leon?" "Look if I have to leave, I promise I will find somewhere for you and Sugar Pudding to go until Ms. Emma comes home. Don't say nothing to no one understand. I want you and Sugar Pudding to stay out of Ms. Ruth way. I'll find somewhere for you go everyday if I have to. You can't stay in the house hiding from her and afraid to walk around. I can't be here all the time. You girls watch what you say to her. No smart mouthing Myrtle, understand!" "I understand Uncle Leon. What time is it?" "It's a little after seven, come on let me get you something to eat," he said.

Chapter 18
The search…

"Come on Clemmons, I got the key to Ms. Emma's house, we gonna look all over the place for them damn papers. The doctors said she maybe able to come home in a few weeks. Hell! It could be a few days. Once she comes home, we can't get in to find those papers. She needs to sign those papers as soon as possible. I found out the construction on the road won't start until a few years from now. We can't take any chances on Ms. Emma living to be Grandma Moses age," ol' Willie laughed. "Let me get my cigarettes and some matches. I need a smoke. Hell Willie it's dark," Clemmons complained. "Ms. Emma got lights in her house?" he asked as they walked to the truck. "Would you stop complaining, this is all your fault Clemmons," Willie argued. "You should never have seen that colored woman! Let's get out there and back! I don't want no one seeing us!" He started the truck and they drove to Ms. Emma's house in silence.

"Where you gonna park the truck?" Clemmons asked taking a sip out of the bottle of beer he had brought with him. "In the back of the house behind that old broken down milk truck that's been sitting there for years," Willie answered. "We ain't gonna use the lights…I brought two flash lights. Even though there might not be a house close enough for anybody to see the lights, I just don't want take any chances, okay! We here now. Well, lets get out!" ordered Willie. "Damn it's dark as hell out here! You can't see nothing," mumbled Clemmons.

Before he finished his sentence, Clemmons had fell through the hole left by the missing steps. "Oh hell! Willie I think I busted my ankle! It hurt's like hell!" he said as he reached down to rub his ankle. "We got to get in the house Clemmons, quit your playing around! Okay, let's try the key. Good it works!" Willie opened the door and walked in.

He turns the flashlight on trying to see where everything is. "Man! I don't see how blind people get around, mumble Clemmons." "Come on in here...this looks like where the girls sleep," said Willie. "They left a few of their clothes on the bed. Check the dresser drawers Clemmons!" he barked. "Ain't nothing in the dresser drawers. They are empty," answered Clemmons. "There's another room in the back of the house, let's check in there. Come on Clemmons!" called Willie.

As they pushed the door open, and shined the flashlight on the floor. Something ran past Clemmons injured ankle. "Man, let's get the hell out of here! The place been closed for so long, critters done got in here," argued Clemmons. "Ain't no critters in here, look again...down on the floor," grumbled Willie! Clemmons looked down, and saw a piece of silk ribbon with the lace caught on the buckle of his boot that had somehow got caught between his two clumsy feet. "What's this doing here?" he asked somewhat embarrassed. Clemmons picked up the silk ribbon. It looked like it belonged to one of the girls; pink and lacey...something a girl would tie in her hair he thought. Maybe it belonged to one of Rachel's girls he was thinking as he stuffed the ribbon in his back pocket. Clemmons was deep in thought when Willie called his name.

"Man, what are you thinking about? Let's go! I checked the rooms and drawers and the closet, ain't nothing here! I wonder where she hid the damn letter." Willie said loudly! He was angry! "Maybe she threw it away or used it for firewood Willie," said Clemmons. "Hell, what are we gonna do now! We can't ask her for the letter Willie, she'll know you had something to do with it," said Clemmons getting back in the truck. "Would you shut up for a minute! Let me think on this, all right! I'll figure out something!" Willie said angrily.

Clemmons sat there saying nothing. Not even conscious that the cigarette he was holding was burning his fingers. He had something else on his mind, the two houses and all that land. He has got to find away to get them houses back, and move into one of them. He had plans...plans for all that land just sitting there. While he was in jail, that's all he thought about. He was coming home and starting all over again. He didn't want to stay with Willie. Even if it means owning up to fathering them girls he would do it. Damn right he thought, I could say I am their daddy and their mama abandoned the girls. I'll file for custody. I don't want to make any mistakes he thought to himself.

Chapter 19
The protector…

      I have to figure out away to stay in this house to save those girls from Ms. Ruth trying to take them, Mr. Leon was thinking to himself. I won't like it, but maybe I have to try to be a little nicer to her until I can find out what she is planning to do with those court papers. He was deep in thought, when Ms. Ruth walked in the kitchen that morning. "Mornin, Ms. Ruth," he spoke nicely. "Oh you still here?" she questioned, her voice still dripping with anger from the night before. "Look Ms. Ruth, I like them girls, and I want you to treat them right," he begged. Maybe I can help out a little more around the house or …maybe at the club. The girls can stay here at night by themselves. I don't think anyone will bother them. Whatcha' you say, I help you out at the club?" he looked her straight in the face. "Well, you have been here a long time Mr. Leon, and you ain't got no where else to go. We'll see," she said as she walked out the kitchen holding a cup of coffee he had just made that morning.

      Mr. Leon waited until Ms. Ruth had left for her cleaning job. He had to search the house and find Ms. Ruth's court papers before the girls wake up. He got the letter the court mailed to her two weeks ago and burned it in the stove. Now, he had to find the papers so she can't take the girls away from Ms. Emma. He knew Ms. Ruth was always changing her pocketbook. She is the only woman I'd ever seen wearing high heels shoes, a Sunday church hat, and carrying a pocketbook trying to look fancy while she cleaned for them white people, he chuckled to himself. He went down the hall to her room. He had never been in there, so now was as good a time as any. He went straight to the little closet. It was packed with all kinds of bags and shoes. He went through each bag carefully putting it back where he had gotten it.

The last bag was black with a large tassel on the front. He opened it, and there before his eyes was a large brown envelope. He opened it quickly. Inside were the court papers. He didn't bother to read them, just stuck them in the front of his shirt and hurriedly put everything back in place. He went into the living room, and opened the door to the potbellied stove and lit a small fire. It was a cool morning, so the girls wouldn't think twice about a fire burning in the stove. He placed the envelope on the smothering fire and watched as the flames turned it black and finally into ashes. He put the fire out and went into the kitchen. He had a plan, but he needed the girls to help too.

He knocked on their door. Myrtle was already up, and she was brushing Sugar Pudding's hair. "Good morning Uncle Leon," Sugar Pudding said with a smile. Mr. Leon noticed the pink and pretty lace ribbon Myrtle was tying in Sugar's hair. "I like your ribbon Sugar Pudding," he said smiling back at her and playfully tugging on one of her curls. "We had two just alike Uncle Leon, but I guess I left one in grandma's house, you know, the night she got sick." Sugar Pudding explained, all the while fidgeting and bouncing around as Myrtle tried to tie the ribbon in a large bow. "I am going to wear the yellow one today, because it reminds me of the ribbon Anna gave me," said Myrtle. When she thought of Anna, it made her feel very unhappy. She had lost her friend forever, she thought.

"Well," Uncle Leon spoke very slowly… "Girls I gotta talk to you this mornin'. You gotta listen now, what I have to say is very important, and you cannot tell nobody understand," he said in a very low voice. "We understand Uncle Leon." "You know Ms. Ruth and me were arguing last night but we fine for now! I need you girls to help around the house as much as you can, you know washing dishes, sweeping the floor and maybe dusting. I'm gonna help out at the club where she works at night. I gotta leave you for a little while by yourselves, just don't open the door for nobody understand? Myrtle, watch Sugar Pudding and keep her outa Ms. Ruth's way….he warned!" "No, Uncle Leon, it's Ah...ah…Aunt Ruth," Sugar Pudding stammered trying to correct him. "You are right, and don't you forget," he playfully reached up and pulled her pink bow loose, and smiled at her. "Remember you girls be good until I get back. I got to handle something very important, okay."

We watched Uncle Leon leave, until he was out of sight. For once, I was feeling real good. I was not afraid of doing anything wrong to make Aunt Ruth mad. However, my good feeling did not last long. Later that day, Aunt Ruth accused Sugar Pudding and me of going into her room, and taking her papers. "I want you to look all over this house and find them!' she yelled. I know you half-white girls took them!" Sugar Pudding ran as fast as she could to the room we shared. I looked everywhere she told me to look, but the papers were nowhere to be found. She finally gave up and went back to her room. I went to our room and found Sugar Pudding curled up like a small kitten, under our bed asleep.

That afternoon, Aunt Ruth left Sugar Pudding and me alone. She did not say where she was going. When Uncle Leon returned later that afternoon, I told him what had happened. He did not seem too worried. He said don't worry everything gonna be fine. He went in the kitchen to fix us something to eat. We ate and went to our room.

Chapter 20
Ass in hot water…

"Good afternoon, Mr. Sheldon I lost the papers the judge gave me. I know they is somewhere in the house, but I can't find them," explained Ms. Ruth with growing frustration. "I am sorry Ms. Macklin; the papers had to be in last week. You should have received the notice in mail a few weeks ago. Unfortunately, you will not have enough time to re-file for custody. Your court date is one week from today. If there is nothing else, I have another client waiting to be seen. Good Afternoon, Ms. Macklin." Mr. Sheldon was ending the conversation when Ms. Ruth abruptly interrupted him. "Notice! What notice! I have not received any mail from you!" She yelled waving her hands in the air. What do I do now?" she questioned angrily. "One thing you can do immediately is to calm yourself down, Ms. Macklin! You can keep the girls until their grandmother gets better, or you can turn them over to the court. That's up to you Ms. Macklin. Oh, by the way if the papers are not filed in one week, the financial support of $25.00 is cut off for next month," he said sarcastically.

Mr. Sheldon opened the door for her to leave. She stumbled slightly, fumbling frantically in her bag looking for her cigarettes. Ms. Ruth was angrier than she had been in a long time. She could barely think. There is nothing I can do, she thought to herself, until I find out who stole those papers and who took my mail. Her hand shook badly as she tried to light the cigarette.

Chapter 21

A letter of discontent...

Ol' Willie heard a knock at his front door. Opening the screen door, he recognized Mr. Baylor Tyner, his grandmother's attorney who read the will a week after her funeral. Willie's hair stood out on his arms, and somehow he suspected bad news from this old guy who dressed like a preacher, looking holier-than-thou. "Come on in Mr. Tyner, what brings you out here this late in the day?" he asked cheerfully. "Morning, Mr. Hayden, or can I call you Willie?" "No...Willie is fine, here have a seat," Willie said pointing to an over stuffed mustard colored chair sitting by the door. "Willie, I'll get down the business of why I am here." He was clearing his throat, and wiping his brow with a handkerchief he suddenly, as if by magic had pulled out of the air. Damn! This gotta be bad news Willie thought, the man looks like he gonna pass out at any minute. "Can I get you some water or a drink?" asked Willie. "Yes, Willie maybe some water. Thank you, it must be the heat!"

Willie gave Mr. Tyner the glass of water. He took a few sips and wiped his head again. "Willie, sit down, I really don't know how to tell you this, except to come right on out with it! This morning one of the new clerks was reviewing your grandmother's will. You know it's been several years since the will was filed and evidently, during the haste to have the will probated for clarity we failed to see...some papers were misplaced" He paused again to wipe his brow. "Your grandmother left a mighty sizable insurance policy." Willie's heart started to pound with anticipation. "Uh...what policy?" He asked nervously wringing his hands.

Mr. Tyner continued. "The policy was updated before the time of her death. Somehow or another it was misplaced in my office and should have been included in the reading of the will. Your grandmother also left a letter and another will to be read after her death. If you like, I can read it to you now, or we can go in town to my office for a formal reading of the will and the newly found attachments. Well, what do you want to do, Willie?" Mr. Tyner pretended to look for something in his briefcase, all the while trying to avoid looking directly at Willie. "I'm not sure Mr. Tyner; you see my brother is home now. He just got out of prison, and he didn't take too well to the news that the houses and land were left to his two girls and their colored mama," he explained in an agitated tone of voice. "Well, Willie maybe it's best he's not here right now…the news is not that good and he reached for the glass of water. "Go on Mr. Tyner, read the letter," said Willie anxiously. Willie sat down on the old couch and held his head between his hands. Mr. Tyner opened the newly found will, and began to read.

"On this day, June Twelfth, Nineteen Hundred and Fifty-five:

I Stella Louise Hayden being of sound mind and body leave the following property and monies to Rachel Jackson, and her two daughters, Myrtle and Sugar Pudding, my two great granddaughters. All monies in my financial accounts are to be distributed to Rachel Jackson to place in a trust fund for the two girls. The houses and land she can do as she wishes. There is also a $500,000 dollar life insurance policy to be included and Rachel Jackson and her daughters are the sole beneficiaries of that and any other financial holdings I may have inadvertently left out. Mr. Baylor Tyner shall be the overseer of my estate and carry out my wishes as instructed in my will.

My only child is dead due to an unfortunate hunting accident. I leave not one dollar to my grandsons. Arrangements has been made to pay the taxes on the two houses and land not to exceed three years after my death or three years after Rachel takes ownership of the houses. The houses, and land shall be recorded, as such and no amendments shall be made to this will.

"Willie it was signed, Stella Louise Hayden and it contains two witnesses' signatures and a seal of authenticity," Mr. Tyner finished slowly, trying not to look directly at Willie. He began to explain.

"I'm so sorry Willie. It's evident your grandmother was a very smart woman," he said apologetically. "Willie there is nothing really you can do. This is the most recent Will, and all she has done is added the life insurance policy and other financial requests. It will hold up in any court. As far as the up and coming highway, the state will hold up on the building of the highway, because it's caught up in a lot of red tape that could go on for years. The problem is the state can take the houses and land, and unfortunately the money as well if the girls and their mama cannot be found. I have done some calculating of my own. I have a little over three years, to find Rachel or the grandchildren. In the mean time, the houses and land will remain in my care, and as the attorney for your grandmother, who has authorized me as the legal caretaker of the houses and the land as well as the financial part of her estate. I will do everything in my power to carry out her wishes."

Pausing and hearing no response from Willie, he continued. "I know you are still watching over the estate, but you don't really have to Willie. I can take care of that. I know it hard for you to let go, but… Look Willie, it's a sad thing your grandmother did. I think you should try to find Rachel and the two girls. Maybe your brother and you can patch things up with Rachel. I can't tell you anything else," he said solemnly staring at the will. "You telling me both the wills are legal!" Willie yelled as he walked around the little room knocking and throwing things around! Mr. Tyner jumped out of his way a second time to keep from being hit with something. "Please calm down Willie," he begged. "There was nothing I could do or anybody could have done. Your grandmother had her mind made up!" Mr. Tyner yelled trying to get closer to the front door. "But why would she leave all that money to a colored woman she didn't like? Hell, she ain't never had no use for niggers! Why now, Mr. Tyner!" Willie was crying and holding his head in his hands. "I can't answer that Willie. I have to go now, it's getting late." Mr. Tyner had one foot through the door and the other foot on the first step. "Please stop by the office tomorrow and I will give you a copy of the will," he called back running down the steps.

Mr. Tyner walked quickly to his car and drove off with the door half open. He was sweating profusely and trying to get control of his thoughts. He was too old, much too old and he had a high blood pressure problems. He had to get back to his office.

Baylor Tyner had wished repeatedly that he had never ever met the Hayden family. They were awful people, hateful people. They paid off or bought people with their money. Nevertheless, this was the worse he had seen and been involved in. The grandmother was finally dead, but she was still in control and ruining what was left of her family and their lives from her grave. Thoughts ran through his mind. He remembered when the problems first started.

The old woman called him late one evening. He had just finished dinner and had poured himself a snifter of brandy to relax. The telephone was ringing, and he had thought twice about not answering it. He wanted some peace and quiet. He answered the telephone, recognizing immediately the voice on the other end as 'Mrs. Hayden.' She was upset and very angry. Her daughter Elizabeth had told her she thought Clemmons, her favorite grandson, was seeing a colored girl. Elizabeth had caught them twice together, but Clemmons didn't know it. She wanted to put a stop to it as soon as possible, even if it meant running the colored girl out of town and threatening to leave Clemmons out of her will.

Baylor lean back in his chair remembering how much Mrs. Hayden was quite fond of her grandsons and gave them anything they wanted. She often told them, "When I die, you boys will get everything!" Shit the oldest boy Willie never worked a day in his life. Clemmons wanted to work to get from under his mama who worried the hell out of him because he was the youngest and reminded her of her husband. Their father Luther Wright, a wealthy land developer, ran off with a pretty girl half his age, never to be heard from again. Elizabeth treated Clemmons differently from Willie. Clemmons she showed mountains of affection and Willie was lucky if he got a friendly hello. Their mom went through a lot of pain and sadness during the divorce and eventually changing the boys' last names from 'Wright' to 'Hayden.' She didn't want any part of Luther Wright's name. She settled into a deep depression, spending most of her time alone and traveling when she felt like it. When she returned from France, she was upset to find Clemmons was seeing this colored girl, Rachel Jackson.

Clemmons so-called friends told his mother and better yet, she offered money to them to rat on Clemmons, and they did. His friends kept his mother informed, even up to when Rachel had the first girl. The grandmother was beyond angry, thought Mr. Tyner as he remembered what she said. "Baylor, I want you to find this colored girl and offer her some money to leave this county! I can take care of Clemmons. I will forbid him to see her again. I won't have it, Baylor! No grandson of mine will marry a nigger! I never had any use for those people! My heart is breaking Baylor!" she cried waving a dainty lilac and lavender scented handkerchief in the air.

He regretfully remembered going to Rachel's apartment. Mrs. Hayden gave him fifteen thousand dollars, five thousand in each separate envelope. One envelope he was to give to Mr. Michael and Nadine Simms to evict

Rachel if she did not move out of Southend. He waited for Rachel to move, but she didn't. He reported this back to Mrs. Hayden. The old woman said, "Pay them niggers off! They will take the money. I just want to get rid of her Baylor!" Sure enough, he talked to the Simms in private and gave them the second envelope with the five thousand dollars in it. Nadine, Mr. Simms wife, started to cry, and told her husband he would burn in hell if he did this to Rachel and those little girls! She ran out of the room.

  Baylor remembered pocketing the other five thousand in the third envelope. That money was for his time and trouble. However, it did not stop there, he remembered, with a pained expression on his face. Mrs. Stella Louise Hayden had a surprise for us all, including him. Shortly after that, she became ill, and asked him to redo her will. He will never forget the night he came to her 'mansion' as she called it. She was sitting up in bed fully alert. "Good evening Baylor," she said in a raspy sounding voice. "Here are the changes to my will and I want them to go into effect immediately, you understand." He took the changes and proceeded to read them. They were written with the neatest handwriting he had ever seen. He was sweating, and coughed a little as he read each change. "Are you sure you want me to type this up?" he asked confused and shocked. "Yes, I do Baylor. This is no joke. Have the papers ready for me to sign tomorrow, and don't forget to bring the clerk from your office and Mr. Steed the vice president of the Bridgefield Bank. I want them as my witnesses when I sign the will. Do you understand?" She looked at him; her eyes conveyed the seriousness within them.

  Baylor listened and watched the saliva creeping slowly down the right side of her bottom lip, dripping onto her wrinkled chin. She softly patted the corner of her mouth with the dainty silk handkerchief he had grown accustomed to seeing in her hand. It was as if the silk handkerchief attached to her hand was an appendage, a permanent fixture. He could not remember ever seeing her without it.

He sat there, completely in shock. She had left everything to Rachel and her children! Not one dollar went to her grandsons. He knew better than to challenge her or ask questions. "Yes, Mrs. Hayden, I understand and I will have them ready for you tomorrow. Will there be anything else, Mrs. Hayden?" he asked cautiously. "No, you can leave now. I am tired and want to get some rest." He left immediately. The next afternoon, he had the papers ready for her signature and he had brought the clerk and the bank's vice president with him. They signed the papers and he took them back to the office.

Two years later, she died. He did not want to read the new will to the family after the funeral. He felt, since Mrs. Hayden had appointed him the executor of the will, and overseer of the houses, land, financial distribution of her estate, and the fact she paid off all of his debts by sending him more clients then he could handle, he felt it was only necessary to read the first will. Mrs. Hayden had indicated in both wills, she left the houses and land to Rachael and the girls. That was shocking enough, he thought. He just could not dump all those changes on the grandsons, especially Willie. Willie had a temper as well as his brother, Clemmons.

He decided to put the new will away, and hope that he would never have to read it again. Nevertheless, as luck would have it, the old lady had sent a letter to the bank before she died, authorizing Mr. Steed to pay the property taxes on the houses and land exactly as she had specified in the new will. Baylor knew he had no choice but to go out to Willie Hayden's place and informed him of the new will. Hell, the Pinewood prison had notified him a few months ago, Clemmons was getting out soon, and he could not keep this information hidden any longer. He knew Clemmons would challenged the old will when he got out, so he made up the story of the new will being misplaced and the clerks found it. He knew Willie would tell Clemmons of his visit today, and he will rant and rave and probably break everything in their house, and come looking for him with a rage to kill.

Baylor realized in his heart he had to find Rachel first. He could not do anything about the girls. But he knew if Rachel was to come back this will put an end to Willie and Clemmons trying to challenge the will and take what is rightfully Rachel's and the girls. He stayed in his office all night trying to figure out a plan to find Rachael.

Chapter 22

Picking up the sordid pieces...

When Clemmons returned he found Willie dead drunk, and the place looked like it had been trashed and robbed. He had ridden around all day and all that evening trying to figure out his next move. He was in no mood to deal with his brother Willie. He had to find out if he could get custody of his girls. Willie told him the state would take the houses and land if no heirs appeared to claim ownership of the houses and the land.

Now, if he finds Rachel, will she be agreeable to give him the houses... "Hell No!" He answered his own question loudly. Rachel was no dummy, but why did she abandoned the girls? He has asked himself that question over and over since he found out they are living with Ms. Ruth at her boarding house. Hell, he thought I can't just go over there and say, "Give me my girls back!" Shit, I still can't get the houses or land, because Rachel is the beneficiary of the houses and land. Suddenly, he sprung up from his chair and walked across the floor where Willie was laying. Clemmons yelled down at his drunk and passed out brother, "I've got to talk to a lawyer and find out what my rights are. I am not giving up! You hear me Willie!"

Chapter 23
A change of grace...

"Ms. Emma, we got good news for you," announced her caretaker Ms. Ella. "The doctor said you can go home in a few days!" Ms. Ella announced cheerfully as she adjusted the pillows behind Ms. Emma's back. She noticed Ms. Emma was crying softly. "Wait now, Ms. Emma, this is a happy occasion. Don't you want to see your granddaughters you have talked so much about these past few days?" "Yes, I am ready to go home." Ms. Emma paused for a few seconds. She reached over to the small white metal dresser; the top drawer stained, rusted with age and constant use, pulled out the top drawer, and grabbed a little piece of paper. "Ms. Ella, please call this number and ask for Mr. Leon...if he don't answer, don't leave no name understand, we can try again tomorrow morning, okay," said Ms. Emma excited to be going home.

Ms. Ella went down the hall to the nurse's counter, and called the number written on the piece of paper. It rang once, twice and finally someone answered. "Hello"...Mmm...a man's voice. "May I speak with Mr. Leon please?" "This here is Mr. Leon, who are you?" He asked. "This is Ms. Emma's caretaker Ms. Ella; she is ready to go home." Ms. Ella spoke cheerfully into the telephone. "Oh! That's fine, Thank you, Thank you! When will she be able to leave?" asked Mr. Leon. "The doctor said she can leave this Friday sir. Can you pick her up around eleven 'o' clock in the morning?" Ms. Ella asked. "I show can, Thanks again for calling!"

Ms. Ella went back to Ms. Emma's room and told her she spoke with Mr. Leon and he will pick her up Friday Morning. Ms. Emma wanted to go home now! Nevertheless, she knew she had to wait until Friday. She thought to herself, I've got to talk to Mr. Leon about them papers I signed. I got to get them girls' outa that house. I thought Ms. Ruth was my friend. Well, she thought, the Bible said Judas sold Jesus out for thirty pieces of silver. I can't expect she be any better than Judas.

Mr. Leon held on to the telephone receiver, his chest swelling with a good feeling. I got to tell the girls. It's late he thought, they might be asleep. No, on second thought, I'd better tell them now before Ms. Ruth gets home. He knocked on their door softy and called Myrtle by name. "Uncle Leon, I'm not sleep," she said. "I am writing a letter to grandma." He walked in and shook Sugar Pudding. He wanted her to hear this too. "I've got some good news," he said as he sat down on the only chair in the room. "Your grandma is coming home this Friday." The look on their faces told him they missed their grandma. He gave them a hug and told them not to say anything to nobody. "Start packing your bags. We will leave early Friday mornin' to go pick her up. We got to take the bus, unless I find someone to give us a ride, okay." The girls were so happy they were talking a mile a minute. "Shhhhh! be quiet now. Go back to sleep, I will talk to you tomorrow." He closed the door behind him.

Uncle Leon looked at his pocket watch…eight-fifteen. Well, I will wait until around ten tonight and go to the club to help Ms. Ruth. I don't want her to suspect a thing he smiled to himself.

He went in later to check on the girls and to make sure Myrtle locked the front door behind him. He didn't like walking on the roads at night so he took the short cut through the woods. That was not half as dangerous as being snatched up by them men in the white sheets. He had heard frightening stories about them Klu Klux Klan, but he ain't never actually seen one.

He got to the club around twelve thirty a.m. The club didn't usually close until twelve o'clock or until the last person leaves. Old man John Raye runs the club and has a deal with the police to give him a cut of the money from all the moonshine they give him to sell in the club after hours. Mr. Raye made a lot of money on the side and paid the two women who worked for him quite well. That included Ms. Ruth. She made her money too. She had two young girls that used the back room in the club for prostituting. Half of what they made went in Ms. Ruth's pocket. Hell, Mr. Leon thought to himself, she maybe taking a few men back there herself. She ain't never ask him for no money the whole time he been living in her boarding house, and he ain't ever been to bed with her.

Mean as she is, he thought he couldn't imagine himself going to bed with her. He tried playfully…to conjure up in his mind what it would be like to screw this woman! Ms. Ruth had a nice shape to be as old as she is….what maybe fifty-five or sixty years old. Hell, it didn't matter how old she is. She wasn't bad looking for a big woman. She has large breast and a wide ass that would move up and down and jiggle as she walks. Nice full legs, but some of the biggest ass feet he had ever seen on a woman. Probably wouldn't be so bad screwing her if it wasn't for that nasty mouth and the odor of cigarette smoke that circled her body like a cloud. On top of that, she could drink and hold her liquor better than any man he knew. Mmm…screwing Ms. Ruth…hell he couldn't imagine it, and neither did his penis. He reached in his pocket and felt it…hell he couldn't even get it hard thinking about her! He laughed to himself; I wouldn't mind getting a piece a ass every now and then.

He remembered Helen the last woman he had screwed and she left him for another man. Said she didn't want no jailbird for a boyfriend. He stopped trying to find a woman because of the fear of being rejected. Hell, he thought, I'm not a bad looking man, just had a few problems, but I don't do none of those thing now…his thoughts trailed off when he reached the club.

He walked in, the smell of liquor and stale cigarette and cigar smoke made him cough a few times. He stopped drinking and smoking when he went to prison, and never picked up the habit again.

As his eyes adjusted to the darkness and dim lights in the small place, he spotted Ms. Ruth. She was leaning over a chair, her large brown breast exposed, and flirting with some old man grinning at her with no teeth in his mouth. He ignored her and kept walking. He paused every now and then to speak to someone who was leaving or trying to come in and get a drink, always asking the same question "Is the club still open?" He couldn't figure out why they called it a club. Mr. Reynolds had an old shack on his land about two acres from his house where he grew tobacco and at one time cotton.

Some of the colored men helped James Raye build another room onto it and sold fried fish sandwiches, bar-b-que ribs, and pig's feet on Friday and Saturday nights. Mr. Reynolds caught wind of it and turned it into a grill. He got a liquor license and sold beer. Mr. Reynolds told James Raye if he ran it for him, he would give him a cut of the money. That lasted a while until old man Raye had an idea of his own. Raye and a few men opened the back of the grill and built another room. They put some chairs and tables back there, stuck a few candles in some old green mason canning jars, and sat them on the tables for light. Word of mouth spread about the place, and it became known as 'Raye's Club.' James Raye knew the longer they stayed, the more money they spent. This didn't last too long either. When Mr. Reynolds caught wind of the new idea, he wanted a part of that too.

Hell, everyone in Tapasalle knew Mr. Reynolds did not like colored people, but he recognized the 'club' as a way to make some more money and sell his moonshine on the side. Like most juke joints, this one was a level higher because it not only provided food, drink and entertainment but sex too. Truly, people crowded the little joint, some were shoulder-to-shoulder, grinding, swaying and shaking. The piano and guitar sounds played, were soulful and bluesy. It made you want to dance. If you were standing close enough to the backroom, you could hear groans and guttural sounds coming from the small back room in the back of the kitchen. The room was conveniently built right next to the back door. Hell, on a good night the back door was just as crowded as the front. Mr. Reynolds and his brother Louis were known, to frequent the back door messing around with Ms. Ruth's colored girls. Across the small and dusty dance floor, over in a corner, men oblivious to the activity around them were hunched down throwing dice. Occasionally someone was cut or had the shit beat out of them for cheating, but they always came back for more.

Mr. Leon brought his reminiscing to a halt as soon as he reached the kitchen and saw the mess left from tonight's crowd. He started cleaning up the dishes. He wanted to be home by four 'o' clock am. Ms. Ruth came back there a few times to see if he needed anything. Most of the glasses were done. The only things left to clean were the ashtrays. That was easy enough to do. They were only sardine cans washed out and used for ashtrays. Ms. Ruth said they spent too much money replacing the glass ones that kept falling to the floor because some drunk wasn't watching what he was doing.

Ms. Ruth was collecting the tablecloths to take home and wash. The dishtowels on the counter she threw in a separate bag because they were usually very greasy and stained very bad. She didn't want to mix the dishtowels with the tablecloths. She thought, she would never be able to get the tablecloths white again.

The last customer finally got up and left. Mr. Leon looked at his watch; it was two-thirty. Ms. Ruth pulled the shade down at the front door and locked it. She always left one light on when she locked up. She was tired tonight. She had a lot on her mind. She had to find those papers that had mysteriously disappeared. Someone was taking her mail. Maybe it's those little half-white girls, but what could they do with them, she wondered. She knew it wasn't Mr. Leon because he did not know about the custody papers...wait a minute, unless the girls told him. Nah! She thought confidently, they is scared to death to cross her. Didn't that little young one feel the pain of her backhand a few weeks ago? I won't mention the papers again. I'll just look over the whole house myself maybe I misplaced them.

"You ready Ms. Ruth. I locked the back door, and put the trash out," said Mr. Leon. Interrupting her train of thought she answered, "Yes, I'm ready, let's go." They walked home in silence.

Chapter 24

1957, the missing pieces of a puzzle...

"How long have you been in New York?" Joanne asked Rachel. "Well, about a year or more. Are you from New York Joanne?" Rachel asked. "Yes, I lived with my mama in Long Island until she died two years ago. I still live in the same apartment, but with lots of cousins. That's how we manage to pay the rent," answered Joanne as she threw another box of crackers in her grocery cart. "Look Rachel, I have been doing all the talking tell me something about you." "There's not much to tell Joanne. I live in a rooming house on Fillmore and Grant Avenue, and I work for Delman's Cleaners right around the corner. I came up here a few years ago on a bus, and met this woman name Cecelia who told me where to find a room and she helped me find a job a week later. She was kind enough to let me stay with her for a few days. I really didn't have anywhere to go. I go to work and come back home and watch a little television with the old woman who runs the rooming house. I run a few errands for her, because she has arthritis in both legs and can't get around too well. She knocks off the rent for the room. I think that is so nice of her," said Rachel.

"You got any family?" Joanne asked. "Only a mother I haven't seen in years. I don't know if she is alive or dead. My mama told me she has a sister, but I never saw her. I remember her saying they didn't get along too well. They used to live together, but my mama left before I was born. I have no idea really, who my daddy is. Mama never talked about him and to tell you the truth I didn't ask. My mama finally left North Carolina when I was around seventeen years old. She told me she was not happy living there and as soon as she found some place to live, she would come back for me. In the mean time, I lived with my uncle for a while in his apartment. At least mama said he was my uncle. He had a stroke a few months after she left, and was placed in the state nursing home. He died there. I have been on my own ever since." "Well Rachel, you and I have quite a few things in common, we shop at the same grocery store and attend the same classes. However, I've got news for you; we are not going to sat around this weekend with nothing to do. There is this nice".... Rachel interrupted her. "Maybe some other time Joanne, I have a few things to do this weekend, is that all right?" "Sure Rachel, I'll see you in class." Joanne waved good-bye and went back down another isle looking for some saltine crackers.

Rachael left the store in a hurry. She felt bad lying to Joanne about her family. She thought I do have a family, two wonderful girls that I have not seen in over two years. I can't go back to get them until I find a place big enough for all of us. She didn't want to leave Tapasalle County. The Hayden family wanted her and her half-white kids out of Southend. People described her as shameless and a stupid ass nigger, whispering behind closed doors and sometimes in her presence. Ain't no colored man gonna want her cause she is damage goods. The only thing I did wrong was to fall in love with a white man, she thought sadly, as the happy and painful memories took over her conscious mind.

She remembered how she first met Clemmons. She was walking back home one warm and breezy evening from a church picnic over at Greater Mount Zion Devine Rock Baptist Church in Southend. A truck whizzed by and then backed up and came to a complete stop. She kept walking swinging her bag of left over food from the picnic. Suddenly the truck was behind her. The driver gunned the motor, and blew the horn and drove by her again. Frightened, she ran into a yard full of tall dried up cornstalks and ducked down behind the stalks and the tall wire fence. Her back was turned and she did not see the young man run up behind her. He snuck up from behind and tapped her on her shoulder. "Hi There," he said. "Did I scare you? If I did, I'm sorry. My name's Clemmons," he said with a beautiful grin that showed perfect straight white teeth. "Hi, Clemmons and yes you did scare me!" "Can I give you ride? How far do you live?" he asked still grinning. "I don't live far. I live in Southend on Carver Street. Are you going that way?" "I am now," he laughed offering his hand to help her up.

Rachel was a little hesitant and frightened at this white boy staring down at her. He has some nerve offering me a hand! Shit, white men won't even hold the door open for you especially if you are colored, she thought. "Come on I won't hurt you. My truck is over there," he said pointing to a blue pick up with the back window broken. "Here let me help you up, you'll get all dirty," he said as he extended his hand to help her up. Reluctantly Rachel let him help her get up and they walked over to his truck. "You sure it's okay for me to ride up front with you?" "Yeah it's okay. What did you said your name is?" asked Clemmons. "It's Rachel, Rachel Jackson." "Well Rachel, this is my truck and you can ride up front with me. It ain't nobody's business who I ride in my truck!" He laughed.

Clemmons drove her to Carver Street. Rachel thanked him for the ride. As she struggled to open the door, Clemmons jumped out, and ran around the passenger side and opened the door for her. He grabbed her hand and helped her out of the front seat of the truck. As she turned to leave, he ran to catch up with her.

"Rachel look, I have never been out with a colored girl. I…like you and want to…well take you to the movies sometimes." "I don't think people will like that very much Clemmons. That could be dangerous for you as well as me. What would your parents think about you taking a colored girl to the movies?" "They would think I am crazy and probably disown me," he laughed again. "Don't worry Rachel, we will be careful okay." Rachel couldn't resist the warm glow of his smile. "Okay, the movie does sound nice, what..." Before she could finish, Clemmons said, "Tomorrow we go to the movies. Where should I pick you up?" "Here, at Carver Street. You know we can't sit together. Colored people have to sit in the balcony and whites sit down stairs in the movie house, she explained." "We can meet when the movie is over." "Okay," Clemmons agreed.

The next day couldn't come fast enough. Rachel. was up all night thinking, I am going to the movies with a white boy. I must be crazy! The next day we met at Carver Street and Clemmons slip me a ten-dollar bill. "Here, pay for your movie and buy all the popcorn you can eat. I'll see you after the movie." Rachel was so excited, she couldn't remember what the movie was about, or the popcorn she ate. Her mind was on Clemmons, the white boy with the beautiful smile, sandy colored hair and brownish gray eyes. Rachel remembered after the movie, they met at an agreed upon spot. Most of the evening, we sat in his truck eating sandwiches and drinking sodas. We talked about leaving North Carolina, going up north, maybe to New York. He told me about his mama. She was okay, but didn't like him hanging around the colored boys all the time. Hell, he would say... "We are just friends' mother," or lie and say he gave them a ride.

Clemmons said his family believed colored people should stay in their place and everything would be all right. He said he didn't necessarily agree, but he didn't argue the point either. He said he would do what he wanted to do, and be friends with who he wanted to have as a friend.

Knowing all of this did not change my mind about seeing Clemmons. I like him from the beginning. I didn't see a white boy, I saw someone who liked me and wanted to be with me.

I was happy. We had to sneak around in other parts of the county, in the dark, abandoned houses, and barns.

You name it we tried it, so we would not be seen together. Early one morning Clemmons had picked me up and we were going fishing. His mama was driving into town early that same morning and spotted us together in the truck. Later that evening after he returned home, Clemmons said she asked him all kinds of questions, and most of all, why was he driving around with a colored girl in his truck.

He said he lied and told her I was Carl's sister and he was just giving me ride into town. She must have bought the lie, because Clemmons later told me his mama said she did not see anything wrong as long they were not seen together; at least that's what Clemmons always said. I insisted that we should be very careful when we met, especially the back roads Clemmons often took in order to pick me up in Southend.

Waiting to see Clemmons and hiding their friendship was beginning to take it's toll on Rachel. A few times, she tried to avoid seeing him. Once he ran into her in the grocery store. He wanted to give her a ride home, but she told him she had not finished shopping. It took everything in her heart to tell him that lie. She was tired of hiding and ducking. She really wanted the whole world to know about her and Clemmons. Keeping it to herself was like a huge cement rock tied around her neck.

On her days off at the Dumphrey's grocery store, she stayed inside or slept to avoid seeing Clemmons and to make the days go by quicker. As fate would have it, Clemmons came into the store one morning being careful not to let on to Mr. Pickett that he knew me. I was putting some can goods on the shelves when Mr. Pickett called me and asked if I saw that customer standing there. "Rachel, you want to stop what you are doing and help the young man find what he is looking for," his eyes displayed a can-you-move-quickly look. As I walked around to the front of the store, there was Clemmons standing there smiling. "Uh, Miss can you help me find the sandwich bread?" I walked over and pretended with all my strength to show him which shelf the bread was on. As I turned to leave, he quickly dropped a piece of paper on the floor, and walked up front to the cashier. I bent down to pick up the paper and put it in my pocket, and quickly went back to the stocking the shelf I was working on. When no one was around, I took the piece of paper out of my pocket and read it.

"Rachel meet me this evening at 5:30 at the corner of Carver Street. I miss you!"

    I did not think twice about meeting Clemmons. I missed him as well. I would meet him, and let him know how I feel about hiding our secret. Mr. Pickett told me I could leave early, because it looked like a storm was coming up and the store wasn't that busy, so I left around four 'o' clock that evening. Lucky for me the store was just a few blocks from where I lived. I quickly walked home showered and changed my clothes. It was getting dark outside and I didn't like thunderstorms. The noise and lightening always frightened me. I left anyway and ran to the corner of Carver Street. I didn't have to wait. Clemmons was parked across the street. He saw me and started up his truck. He swung around and pulled up in front of me. Being a gentleman, he jumped out the truck and came over to help me get in the truck. We didn't hug and kiss at first. It was still daylight and someone may see us. Clemmons drove to an area in the woods and parked the truck.

    "Rachel I brought some sandwiches and cokes. We can eat and talk if you like," he said. "I haven't eaten all day and I am kind of hungry." "What did you bring?" I asked removing the wrapping around the package that lay between us on the front seat. Clemmons reached over and took my hand, brought it to his mouth and kissed it. He caught me off guard. Suddenly I had lost my appetite and before I knew it, I was in his arms and kissing him deeply and passionately.

Bolts of lightening and the boom of thunder brought us back to the present. "It looks like the storm is getting worse. Come on we had better go," he said. I thought Clemmons was taking me home, but when I looked out the window, the rain was coming down real heavy, and we were turning onto a gravel road. There was a large white house up ahead. "This is my grandmother's house. I thought we could go inside for a while until the storm is over," he said very casually. "No! Clemmons, I will sit in the truck. I really don't want to go inside your grandmother's house. I feel very uncomfortable, what if someone sees us?" "It's okay Rachel. Granny is sleep; anyway, she lives on the other side of the house. She will never know you were here," he answered calmly. I live in the house with my granny and my mother. My mother is out of town and granny is the only one here," he said trying to convince me that it's all right for us to be there. "Okay Clemmons, but we are going to get soaking wet when we step out the truck," I protested trying to act as if I was all right with this!

We ran for the side door. Clemmons opened it and we walked in. Clemmons led me through a long hallway that was partially lighted. The house was beautiful. Pictures were hung on the ivory painted walls of very old white people dressed in very long dresses and holding umbrellas with ruffles around them. Pictures of horses, and various dogs also lined the walls. I paused for a closer look, and Clemmons opened a door to a room that was decorated in white and beige with two large windows with gold colored curtains that hung from the ceiling down to the floor. A very long chair that resembled a couch with no arms sat in one corner of the large room. Clemmons walked over and sat down on a large white bed that had four posts the size of tall oak trees, and a blue satin spread with matching pillowcases embroidered in the center with tiny white and yellow flowers.

"Who's room is this?" I whispered. "It used to be my Aunt Helen's room when she lived here. She died of some kind chest illness two years ago. It's my room now," he said quietly. "Don't worry Rachel; granny's room is on the other side of the house where the servants stay. "Here", he patted the bed... a motion for me to come over and sit beside him. "My clothes are wet Clemmons, and I don't want to wet up your bed covers." "Look, I know you are scared, but you have nothing to worry about. I would not have brought you here if I thought we would get caught. We will just stay until the storm is over and then we can leave, okay."

Clemmons was pulling Rachel toward the bed. "Take off those wet clothes before you catch cold or something." He pulled the corner of the blue satin spread up and around her shoulders. As Rachel began to remove her blouse, Clemmons playfully tugged at her bra strap. He slowly moved over to help her. She felt nervous but excited. Rachel thought, they had fooled around in the truck, a coupled of times, but they never had the opportunity to really make love. She knew tonight would be different. She was no longer afraid of the lightening and thunder. As each bolt of lightening lit up the sky and the sudden boom of thunder shook the house, she snuggled closer to him.

He pulled at my panties and whispered gently, "everything will be okay." "Rachel," he whispered my name softly, as he gently stroked the sides of my neck with his fingers, and worked them toward my breasts. I moved in closer to feel his warm body close to mine. He coupled my breasts in his hands... kissing each one and lingering... just slightly sucking and tugging at my nipples. I didn't want him to stop. As if he read my mind, he began to softly caress and stroke my thighs, his fingers probed and touch areas that had never been touched before. As if the storm was getting ready for it's final bolt of lightening and rumble of thunder, I felt the warm passionate thrust of his penis sending the quick sparks of lightening and rivers of pleasure through out my body. At last, reluctantly, we parted a few inches. We laid there, together in each other's arms in sweet silence.

Before we left, Clemmons check the property for damage from the storm. A few small trees were down, but nothing serious. Clemmons did not drop me off on Carver Street as we had previously agreed. He took me all the way home and waited until I opened the door and walked inside my apartment. Thank God, no noisy neighbors were up to see me get out of a truck with a white man. We spent a lot time together after that night, but the hiding and sneaking in and out of his granny's house continued.

After about six months into the relationship, I started to feel tired and my stomach was giving me a problem. I felt like throwing up much of the time, and I was rarely hungry. I knew I was pregnant…no period for three months and I slept constantly. I dreaded telling Clemmons. I really didn't know how he would react. We had enough problems trying to keep our relationship a secret. I finally told him one night he came to pick me up. The look on his face was something I was not expecting. I knew he was not going to jump for joy. However, he just held me and told me everything will be all right. "Don't worry Rachel, we'll work something out," his voice void of the confidence he normally displays.

Weeks went by and I continued to work until one morning, I felt weak and my head was spinning. I tried to make it to the little stool; I sometimes sat on when I was wiping down the bottom shelves. I missed it and fell to the floor knocking over the bucket of water I was using to clean the shelves. When I looked up, there was Mr. and Mrs. Pickett the storeowners, staring down at me, and Ms. Pickett was wiping my face with a cold washcloth. "Shhhhh…don't say anything Rachel; take your time getting up." She pulled a chair over for me sat down. "Mr. Pickett has gotten up the water and returned up front to help some customers," she said in a very caring tone of voice.

"Look, Rachel I know you are pregnant. I don't want to fire you, but we really need someone to help out, and work longer hours. Mr. Pickett and I was going to ask you to do it until the incident this morning. I am so sorry Rachel, but we can't be responsible if something happens to you and the baby." Ms. Pickett had tears in her eyes. I liked her and Mr. Pickett because they gave me a job and treated me good. I managed to stand up and used the back of the chair for support. "I understand Ms. Pickett, I'll leave now. I can get home." "No, wait until you are stronger Rachel, there's no hurry. Sat back down and get yourself together honey. I will pay you for the full week. I'm sure you can use the money." Ms. Pickett patted me on the shoulder and went up front with her husband.

A few days later, Clemmons came over and I told him I had lost my job because I passed out in the store. The owners knew I was pregnant and didn't want anything to happen to me. I was crying and I had a terrible headache. "Rachel, I can help. I have some money, and I will get you what you need. It's my fault too," he said smiling holding me close, kissing the side of my neck. I playfully struggled, pretending to get away. He pulled me closer, running his hand between my legs, whispering in my ear, 'I need to be close to you, Rachel."

Clemmons gave me money to pay the rent and buy food, and a few extra dollars for myself. At that time it never occurred to me that, his family was rich. I assumed he had a job, so I never questioned where he got the money. When it was time to have the baby, Clemmons took me to the county hospital in Southend, that's where most of the coloreds went to have their babies if they didn't have them at home. We walked through the hospital door and the nurse ran over and asked, "Is she ready to have the baby?" I answered, "Yes." I listened to Clemmons babbling on to the nurse how he was helping me out as a friend. Yeah, that white nurse didn't believe that crock of shit for one minute. I was in pain but I had to laugh silently to myself. The look on the nurse's face was one I would never forget…contempt!

Myrtle Ilene Jackson came into the world, white as new fallen snow and light brown hair and grayish brown eyes. Three days later, I was home. I knew I would have a lot of explaining to do, But that could wait. I wanted to enjoy the happiness I felt holding my little girl, and could not wait for Clemmons to see her. It was two weeks before Clemmons got up the nerve to come to my apartment. That morning when he saw Myrtle, his eyes became moist with tears. He kissed her head and held her for a long time. Later that afternoon, he left some money with me, and said he would be back later.

Rachel! Rachel Jackson! Someone was calling my name. I laid the baby down and went to the door. "Who is it?" I asked. "It's Mr. Simms" and me, "Nadine his wife!" I knew who they were now. The Negro owners of the apartment building, and they did not mind bragging about it to other Negro people. "Just a minute," I called out, hesitating a little before I opened the door. "Hi, you kind of caught me at a bad time," I lied. "Can we talk to you for a moment?" Nadine asked fiddling with the buttons on her coat. "Can we come in, please?" "Sure," I answered and opened the door for them to come in. "Look Rachel, I will get to the point. We know you had a baby a few weeks ago, and we just want to let you know, if you need anything please let us know," said Nadine. Mr. Simms just stood there with this sick smile on his face. "Thank you," I manage to say, though I was surprised. I always felt Nadine didn't like me. After all, she was not too friendly when we pass each other in the hallway or in the back yard taking out trash. "Can I see…we see the baby?" she asked with a little hesitance in her voice. "Yes, she is sleeping now. That's her lying on the bed." Nadine tiptoed into the bedroom and pulled back the blanket, and tiptoed back in the front room. "She is so precious. What did you name her?" Nadine asked trying to keep a straight face. "I named her 'Myrtle,' Nadine." Mr. Simms didn't look in the room. He just stood there by the door, where he had been standing for the past fifteen minutes.

"We'll better go now we don't want to wake her up," said Nadine. Well, that wasn't too bad… I thought a little too quickly. Nadine had gotten halfway through the door, and she turned and said, "Before I forget, we will have to go up on the rent. If you are a little late it's okay." I stood there and just looked at Nadine. I was angry, but I was in no position to make them angry with me. "It's okay Nadine, I understand. I will pay the extra rent, and by the way we won't be any trouble." I tried to sound normal as if their sudden piece of information did not knock me to my knees. They said their good-byes and left.

I closed the door and sat down at the kitchen table. Now, I have to ask Clemmons for extra money for the rent. I wasn't happy about that because he was already paying for everything. I knew I had to get back to work and soon. I gave Clemmons the news a few days later. Again, his famous words, "don't worry Rachel, I will take care of it," and he did for five years, but odd as it sounds Myrtle never saw much of her daddy. She was only two years old when he stopped coming to the house and Clemmons frequently asked that I meet him without the baby. This arrangement went on for about three years.

As if I had enough to worry about, I had missed my time of the month for the last two months. I had said nothing to Clemmons. Here lately, he seemed to have a lot on his mind. As fate would have it, around nine 'o'clock one evening, Clemmons came over unexpected. I knew something was wrong when I opened the door and saw his face. He walked in quickly as if someone was after him. "Is everything all right?" I asked reaching out to him. Avoiding my outstretched hands, and walking away from me, he answered, "Yes and No... Rachel, look I have to stop seeing you for a while. I have some things I have to work out. I will continue to give you money for you and Myrtle. I just can't explain it now. You got to trust me, okay!" He sounded upset and angry. "Look Clemmons, Myrtle is five years old and does not know you," I cried. "How long are we supposed to live like this? My whole world has fallen apart. I do not know what to do, and to make matters worse, I just can't have another baby! I can barely take care of Myrtle!" I shouted at him. His final words were, "I don't need anymore problems, I have enough of my own!" he sounded bitter. I didn't care anymore, I was angry too, and lashed out at him. "I am pregnant again Clemmons," and I sat down on the bed and cried. He quietly left the room. He opened the front door and never looked back. I never saw him again. The baby was born on Christmas day. I had not named her. I was depressed and couldn't figure out a name, so I called her my little 'sugar pudding.' I guess the name stuck, because I finally signed the birth certificate before I left the hospital, Sugar Pudding Jackson, father; Clemmons Hayden.

    I received money from Clemmons for a while and all of a sudden, it stopped. I had a little saved but not enough to last me. I knew I had to find a job. One afternoon when the girls were napping, I knocked on Nadine's door and asked if she could help me. I really didn't want to ask her for nothing. However, I needed some help. She invited me in. "Nadine, I can't stay long because the girls are sleep. I am going to run out of money soon, I really need to find a job but I don't have anyone to watch the girls while I work. I was wondering if you could watch them for me. I can't pay much." Nadine interrupted before I could finish. "You don't have to pay me now; I can wait until you get on your feet. Sure you can bring them here." "Thank you Nadine," was all I could say."

Nadine kept her promise and watched the girls while I worked various jobs. However, the good jobs were not for colored women. Most of my friends worked in restaurants as waitresses, washing dishes, maids or cleaning white folks home. I began to tire very easily and a few times, I lost my jobs because of my health. When I thought things could not get any worse, and on Sugar Pudding's second birthday, I answered a knock at the door. I asked, "Who's there?" "I am looking for a Rachel Jackson!" I opened the door, and saw this strange white man, who looked, as he was dressed for church and he held a briefcase in his hand. "Are you Rachel Jackson?" he asked quickly, looking all around him as if he was being followed. "Yes, I'm Rachel Jackson, and who are you, and what do you want with me?" "My name is Baylor Tyner. I represent Mrs. Stella Louise Hayden. I believe you know her grandson Clemmons Hayden." "What is this about Mr. Tyner?" I was getting very nervous and I did not like the way he stared at me! "Ms. Jackson, May I come in Please! This is very important and I would rather we speak in private." I asked him in and closed the door. "Ms. Jackson, I don't know quite how to say this but," he paused a moment. "Mrs. Hayden wants you to stop seeing her grandson Clemmons. She is prepared to pay you a small sum of money monthly if you deny the children…the girls were not fathered by Clemmons, and you and your family move to another county or city of your choosing." Silence, for a brief moment engulfed the small room.

Suddenly it occurred to Rachel and it was beginning to make sense now…why Clemmons stopped seeing her. It was the grandmother! Now, I understood why Clemmons said all those hurtful things to me. "Well…Mr. Tyner, I haven't seen Clemmons in two years, as a matter of fact today is his youngest daughter's second birthday." She was trying to remain calm, but the tears kept coming. She forgot the girls were napping, and suddenly she heard Myrtle call her. Myrtle walked out first and Sugar Pudding close behind her. They walked slowly over to her. Sugar Pudding hid behind her and Myrtle stood defiantly and stared at the white man. "Hello," Mr. Tyner said, reaching out to shake their hands. The girls did not respond. "Myrtle, take Sugar Pudding back in the bedroom and you stay there. I'll come and get you in a minute, okay."

They went quietly back to the bedroom, I turned to face him, "Mr. Tyner, I will have to ask you to leave. I don't want to hear anymore about Clemmons, or his grandmother. You tell her for me Mr. Tyner, Clemmons walked out on his family," she said fighting back tears. "I haven't seen or heard from him in two years," she said turning her face away from him. "I understand," he said sympathetically. Rachel walked over to the door and opened it as wide as it would open. She wiped back tears with the back of her hand. Mr. Tyner took out a large brown envelope from the briefcase he was carrying and laid it on the table. He walked hurriedly out the door. "I am sorry Ms. Jackson," he trailed off as he walked down the steps.

Rachel opened the envelope and looked inside. There were three small bundles of money wrapped together with a red rubber band, and a letter lying on top. Rachel reached for the letter first. Her hands shook as she unfolded the light blue paper. A light fragrance seeped from it. It smelled like lilacs and lavender. The handwriting was neat and looked as if who ever wrote it, took pains to make the letters as even as possible. As she read the contents of the letter, hot tears continued to flow down her cheeks. Tears dropped on to the letter, forming greenish blue circles that resembled ocean water.

"Dear Ms. Jackson, Please contact Mr. Tyner with your new address. I will continue to send you some money until

you are able to make it on your own." Stella Louise Hayden.

Mr. Tyner's name and telephone number was written at the bottom of the letter. Rachel sat down at the table, staring at the birthday cake Nadine had baked for Sugar Pudding. The envelope contained five-thousand dollars to leave the county of Southend with her daughters. Rachel had felt hurt before, but not this magnitude of sadness in her heart. The letter and the money made her realize to what degree she was 'really alone' and had no one to turn to or help her in her time of need.

"Mama!" "Mama! Can we come out now?" Rachel quickly wiped her face so the girls would not see her crying. "Yes, come on out. Sugar Pudding is going to cut this cake and we are going to eat some ice cream," she answered trying to sound as if nothing…nothing on this great earth was wrong with her.

After the girls ate their cake and ice cream, Rachel could hear them in the bedroom singing "Happy Birthday to you." After a while, it became very quiet. The only sounds you could hear were the loud ticking of the alarm clock that sat on the table, and the hum of the radio that Rachel had turned down, so she could think. She knew she had a decision to make, and she could not get any rest until that decision is made. She heard a voice, a strong voice, "You are not leaving, and no one will chase you out of Southend! She was angry, the hell with Mrs. Hayden and her hatred of me, and to hell with that no good bastard Clemmons!" It was her own voice supporting her decision to stay in Southend.

A few months later, while shopping for groceries, Rachel bumped into Carl a friend of Clemmons. She remembered Carl was friendly and treated her nice. Even though Carl is colored too, he didn't seem to mind that she and Clemmons were seeing one another. She asked Carl if he had seen Clemmons. "No I haven't…but ain't you heard? Rachel, Clemmons was arrested for involuntary manslaughter, carrying and using an unlicensed rifle and shooting deer out of season. Clemmons and some of his friends were in the woods hunting for deer. Clemmons spotted the antlers, as well as the others and began shooting. One of their bullets strayed and hit his mama. No one knows to this day, what his mama was doing in the woods that awful day. The police thought she was out taking a walk and may have gotten lost in the woods," Carl finished quickly. Feeling as though he had said too much, he said he had to go and waved good-bye to Rachel.

  Rachel processed the information in her mind, as God getting back at that mean old woman for trying to run her and her babies out of Southend. She didn't feel anything but contempt. She still had quite a bit of the money the old woman gave her to leave Southend. She had it hidden away in a safe place. She had planned to use it carefully until she found a job. Her rent was paid and there was plenty of food to eat and they had clothes to wear. Yes, she thought we would be all right.

  A few months later, Sugar Pudding started running a fever and vomiting up her food. She said her chest hurt. Nadine and I took her to the same county hospital where I had Sugar Pudding. The same old stares and questions greeted me as I walked in the door carrying Sugar Pudding in my arms. A large white nurse around my age, asked what was wrong, and I explained to her Sugar Pudding was sick and was breathing funny. The nurse quickly took Sugar Pudding from my arms and walked down the hall to an open room. Nadine and I had to walk fast to keep up with her.

  As we reached the open door, a doctor was just beginning to exam Sugar and asking where is the mother? "I am her mama, Rachel Jackson!" The doctor looked at me and continued to examine Sugar Pudding. I stood there waiting for the doctor to tell me something. I was afraid to ask what is wrong with my little girl.

Finally the doctor spoke. "Ms. Jackson we will have to keep your little girl. I am afraid she may have pneumonia. Go back to the nurse's counter and fill out her admission papers please. She will be fine. We will have her just like new in a few days."

Rachel was relieved and went back to the nurse's counter. After she filled out the papers, the nurse told her she could only see Sugar Pudding for a few minutes, because they were taking her to her room shortly. Never been separated from her girls before, Rachel was trying hard to hold back her tears. The nurse noticing Rachel's facial expression cheerfully said, "You don't have to worry, you can come back tomorrow morning," she smiled and lightly patted Rachel on her shoulder. "I want to stay with her. You don't understand, I have never been away from them, not even a day!" She was rambling on and crying and didn't care who saw her. The nurse stood firm, "She will be okay, and Ms. Jackson please don't let your daughter see you like this. Try to get yourself together!" Nadine walked over and grabbed Rachel by the arm. Rachel forgot Nadine was there. "Come on Rachel we can come back tomorrow. Let's go, she's asleep and wouldn't know you were in the room anyway," she said slightly agitated.

Nadine kept Myrtle and sent her to school while Rachel went to the hospital every morning to help the nurses' bath and take care of Sugar Pudding. Rachel was numb to the hurtful words, often said in her presence. As she walked down the hall each morning on her way to Rachel's room, she had to listen to the same old questions. "Is she the child's caretaker? Is she the nanny? Does she ever go home?" the nurses said, as Rachel walked past them to get to Sugar Pudding's room. Before she had reached the room, she overheard another nurse discussing Sugar. "Is the child white or colored?"

One morning after Sugar Pudding had been in the hospital a week, and as Rachel approached her room, she noticed the bed was empty. She did not panic; she simply thought her child went down for another x-ray. She was still standing in the room by the empty bed, when a nurse walked in asked her was she lost. "No, I am not lost. I am waiting for them to bring my daughter back to her room," Rachel said and walked over and sat down in a chair by the window. "You must be on the wrong floor," the nurse said indignantly. "I am not on the wrong floor! I have been coming here to this room everyday to help take care of my child," Rachel responded in frightened voice. Just as the nurse was leaving the room to find out what was going on, another white nurse who recognized Rachel coming in and out of Sugar's room, walked in. "Good morning Ms. Jackson, we moved your daughter down the hall to the colored section. She was put in this room by mistake. If you come with me I will take you there."

The nurse motioned for Rachel to leave. Rachel stood up, and walked over to the nurse and followed her down a long hall. Rachel noticed the walls in the hallway were not decorated; as nicely as the walls, where Sugar Pudding had been. An elderly colored nurse approached the white nurse that was standing next to Rachel. "Good morning Nurse Ellen," the colored nurse clapped her hands together, greeting the nurse enthusiastically. "Precious Jesus! Is this one of the church ladies you bringing to help me today," she asked walking toward Rachel to greet her.

Before the colored nurse could say good morning, Rachel looked disappointingly at the much older and deplorably large and untidy colored nurse and responded angrily, "I'm not a church lady! Where the hell is my child? Why is she being treated so awful?" Rachel stared at the colored nurse with pain and confusion on her face. The white nurse turned and walked quickly down the hall and was completely out of sight before Rachel noticed she was no longer standing next to her. The colored nurse walked over and spoke very kindly to Rachel. "I know you don't like what happened honey, but the hospital got rules. We don't put white and colored kids on the same floor. There was a mistake Ms. Jackson. You are Ms. Jackson?" She asked knowingly. "Yes, I am Rachel Jackson. Where is Sugar Pudding's room?" she asked still angry and upset. "She is in a room with four other little colored girls," the nurse answered without looking directly at Rachel. "She is being taken care of. She will be well enough to go home soon." It was evident the colored nurse was trying to make conversation with Rachel, and she was not in the mood to talk to this woman.

As Rachel reached the room, her heart dropped to her stomach. There were five beds in a row. In between each bed were white wooden partitions, cracked and peeling, and badly in need of a fresh coat of paint. Yellow faded curtains hung from each window, with hemlines tattered and worn from years of laundering and being pulled back to let the sun in. Old newspapers spread about the floor created a very bad illusion of covering up a spill. Balled up and used toilet tissues covered the floor. A few wooden chairs sat against the opposite side of the room. The only picture on the huge wall is a fat white naked baby with pink cheeks holding a washcloth sitting in metal tub advertising "Bright as White Soap Flakes."

The little colored girls have on gowns that were much too big or too small for their little bodies. Her eyes fell upon one little girl sitting on her bed with her thumb in her mouth and snot running down to her top lip. Her hair was nappy, and so full of bed lint you could knit a scarf. It looked as if it her hair had not been combed in a while. Another child was throwing what looked like oatmeal on the floor and another child with dried up oatmeal on the front of her gown, was rubbing her toe in the horrible mess. Another little girl was just lying there staring into space with a tube attached to her arm and a glass bottle filled with a clear yellow liquid hung over her. The room smelled like pee. Rolled up towels were lined in a row on the ledges of the three windows to keep out the cold air. Rachel's eyes fell on Sugar Pudding, who was in the last bed next to a metal table with some old wooden blocks sitting on it. Rachel rushed over to the bed, and picked up Sugar Pudding. Tears ran down her face. Sugar Pudding laid her head on her mother's shoulders, and looked up at her and smiled. "We going home mama?" she asked weakly. "Yes, as soon as I can talk to the doctor," and she kissed her on the forehead and brushed back her hair. She assumed the nurse had combed her hair and plaited it in the one long plait that hung down to the middle of her back.

Rachel stayed as long as the floor nurse would allow. She helped the elderly colored nurse, Ms. Lee; take care of the other girls until it was time for her to go. Rachel was afraid to leave Sugar Pudding in this room. She wasn't afraid that the girls would not get along, she was afraid they might not get the same care the white kids get on the other side of the long hallway. She stayed late enough to meet the evening colored nurse who also struck her as being rather slow and lazy. Rachel couldn't remember ever seeing her cleaning the room or straightening the bed covers over the children. The room was chilly and she noticed they slept curled up, little brown legs drawn closed to their chest, trying to keep warm. An old radio sat in one of the windows. A very low and persistent humming is the only sound coming from it.

The rest of the week, she watched other mothers come and go. They hardly said anything to her or Sugar. Just staring and making awful comments about the color of Sugar Pudding's skin and hair. One mother had the nerve to scold her daughter for sharing a pack of cookies with Sugar Pudding. The ignorant ass woman pulled the little girl over to her and said, "Don't let her touch your cookies; you don't know where her hands is been!"

Finally, Rachel had reached the point where she could not take another day of the way her child was being treated, the dirty smelly room, listening to the nasty remarks the other kids mamas made right if front of Sugar, and the nurses ignoring everything but their feeding time. She had made up her mind to take Sugar home immediately. Interrupting her thoughts, the doctor came into the room and said, "You can take Sugar Pudding home today."

The morning nurse, Ms. Lee, came in shortly after the doctor left, and gave her some instructions about how to care for Sugar Pudding and a bottle of medicine for her to take twice a day. The nurse turned to Rachel, grabbed her hands gently and said, "thank you for helping me with the other kids. I'll let the doctor know of your kindness and maybe they will knock a little off your hospital bill." The elderly nurse paused a minute…and she handed a little white bag to Sugar Pudding, smiled and patted her head. "Thank you Ms. Lee for taking care of Sugar Pudding, and I didn't mind helping. It kept my mind off the ugly things people were saying about my child."

Sugar Pudding tugged the nurse's uniform and said, "thank you!" They both smiled down at Sugar. Rachel was feeling much better she was taking her baby girl home today.

Rachel was happy, and relieved Sugar Pudding was fine. Myrtle made a get-well card for Sugar Pudding out of a brown paper bag, and she had drawn a pretty, yellow flower on it. She quickly handed the card to Sugar Pudding as she walked through the living room door. Sugar took the card and gave Myrtle a kiss on the cheek. She then grabbed Myrtle's hand and held on to it as if Myrtle was going to leave her. Myrtle reached down, and hugged Sugar tightly and kissed her baby sister on the cheek. Rachel saw this close bond and hoped it stayed with the girls for the rest of their lives.

Sugar's was running out of medicine again and the money Clemmons grandmother gave her to leave the county was almost gone. She used a large portion of the money to pay Sugar Pudding's hospital bill. Rachel found herself without money, and falling behind in the rent. A few times, she had to ask Nadine to feed the girls because there was not enough food to go around. Nadine fed the girls daily and made Myrtle's lunch for school.

She found jobs, but they weren't paying enough for her to catch up on her back rent. She was more than three months behind. Nadine was kind, and to her husband's dislike, Nadine let her pay what she could. This went on for about three years.

She tried to survive off friends, mainly men she had met working on her last job, Nelson's Packaging and Box factory over in Odenton County. Some treated her nice and others treated her badly when they found out her girls were by a white man. Tony was the exception. He loved her unconditionally. He would give her the world, but she couldn't love him. He had a good job and a limp. Not a bad limp, but a limp all the same, which some people who didn't know Tony thought he was a little slow or simple minded.

He explained the limp. He said he fell off a horse when he was small and his ankle never healed correctly because his mama never took him to the hospital to have it looked at. Tony wasn't the most handsome man; he was very dark, his skin the color of burnt firewood. His body is thin and short. It was bad enough that colored and white people stared at her kids, and when they were together, on the streets, they stared at him as well. Rachel thought, I guess we did look sort of out of place, a brown-skinned colored woman, two kids who appeared to look white, a very dark-skinned man five feet tall with a damn limp.

Shit! Rachael laughed to herself. "I can do a hell of a lot better than this!"

Nadine was always helpful and tried to understand what Rachel was going through. Days went by and suddenly Nadine started making excuses for not visiting, and had started complaining about feeding the girls. She knew something was awful wrong when Nadine wouldn't take the partial payment for rent. Rachel was worried and confused. She could not understand why Nadine was avoiding her and her girls. When she was between jobs, she barely got up to get Myrtle ready for school. Weeks went by and Rachel began to lose her appetite. She slept all day and was depressed most of the time.

Rachel remembered with sadness that fateful night, November 3, 1955. Nadine and Mr. Simms came to the apartment. "Rachel this is very hard for me and Mr. Simms. I know you have gone through a lot but you are several months behind in your rent and Mr. Simms and I can no longer let you stay here and not pay. You will have to leave as soon as you can. I am sorry but you leave us no choice Rachel," she said hanging her head down to avoid looking directly at her.

"I don't have anywhere to go Nadine! Where would I go with two little girls and no money? I can't leave just now, not until I find a home for my girls! I know very few people and I could not just leave them with strangers," she pleaded wearily. "You may as well! Rachel you can barely feed and clothe them yourself!" snapped Nadine, dragging on her cigarette like it was last one! "Than you take them! I can't keep them any longer! Can't you just keep them Nadine? Please… until I find a place for them." She begged, crying uncontrollably. Rachel's head was hurting awful bad. She sat down at the table and held her head in her hands. She couldn't argue anymore. Mr. Simms grabbed his wife by the arm. "Let's go Nadine. She will be out by tomorrow!" and he abruptly closed the door behind them.

Rachel quickly brought herself back to the present, trying desperately to tuck the sad and lonely memories in the back of her mind, and concentrate on the present moment, grocery shopping and answering Joanne's question. She knew she could never tell Joanne why she left the girls. Joanne would not understand that leaving my babies in that cold bus station was the hardest thing I ever did in my life.

I've got to find them and see how they are doing. Whoever found them in that bus station, I hope they read the note I pinned on Sugar Pudding. Rachel's thoughts raced back again, to the past. She stood there, in the middle of the store, remembering the last time she saw her girls. They were sitting in that cold bus station. Sugar Pudding curled up close to Myrtle to keep warm. Not wanting to take my eyes away, I had to try one more time to find a home for my babies. She remembered gently touching an old colored woman sitting on the metal bench next to her.

"Ms. Lady, Please wake up! My girls and I need somewhere to stay," I whispered. The old woman slowly raised her head up. "My Lord, miss why you got them girls out on such a cold night?" she asked looking down at Myrtle and Sugar Pudding. "We…we…need, they need a place to stay," I stammered. "Honey, I can't help you, but I hear this colored woman will take in people that ain't got nowhere to live. Her name being Ms. Emma. I hear people talk about her where I go to church. Let me think. What is her last name?" The old woman's brown eyes narrowed, "I remember now, Ms. Emma Jackson! Yes that's it, Emma Jackson! Now, I don't know her address, but everybody knows her." The old woman gave a long yawn patted, my knee, and dropped her head down to nod off again.

Rachel thought about the girls' everyday. She also wondered if Clemmons ever got out of jail. He had a brother, an older brother but she could not remember his name.

Chapter 25
Just being a daddy…

"My name is Mr. Sheldon. I am the county clerk. How can help you today," he asked standing there with both hands in his pockets and chewing on a half lit cigar. "Mr. Shelton, my name is Clemmons Hayden. Where can I file papers to get custody of my daughters?" he asked, nervously shifting from one leg to another for support. "Who do your daughters live with Mr. Hayden, and do they live in this county?" Clemmons watched as Mr. Sheldon removed the chewed up cigar from the corner of his mouth and dripping spit on his fingers as he laid the cigar in a ashtray.

"They live in this county with some friends," he lied. "You see their mama left them," he paused waiting for Mr. Sheldon to interrupt him but he didn't. Clemmons continued, "She abandoned them about a while back. I just found out today." He was trying hard to keep his story together. "Come into my office and I will give you some papers to fill out." Mr. Sheldon motioned for Clemmons to have a seat. He sat down at a small table covered with lots of papers and a lamp. Clemmons glanced at the lampshade, it was so thickly covered with dust, you really couldn't tell what its' original color was. Mr. Sheldon sat down across from him, pulled out his pen and began to date the papers lying on the table. "What is the mother's name Mr. Hayden?" "Do we need to use her name?" Clemmons asked rather cautiously. "Well, yes Mr. Hayden. We have to try and find her and notify her that you are asking for custody of your two children," he looked strangely at Mr. Hayden. "Is the mother alive Mr. Hayden?" he asked as he impatiently tapped his pen on the desk. "Yes, she's alive, I think…I'm not sure," he mumbled. "Look, can I just take the papers with me and bring them back tomorrow?" he asked anxiously. "No, you have to fill out this form first,"

Mr. Sheldon explained as he pushed the paper in front of Clemmons. He stared at the form. The first thing he laid eyes on was the questions asking the name of the mother and of the children.

He thought, I have come this far and I can't go back. I want the houses, and the land. "Mr. Sheldon, the mama's name is Rachael Jackson, and the two girls' names are Myrtle and Sugar Pudding, and I think their last name is Jackson too," he answered flatly. Mr. Sheldon was writing very quickly. He was nervous and didn't want Mr. Hayden to notice. Early this morning a colored man filed custody papers for two girls with the same name. Is this a coincident? Mr. Sheldon, thought for a few moments, allowing himself time to regain his composure.

"Mr. Hayden do you have an address for the mother and I will," he paused again… clearing his throat…need one for the two girls as well." "I don't know the address where they live, but I can find it. I have no address for the mama, just the address where she used to live," Clemmons answered. "Can you bring the information back tomorrow? We can't do anything until we get an address, you do understand, Mr. Hayden?" "Yes, I will try to get the information and bring it back." "If not tomorrow, you have until Friday, Mr. Hayden. The courts are not open on the weekends. If I am not here, give the information to Ms. Davis. If that is all Mr. Hayden, you can leave. Have a good day!"

Clemmons started down the hall and out the door, madder than he was when he first arrived. How in hell am I going to get that kind of information? I know Willie knows, but I don't want him to know what my plans are. Maybe I can ask Willie where the girls are. I'll tell him I'm just curious. He may buy it, Clemmons thought as got into his truck. He sat there for a few minutes thinking how he would bring up the subject of his girls…that is, without Willie getting suspicious. He reached in his pants pocket and pulled out a crumpled pack of cigarettes, lit one and pulled off.

Chapter 26
The hangover...

  Ol' Willie finally woke up from his drunken binge. Damn, he thought trying to swallow. His throat was dry and felt gritty. "Oh," he suddenly remembered. Mr. Tyner, that bastard came here earlier today with some bad news. What time is it? He was trying to find the clock. It was lying over in the corner in a heap of trash. Shit! The damn thing was still working. He looked at the clock. It was only seven 'o' clock in the evening. I must have passed out from all that drinking.

  Ol' Willie stumbled into the bathroom to take a shower. He smelled damn awful and felt the same. Ol' Willie was in the shower when Clemmons came back home. Clemmons called out to his brother. Willie! Willie! "We got to talk right now!" He was still hollering when Willie came out of the shower. He had a raggedy towel wrapped around his waist and a hole the size of a dinner plate exposing his penis. "Damn Willie, put on some clothes. The last thing I want to see right now is a half ass dressed man with his penis hanging out of a hole in a towel."

  Willie kept walking as if he did not hear Clemmons. He put some clothes on and came into the room to pick up the things he had trashed earlier. "What happened in here Willie?" asked Clemmons as he looked around the messy room. "Did somebody break in? You get in a fight with somebody?" "Look, Clemmons, one question at a time. No, I didn't get in a fight. Mr. Tyner... grandmother's lawyer came by that's all. He just pissed me off! Ain't nothing to worry about you hear!" Willie snapped. "It had to be awful bad news or something to make you trash the place." Clemmons kept his voice in a humbling and meek as hell tone of voice so as not to upset Willie. He needed some information, and if he argues with him over the mess in the house, Willie will get in his truck and leave. Willie always ran when he was confronted with a problem, had to tell the truth, or just got damn fed up with everybody and everything!

Clemmons walked around picking up broken things, not saying anything. Willie was standing by the stove waiting for the coffee to get hot. Now, thought Clemmons, this is my opportunity to talk to Willie. Clemmons reached up to the cabinet over the kitchen sink, and grabbed a coffee cup.

"Willie, I think I'll have a cup with you, okay. Here, sit down I'll get it for you old man! Hell, I ain't had no good coffee since I got home from prison. Let me pour that for you," he said cheerfully and patted Willie on his back. "Willie, I was thinking I would like to see the girls," he said quickly. "I've been doing some thinking. I want to see if they are being taking care of, you know like we were."

Clemmons sat down at the small kitchen table and folded his arms in front of him, and stared at Willie. "Well, what you think Willie. You want to go with me? I just want to see them. You know where this rooming house is?" Clemmons was trying to keep from getting agitated.

Willie was sitting there, acting as if he didn't hear him. Finally, Willie spoke clearing his throat the way Mr. Tyner did when he handed Willie the bad news. Clemmons did not like the way Willie was acting. Willie kept swallowing hard as if he was trying to keep the words in his mouth. "Is something wrong Willie?" Clemmons asked wiping his face and the back of his neck with the dishtowel. Willie didn't look at Clemmons. He rather put his head down, as if he was getting ready to pray. "Clemmons I have something to tell you. You may as well hear it from me." The room suddenly became quiet. So silent, Clemmons could almost hear Willie's heart beating. "Now you understand Clemmons what I'm gonna tell you is hard enough as it is to talk about it…so…" He paused holding his hands out to Clemmons. "Now, don't go jumping up and down, wait tell I'm finish will ya!"

Willie was begging. He sounded like a little boy who had done something terribly wrong and was trying hard through tears to tell his daddy what he done. "Look"...Willie paused again for a second time. "The lawyer came to see me today because they found another will and a letter that belong to grandmother. Mr. Tyner said it had been misplaced somehow and one of his office clerks found it this morning during the final processing and filing of grandmother's will."

He was getting angry all over again, and he didn't want Clemmons to react. "Willie, what was in the letter man? Why are you taking so long to tell me? What else can be that bad, shit! She left the houses and land to Rachel! Hell! We know that!" Clemmons voice was rising as he rose from his chair. "Clemmons, please! Let me finish will ya! The letter was a part of the first 'will' read a few weeks after the funeral, but there was more, much more Clemmons!" he explained as he banged the cup down on the table in front of him.

"Grandmother had some money and a few other accounts. In the second will and in a letter grandmother wrote, that the clerk found, she had left all of the money from her life insurance policy to Rachel, and any other money she may have left out." Willie was talking fast; real fast, as if the words were burning his tongue as he spoke them. "Mr. Tyner said…." What did you say!" Clemmons interrupted before he could finish. "Wait Clemmons, Now wait! Let me finish!" Willie pleaded. Clemmons was up on his feet, and pounding his fist into the screen door. "Why! Why! Why! Willie!"…he started to cry. Willie had never seen Clemmons cry. It was more of a wail you would hear at the funeral of a loved one. Clemmons shoulders shook and trembled with each cry and guttural sounds of pure anguish that seem to come from the pit of his stomach, up through his throat and then out of his mouth.

Willie tried to continue. "Clemmons please, get yourself together man! Mr. Tyner is reviewing all of grandmother's finances. He said it looks like there is nothing we can do because it was a legal and binding document and was witnessed a year before she died," explained Willie, walking cautiously over to Clemmons who was still standing. His right hand and wrist covered with blood from the scratches the screen made when he repeatedly rammed his fist threw the door. Blood spattered on the wall, the front door, the chair and the floor.

Clemmons just stood there. His eyes not blinking… just staring at absolutely nothing. Willie left Clemmons ass right where he was standing and got the hell out of the kitchen, fast! He quickly grabbed his shirt, pants and shorts that were lying on his bed. He dressed with the speed of lighting and thought to himself, "I can't talk to Clemmons! No one can talk to Clemmons when he is angry! I can't…and don't want to talk anymore, enough has been said," he mumbled out loudly. Willie hollered as he ran out the door, "Clemmons, I don't want to talk now!" Willie was still talking to himself as he made his way to his truck. "I have to do some serious planning to get back our houses the land and the money! Yeah!" he spoke aloud and with anger, "she gave away all that damn money!"

Chapter 27

Ms. Emma comes home...

Mr. Leon was up early. He didn't say a word to Ms. Ruth and hoped she would not find out Ms. Emma was coming home, at least not until he had picked up Ms. Emma and taken her and the girls to Ms. Emma's house. The girls were waiting patiently, and trying to hide their excitement. They did as Mr. Leon asked. They had packed their clothes, cleaned up the room and was waiting for him.

Now, Mr. Leon thought, I have to get rid of Ms. Ruth while I take the girls to get Ms. Emma. I need a ride, but I don't want to ask ol' Willie. I don't' trust him and the less he know about our business, the better it will be for Ms. Emma and them girls. If I can't find a ride then we will just have to take the bus to get Ms. Emma, and another bus to take them home. It will take awhile but the girls will be happy to get back home and away from Ms. Ruth.

Mr. Leon walked into kitchen, his prayers were answered, he found a note from Ms. Ruth on the kitchen table. The note read she had to go back to the club because she left the bag with the dirty tablecloths in the back room. Mmm...this will take her at least three hours to get there and back. That will give me enough time to go get Ms. Emma, he was thinking.

He hurried to the girl's room, to tell them to get ready, but to his surprise, they were waiting for him. He grabbed the largest bags and they carried the smaller ones. They had to walk a mile to the bus stop. They had been standing a while, and Myrtle notice Sugar Pudding was very quiet. "You okay, Sugar Pudding? Why are you so quiet?" she asked. "You are awfully quiet this morning. Sugar Pudding you sure you okay," Mr. Leon asked agreeing with Myrtle. "I feel fine Myrtle." She paused a little and asked, "Will we have food to eat at grandma's?

"Yes, Sugar Pudding you will have food to eat at Grandma's," Mr. Leon answered. "I will see to that, okay. Come on, here come the bus and remember what I told you do. When we get to the nursing home, you sit down stairs in the waiting room and be good until I come down with your grandma, okay. Then we all can go home," he said joyfully.

Mr. Leon and the girls did not have to wait long. When they arrived, Ms. Emma was waiting for them in the waiting room. Sugar Pudding saw her first, dropped the little bags she was carrying and quickly ran over to her. Not use to out bursts of affection, Ms. Emma didn't know what to do when they all ran over to her and gave her a hug. She stood there and looked at them with tears in her eyes. Mr. Leon knew how she felt. He walked over to where she was standing to help her. When she had regained her composure, she grabbed the girls by the hand and walked out the door with Mr. Leon walking behind them.

They made it down to the bus stop, and prepared for a long wait. They were sitting on the bench, when Mr. Harvey appeared and walked over to Mr. Leon to say hello. "Y'all be needing a ride. I got Mr. Reynolds old truck I can take you where you is going." Mr. Leon jump for joy! "Mr. Harvey, you is a sight for sore eyes! Why yes, you can take us where we is going," answered Mr. Leon. "But I have to ask a favor, could you take us by the grocery store first, I want to get some food for Ms. Emma and the girls." "Yeah, Mr. Leon, we can do that first."

"Nice seeing you again Ms. Emma," said Mr. Harvey. "Been a long time since we work together at Mr. Reynolds house ain't it?" "Yes, it's been a long time Mr. Harvey. It's nice to see you again. You still work for him? she asked." "Yes, I'm is still there Ms. Emma, but I don't work too hard, not like I use to. Look we is at the grocery store. Mr. Leon you and I can go in while Ms. Emma and the girls waits for us, okay." "Sure that will be fine," Mr. Leon agreed. They walked into the store.

"Grandma, I'm hungry said Sugar Pudding." "Wait a minute I think I've got some cookies the nurse gave me. Myrtle hand me that box on the floor of the truck." Myrtle reached down and grabbed the box. It was rather light, and she gave it to grandma. As she handed each of them a few cookies, she look them over with her eyes. She wasn't too sure, but their eyes seemed somewhat distant when they looked at her, and it seem like they had been through a lot since she was gone. She would never forgive Ms. Ruth if she treated the girls badly. After the girls are asleep, I will talk to Mr. Leon and find out what happened in that house, she was thinking to herself.

As the old truck pulled into the yard, Ms. Emma felt an uncomfortable feeling. She was afraid to go into her own house. Mr. Leon helped her up the steps and carefully missing the hole where a step use to be. Ms. Emma fidgeted around in her bag for her keys. She handed them to Mr. Leon, and he opened the door. "Wait now y'all, let me go in first," he announced in a loud voice in the event someone or something was in the house.

Mr. Harvey was behind the kids and helped them carry in their bags. Ms. Emma went straight to her room. She stepped in and quickly stepped back. "Some one has been in here Mr. Leon, I can feel it, and my clothes are thrown all over the room," she said in a frightened voice. Myrtle and Sugar Pudding stood close to Mr. Leon and waited. "Now, just stand here in the front room while Mr. Harvey and I take a look around."

They went into each room, checking the few windows, and walking around in the back yard. They did not see anything back there. As Mr. Harvey was leaving the kitchen, he saw a beer bottle lying in a corner. He almost didn't see it because it was behind the door, and he saw a smashed cigarette beside the bottle and an old handkerchief with dried blood stains on it. He bent down picked up everything and put them in his pocket. He didn't want Ms. Emma or the girls to see them. They sure enough will know someone had been in here, and will think, whoever it was, might come back. He patted his pocket to make sure the items were still there. He thought to himself, "I am trying to be of help to my old friend."

"Well, Mr. Leon if y'all don't be needin anything else, I got to go to work tonight." "Wait a minute Mr. Harvey, I'll walk out with you," said Mr. Leon. "I want to give Ms. Emma and the girls sometime to themselves. They ain't been together for a while," he said as he walked Mr. Harvey to his truck. "Mr. Leon I think somebody done been in this here house while Ms. Emma was gone," he whispered. "I have a feeling someone was here too," said Mr. Leon. I just wondered what they was looking for," he was scratching the back of his head.

"I plan to talk to Ms. Emma this evening about staying here with her and the girls for a while. Ms. Ruth been acting funny and I ain't comfortable there anymore," he explained. "Yeah, I get the same feeling every time I have to go to them big houses at night for Mr. Reynolds," complained Mr. Harvey. "What is going on with the houses?" asked Mr. Leon. "Don't tell nobody, but you know Mr. Leon, I been watching them houses ever since that old white lady died about five years ago.

Every now and then, I see ol' Willie driving around the land. He never git out the truck. He just sits there sometimes all night. Sometimes he be sitting up there with Mr. Reynolds. I don't know what be going on, but one night I heard some arguing. I was sleeping over that night in the large house. They were walking around talking about the old woman who lived there, had died and left everything to a nigger woman. I tell you Mr. Leon I was scared. Then I heard ol' Willie say he had a plan to get them houses. They left after that. I stayed all night in the old servant's room. Mr. Reynolds told me I could bring my old lady there when I stay the night, but don't tell nobody. He said what I was doing was real important. You know that white man pay me ten dollars a week to stay in the old house and twenty-five dollars a month to keep the houses clean and to keep turning them lights on and off, you know like someone lives there," he said as he folded his arms across his large stomach.

Mr. Leon listened to the tone of his voice and Mr. Harvey sounded like he was worried, and didn't too much like the work he was doing for Mr. Reynolds and ol' Willie. "Mr. Harvey, you better be careful. Sounds to me like ol' Willie and Mr. Reynolds maybe be up to something. You could be in a whole lot of trouble. How you know them houses belong to Mr. Reynolds, and what ol' Willie got to do with them houses," he asked Mr. Harvey. "Look, Mr. Harvey don't get in any trouble, but if I were you I would find out all I can. Do you know who the houses belong to?" asked Mr. Leon shaking his head from side to side. "Who knows Mr. Leon, I may find out something tonight, I'll be careful, okay. Talk to you tomorrow." Mr. Harvey got in the truck and left.

Chapter 28

Running out of time…

"Where is everybody," Ms. Ruth called as she struggled through the door with the dirty tablecloths she picked up from the club. "It's too damn quiet. Where is them girls?" she asked out loud looking around the room. "Myrtle! Sugar Pudding! Come in here and help me with these bags!" she yelled. Ms. Ruth walked through the little hall that led to the room were the girls' slept. She opened the door…right away she knew something was wrong. The room looked as if no one had slept in the bed. The dresser was empty and nothing, not nothing was left, not even a piece of clothing. She placed her hands on her massive hips and thinking they must have run away. She'd better find them before Mr. Leon gets home. But where in the world would two half-white girls go to. No…she thought, they didn't run away, and Mr. Leon is not here either. Maybe they is with him, she was trying hard to convince herself that they maybe with him.

    She picked up the bags with the tablecloths and walked out on the back porch. She emptied the first bag in the washing machine. Suddenly without any reason, she remembered how she got the machine. Mr. Leon had helped Mr. Cutter build a ramp on the front porch of his home for his wife's wheelchair. He wanted to roll her out to the yard, and to thank him, gave Mr. Leon the wringer washing machine in place of the money he couldn't pay him. Why would I be thinking of that now? She walked back in the front room and stopped before going into her bedroom to continue looking for those court papers that had somehow and some way gotten lost.

    She was having a problem getting her thoughts and ideas together. Something was wrong she couldn't shake the feeling. Something is missing. Her eyes followed the curtain that served as divider for the front room and the little room where Mr. Leon slept. She snatched back the faded curtain. Her eyes were not playing tricks, Mr. Leon's sleeping cot was folded up and the blankets were folded and stacked on top of the railings. She realized he was gone too. He had cleaned out his room and left.

She left the little room as fast as she could, to go find her purse and get a cigarette. Her hands were shaking and the telephone was ringing. She walked quickly over to the counter where the telephone sat and picked up the receiver and answered, "Hello, Ms. Ruth here!" she barked into the mouthpiece! "What! Who? I can hardly hear you lady! Speak up!" she hollered into the mouthpiece again! Ms. Ruth slowly repeated what the voice said on the other end of the receiver. "Would you please tell Mr. Leon Thomas, Ms. Emma Jackson left a sweater and a pair of glasses, thank…" Ms. Ruth dropped the receiver down on the table as if it was on fire. "Hello, is anyone there? Hello!.." came the words from the telephone receiver lying on the table.

Ms. Ruth never heard the voice. Her eyes were focused on that faded ass curtain that divided Mr. Leon's room from the front room. She picked up the cold black receiver and slammed it down as hard as she could knocking off a piece of black plastic that was around the mouthpiece. She stood there, with one hand on her hip watching the plastic piece twirl around on the floor before it came to a sudden stop. She feverishly searched the inside of her brassier, desperately trying to find a cigarette.

Chapter 29

The point of no return…

Ms. Emma and the girls were busy cleaning up the house, when Mr. Leon walked back in. "Ms. Emma can I speak with you a minute?" he asked. "Sure Mr. Leon, what you got on your mind?" "Ms. Emma I was wondering if I could stay here a spell…I know it sounds kind of strange me asking to stay here, but I just can't go back to that house. Ms. Emma I can be a lot of help fixing anything you needed fixing and watching them girls for you."

"Mr. Leon, you can stay as long as you need. I know somebody done been in here while we was gone. I have that feeling, and I know I would feel better if you stayed, but what you gonna tell Ms. Ruth?" "Don't worry about that none; I won't have to tell her much of anything. She didn't want us there no how. It's best I'm gone. So as the girls won't hear us, can I talk to you later after they is gone to sleep," he asked with a worried look on his face. "Sure we can talk later. The house is dusty and smelly and need a lot picking up before I can go to bed," she sounded tired. Mr. Leon didn't wait to be told what to do. He was looking for a broom, to start cleaning up in the front room.

Ms. Emma had gone to bed and Mr. Leon was still cleaning, putting things away, and only paused a moment to take some food to the girls and check on Ms. Emma…and thinking about his next move to help Ms. Emma and the girls.

Mr. Leon had been living with Ms. Emma for a few days and managed to fix the porch steps and the broken window in the front room. He looked around the house and thought it needed a lot of work. He could understand why the girls wanted to come back to this house, it was all they had, but it was theirs to walk around free without anyone hollering, threatening or smacking them around. He made a promise to himself the first night he stayed; he would make the house as comfortable as possible even if it meant finding some piecework to make some money. I will try to find Mr. Harvey and maybe he can find some work for me he thought, as he piled up the wood beside the old fireplace.

The next day Ms. Emma was feeling more like herself, he thought, and the girls were talking about school opening in a few days.

"Mr. Leon, you know I remember leaving my sweater and an old pair of glasses at the nursing home. Would you mind going up there one day and getting them for me?" she asked. "I can do it this morning Ms. Emma, I got to go in town today to get some nails. I might get lucky and catch a ride." Sugar Pudding heard the word 'ride.' "Where you going Uncle Leon?" She ran up to him and stood directly in front of him as if to stop him from going out the door. "Sugar Pudding you can't go this time, it's too far for you and Myrtle to walk. Stay here with your grandma okay." He reached up and playfully pulled her ribbon loose. He saw that smile and knew she was okay with his explanation. Myrtle was standing there smiling too. "Uncle Leon don't forget to bring us something back," she said. "Ms. Emma do you need anything?" He asked. "I'm fine Mr. Leon, you better be going so you can get back before dark," she warned. Myrtle noticed one very important thing about grandma, she was different, she didn't holler at them and she smiled a little more, and tried to comb Sugar Pudding's hair this morning.

Later that afternoon, Mr. Leon was coming out of the hardware store when he saw Mr. Harvey standing by Mr. Reynolds's truck. He looked around first before he walked over. He didn't want Mr. Reynolds to see him. He called out, "Hey there Mr. Harvey!" Mr. Harvey turned around and almost ran into Mr. Leon. "I'm glad to see you Mr. Leon, you by yourself?" "Yes, the girls are not here," he answered strangely." "You by yourself, Mr. Harvey, he asked?" "Yeah, Mr. Reynolds had me come in town to pick up some things for them houses I told you about. He wanted some chains and locks to put on the fences. He's been acting like something is wrong, him and ol' Willie. I am still trying to find out who them houses belong to. I have to be careful. I don't trust them Mr. Leon." "Mr. Harvey, would it be out of your way to take me to the nursing home where we picked up Ms. Emma? She left her sweater and glasses there." "No, it ain't that far, besides I don't much feel like going back to them houses right now. Come on get in," he said as he patted Mr. Leon on his back.

They were there in minutes. Mr. Leon jumped out the truck and walked hurriedly to the front entrance of the nursing home. He saw the same colored caretaker who brought Ms Emma down to the visitor's room to see the girls when she was here. "Good Morning," he said smiling. "Well, Good Morning to you. It's Mr. Thomas isn't it?" She asked cheerfully. "Yes, that's right," he responded. "What can I do for you today Mr. Thomas?" she asked as she played with a small locket around her neck, all the while looking at him with a little more in mind besides why he is there.

Caught a little off guard, Mr. Leon stammered a bit before he answered. "Oh…uh…Ms. Emma Jackson said she left her sweater and a pair of glasses the day she went home." "Yes, I remember. I called the number she had given me, and tried to tell the lady who answered the telephone to give the message to you sir. I guess we had a problem, we were disconnected Mr. Thomas. Wait here, I'll get her things." "The caretaker came back quickly and gave Mr. Leon a shopping bag with flowers on it. "Mr. Thomas, tell Ms. Emma I said Hello, and don't you forget to bring her back for her appointment next week!" she smiled and patted him on the arm. "Thank you, I will tell her. I have to go now," he said and walked out the front door and got in the truck. Mr. Leon was thinking, it has been a long time since a woman had flirted with him, and it made him feel good. He missed the closeness of being with a woman; however, he could not take another chance, being rejected again by another woman, because he had been to prison.

Making love to a woman was important to him, but not necessarily to go to bed with someone he did not care about. He thought to himself, he had the opportunity to screw one of Ms. Ruth's girls that work in the club, he just could not imagine letting one of them touch him, after they had been with so many men.

Chapter 30
Ambling along…

"Can't you drive a little faster than that Mr. Henry?" Ms. Ruth spoke rudely to the driver. It was the same old dusty looking man, which had driven her to the courthouse with Myrtle and Sugar Pudding when she filed for custody of the girls. This time she was going to the nursing home to find out who came and got Ms. Emma. She had a feeling Mr. Leon picked up Ms. Emma. She thought she was taking an awful chance going back in there. The last time she tried to see Ms. Emma, that nasty old white nurse threatened to call the police on her if she did not leave. Well, she was thinking, I have a reason this time. I'm coming to pick up Ms. Emma's sweater and her glasses. "That ought to be reason enough," she mumbled to herself.

Mr. Henry pulled up in front of the nursing home, and Ms. Ruth quickly jumped out! She walked around to the driver's side and told Mr. Henry to wait a few minutes. "No! I told you Ms. Ruth, for the last time, I have a funeral today and I got to take the car back!" he explained, quite irritated in the manner in which Ms. Ruth tried to boss him around. "Well, go head then, I will get back the best way I can! It ain't like the dead gonna get up and leave!" she yelled at him and walked off in a huff.

She started to light a cigarette but changed her mind. Her hands were shaking and she was in no mood to argue with that nurse if she was there today. Ms. Ruth patted down her dress, adjusted her hat and smooth out the tassel strings on her black satin purse. She had put on her Sunday best. She wanted to give the impression she was somebody important and not to be messed with.

As she went to open the door, and as fate would have it, that same old nasty white nurse was coming out. However, the nurse kept walking as if she did not recognized Ms. Ruth. Caught off guard, Ms. Ruth missed the step and tripped over her big feet. The white nurse hearing the ruckus, turned around, and walked back to Ms. Ruth. "Are you all right?" she asked abruptly. Ms. Ruth tried to turn her face away from the nurse, and mumbled, "I'm fine," and reached out to pick up her purse that had fallen on the ground. When she grabbed the strap, the contents fell out! The white nurse made an attempt to help. As she bent down to retrieve the spilled items, she recognized Ms. Ruth. "Aren't you the same colored woman who came here a few weeks ago and tried to sneak up on the floor? Who are you and what do you want here today?" The white nurse's dark blue eyes were opening and closing rapidly in a display of impatience. Ms. Ruth was pissed but had to keep her temper if she was to get any information. "I...I came here today to pick up Ms. Emma's sweater and her reading glasses. Someone called and said she had left them," she took in a deep breath, trying to control the urge to knock the holy shit out of this white woman. "Well I'll go in with you this time, to make sure you are not going to try anything funny!" The Nurse opened the door and held it wide open to make sure she kept an eye on Ms. Ruth.

    The nurse walked over to the counter and asked Ms. Whitley the caretaker, if anyone left a sweater and a pair of glasses. "Why yes, Nurse Ellis, but a colored man picked them up about two weeks ago. Ms. Emma Jackson left them about two weeks ago," she added. "Okay," the old white nurse said sarcastically. She turned toward Ms. Ruth and with a quick wave of her hand she said, "You can leave now. Someone tried to save you a trip!" she snickered and walked away.

    Ms. Ruth almost ran out the door, for fear that, old bitch of a nurse might change her mind and call the police on her. Hell! It's gonna take me at least three hours to get back home, and I have not found out who picked up Ms. Emma! Suddenly, a thought came to her mind, that caretaker said a colored man pick up the sweater and glasses. Well, it was a man and it had to be Mr. Leon. She reached in her satin purse for a cigarette. She fumbled around for a few minutes before she found some matches. She needed a cigarette badly to figure out what is going on, and do some serious thinking about making her next move. She drew long and hard on the lit cigarette… inhaling the smoke with so much anger, she started to cough.

She walked over and sat on the bench next to the bus stop to get herself together. She had a lot on her mind. She is running Mr. Raye's club all by herself. I could sure use Mr. Leon's help in the club. I haven't seen him in two weeks, and he has not been down to the club. Her thoughts rambled from one thing to another. How did he know Ms. Emma was coming home? It had to be ol' Willie! I'll find out! I'll call him and ask him why he didn't tell me? You can't trust no white people. She quickly lit another cigarette and dragged forcefully on it. The smoke circled about her head like rings around the planet Saturn.

It was close to two o'clock in the afternoon when she finally got home. She opened the door, went straight to the kitchen, and grabbed a bottle of old Granddad whiskey. She needed a drink and another cigarette. She opened the bottle and poured three fingers full into the glass, and emptied it down in one gulp. She leaned back into the kitchen chair and poured herself another drink. Well, she thought first things first. I've got to get another boarder…maybe I will open up the other two rooms. Damn! She fanned the air with her hands in a show of disgust. All of my plans are shot to hell! She took another drink and she lit a cigarette…

Chapter 31
Fall of 1957…

    Myrtle and Sugar Pudding returned to school and most of the kids remembered them and there were some new kids, but by now, they had gotten use to the stares and comments about their skin color and pretty hair. Myrtle heard from some other kids, Mr. Jenkins was sent to prison for raping Anna, and Anna's dad died from a chest illness. Anna, Jonathan and her mama moved to another city. Myrtle got a card from Anna, and a letter saying she liked the school she was going to, and asked Myrtle and Sugar Pudding to write to her.

    Myrtle was doing well and Sugar Pudding was growing out of that baby stage and developing some independence of her own. They still did not have many friends, and some of the girls that attended their school picked on them often, but they managed to stay out of trouble. This was Myrtle's last year at Apple Grove. It was the only colored school in Tapasalle County, which taught up to the eighth grade. Grandma was doing about as well as could be expected, and was getting up in age and napped most of the time.

    The girls still called Mr. Leon, 'Uncle Leon' and Ms. Emma, 'Grandma.' Uncle Leon walked the girls to school some mornings and other mornings he went to find work cleaning yards or whatever needed done to make some money.

    One morning Mr. Leon had to go to the hardware store to get some nails and a hammer, and the only person there was Mr. Fletcher. He seemed rather glad to see him. "Hi there Leon! What can I get for you today?" Mr. Leon was startled. He looked around quickly a little surprised! Mr. Fletcher ain't never spoke to him like that, all friendly and nice like.

"I'm fine Mr. Fletcher. I just need some nails and a hammer and I'll be on my way." "Uh…wait a minute…can I speak with you a moment Leon?" He sounded serious. "Why yes, I suppose you can Mr. Fletcher," Mr. Leon answered with some apprehension. "Leon, I need someone to help me in the store…now it don't pay much, and I was wondering if you could help me out?" Mr. Leon couldn't believe his ears. "Why yeah, I can help you out Mr. Fletcher. When you want me to start?" "I sure could use you today Leon. I got some big orders coming in and I need them on the shelves right away, okay!" "Fine, Mr. Fletcher. I'll start now," Mr. Leon said as he offered his hand to shake on it! Mr. Fletcher was all smiles! Mr. Leon worked until six-thirty that evening. Mr. Fletcher gave him a ride part of the way home. Mr. Leon couldn't wait to get back to Ms. Emma's and tell her the good news.

He knocked on the front door about seven-thirty that evening. Expecting the girls to answer the door, he held up their icy pops in his hand and some cookies he had picked up from the store. Ms. Emma opened the door, and looked as if she had seen a ghost. "I'm glad you is here Mr. Leon," she said wearily. "This is what came in the mail today." She handed Mr. Leon the white envelope and he stared at it. "Myrtle said it came from the court house." "Now Ms. Emma, let me read it and see what it says okay," he said quietly. "Here, come over here to the table and sit down. Where the girls?" he asked. "They is all right. They went to bed early. They got to get up so early in the morning to go to school," she said watching him closely as he opened the envelope, and began to read the letter aloud.

"*Dear Mrs. Emma Jackson, we have received your request to legally file for custody of the two young girls staying in your home, Myrtle and Sugar Pudding Jackson. The court will hear your request on Monday, September 11, 1957 at nine o'clock am. Please be on time and bring the girls with you. Report to room 12A – first floor of the Tapasalle County Court House. Sincerely, Mr. Rawley Sheldon, Court Clerk.*

Mr. Leon gave the letter to Ms. Emma and she just looked at it and quickly put it back in the envelope with the fancy stamp. Mr. Leon reached over and patted Ms. Emma's hand. "Ms. Emma there is no need to get worried. Everything will be all right. I will go with you and the girls. Don't say anything to nobody, understand," he said calmly. "They won't take them girls will they Mr. Leon?" "No this is just to make sure no one can take them from you Ms. Emma. Look, the hearing is just a few days away. We got time to talk to the girls and explain everything to them okay," he answered, giving her a re-assuring smile.

Ms. Emma felt better. Then she asked, pretending to be mad, "where you been all day Mr. Leon?" He laughed and told her what happened to him today when he went in town to pick up some nails and a new hammer. "It's not much money Ms. Emma, but I will use it to take care of you and them girls. I owe you that for letting me stay here," he said. "I'm glad you is here Mr. Leon. Someone came in my house, and I still don't know why or what they was looking for," she said. "Well, I'm here now, and I don't think they will be back. Now let's eat something and put this in the ice box for the girls." He handed the warm soda pops and cookies to Ms. Emma.

Chapter 32

Trying to come to grips...

Ol' Willie had gotten up early, going over and over in his mind this morning, the bad news that Mr. Tyner brought to his house a few months ago. I should pay the old bastard a visit he thought to himself. I want to see all them papers and look at them dates on the two wills, and get some copies. It ain't right that he is handling all grandmother's business. Clemmons and me should be doing that, not him he angrily told himself. I can't talk to Clemmons about this, he won't stop drinking long enough to listen or talk to me. Hell, granny as he called her, probably left the houses, land and money to that colored woman to teach him a lesson about seeing her, and of all things and creatures on earth, had not one, but two kids by the woman! No, he paused. Perhaps, they were purposely left out of her will because Clemmons shot her only child...our mother. Hell, they never figured out where the shot came from because all of them were shooting at the same damn deer!

The sheriff had it in for Clemmons. It was all over the county Clemmons was seeing that colored girl, and if that is not the reason... then why? There are some answers somewhere and I think that Mr. Tyner knows why grandmother changed the last will to include the money...all that damn money he thought to himself as he clinched his fists tightly! He wanted to ram them into something not a screen door as Clemmons did, but somebody's face, jaws, head, anywhere on anybody... Anyway, he could to find some answers to this goddamn mess! It's Clemmons fault, I know it's his fault! Why couldn't he have stayed away from that colored girl! Now, all he talks about when he is drinking is going to Ms. Ruth's house and see the girls. Hell that old colored woman don't know who the hell he is! I think I will go over to her house today…to make sure she don't know nothing. After all Clemmons did spend some prison time with her brother Malcolm before he died. Maybe Clemmons talked to Malcolm about Rachel and the kids. Shit, he thought, it's worth a visit, to talk to the old colored woman and her boarder Mr. Leon to find out what they know.

He walked towards the bathroom as if he was ninety years old. He had a lot on his mind, and knew within himself, it would be a long time before he finds any answers. However, he knew one thing for sure…he was going to pay the old bastard Tyner a visit first. He jumped in the shower quickly, thinking he had better hurry before Clemmons gets up. He didn't want him to know where he was going this morning and mess up his plans. Hell, the less he knows the better.

Clemmons was still sitting in his truck from the night before, too drunk to park it in the yard. He had bought him a truck yesterday. Damn, he thought, it's the best thing he had done since he got home from prison, which was to buy him a truck. Hell, he wanted to feel good about buying something for himself since he got home. After all, he had some money in the bank when he went to prison. What a better way to treat himself.

He sit in his new truck daydreaming. He conjured up visions of driving his truck around his land like the cowboys did, riding on their horses as they checked on the coloreds, and other farm help who worked the crops for them. He visualized rows and rows of tobacco, rows and rows of soybeans and orchards of apples trees, and he had other visions too, of being wealthy not rich! Shit! There is a fucking difference, he thought to himself. "Now all that is gone," he muttered bitterly. He could feel old man anger again rising up in his body, the back of his neck and jaws so tight, the veins in his neck stood out resembling thick tree roots that had surfaces the dirt.

He kept going over in his mind what Willie told him about the two wills, and that one question…yes one damn motherfucking question followed him since he was told about the houses, land and all that damn money being left to Rachel and the girls… Why did granny do it?

He tried desperately to answer the question, keeping in his mind, and remembering the love he had for his granny, so he would not think so terribly bad of her. He loved her dearly because she let him get away with murder! He was the youngest grandchild and got everything he asked for to the point where his mom would get upset with granny. Granny's excuse was always, "Lord knows we can afford it! Why not!" Then she would say a few unkind things about our daddy. "Darling," she would say to my mother, "You know they don't have a father in their lives! Hell, he took off with a woman so young; you could still smell her mama's breast milk on her breath! Elizabeth, baby, wake up! You have not heard from him since!"

Remembering his Granny brought a smile to Clemmons lips. His mind wandered some more. Was she in her right mind? Did she really hate me that much because she found out I was seeing a colored girl! I did promise her I would not see Rachel again, but that was before I knew Rachel was pregnant with my baby. I had to see Rachel to make sure everything was all right. I don't know to this day…who could have told her so much information. If…I ever find out! Wait… am I capable of killing someone, he thought to himself. He shook his head not wanting to think about how his mother was killed and he is sure he did not kill her that fateful day in the woods. He had fired his rifle that morning, but that was before his mother got hit. The sheriff didn't know where the shot came from. He started crying …only softly, like a whimper. He banged his head on the steering wheel of the truck to bring himself back to the present.

He wondered if granny could have been out of her mind, or maybe she was drugged. Who the hell, was with her at the time of her death? "Shit, I don't even know what she died of!" Clemmons was thinking aloud now. He had to hear his voice to make sure this shit is for real, and no one is playing a horrible joke or he has not yet awakened from a very bad nightmare!

He looked in his rearview mirror. He needed a shave, and a bath. He smelled like shit and felt like shit. "I thought you loved me granny!" He cried aloud in the truck. No one heard him through the windup windows. Slowly, he laid his head down on the steering wheel, trying desperately to get control of himself. So many thoughts were going around in his head. As he lifted his head, as if to pray to the Almighty God in the Heavens, he saw Willie out of his rearview mirror, run out and jump in his truck like he was in a sure fire hurry! He ducked his head so Willie wouldn't see him.

After Willie had driven off, Clemmons put the truck in gear and started following his brother. "I wonder where he going?" Clemmons was still talking aloud and to himself. He watched where Willie was going and the road did not look familiar to him. Hell he thought, I've been gone a quite a few years and the county has changed. He saw many colored people. They paid him no attention. Some were dragging heavy bags, others were trying to hitch a ride, and he even saw a few driving their own car or truck. Well, he surmised, I guess they can drive too! It's a free world.

Clemmons noticed Willie turning down a half dirt and gravel road. Old run-down houses lined the street. Discarded car tires painted white were sitting in some of the yards with green plants or some kind of flowers growing from the middle of the tire's hole. He slowed his speed.

Something was wrong! Why were all those people milling around in one spot? He slowed up some more and then he saw it…black smoke, the arid stench of burning wood drifting into his truck, his eyes began to water and his throat felt rough and dry. He quickly lost sight of Willie's old truck. Where did he go? The smoke was so thick he had to windup the windows to keep the smoke from coming in the truck. Damn! There's a fire! Clemmons could see a lot clearer now. Huge tall orange and yellow flames were coming from the front of the door and out of the windows on both sides of the large brown and white painted house. He heard the colored people hollering and yelling, "She's in there! Somebody got to get Ms. Ruth out of there! Where are the girls?" Someone yelled to the firefighters! "Did you see the girls?" a strange woman yelled. The house was engulfed in flames as tall as the old oak trees that grew in the yard.

The fire department had two bright red trucks with hoses lying on the ground. They manage to leave just enough space for a car or small truck to get pass. Clemmons saw two firemen waving their hands, talking to the crowd indicating whoever the woman is, was dead. Another firefighter was frantically telling a white man with a blue jacket on there were no kids in the house. Clemmons recognized the man. It was Willie. He watched as Willie turned around and walked back to where he had parked his truck.

It all came together for Clemmons. So, this is the rooming house where the old colored woman lived that took care of his girls, he thought. Clemmons panicked…he looked around trying to find two girls that looked half-white or with very light skin. Maybe they are in the crowd of people that had formed in the middle of the street. He was sweating beads of perspiration the size of raindrops as he pushed his way through the crowd of people.

He didn't care how he looked or how they looked at him, but he asked over and over as he pushed through the crowd of colored people, "have you seen two little girls that look white?" He knew he sounded like a damn fool, maybe somebody crazy, but he had to be sure the kids…no…his girls had not burned up in that awful fire. Most of the colored people answered him sadly, "no sir, we ain't seen no kids looking like that!" Some asked if he knew the woman that had died in the fire. He answered hurriedly, "No, sorry, I didn't know her!"

Satisfied the girls were not in the house at the time of the fire, Clemmons went looking for Willie. Willie's old truck was nowhere in sight. Clemmons made his way back through the crowd and to his truck. He pulled away from the smoke, the people and questions of how the house caught on fire. There were two very important questions on his mind, where is his girls and why was Willie going to that house?

Chapter 33

Traveling through the past...

This is the best cup of coffee I have had in a long while, Baylor Tyner thought to himself as he slowly sipped and re-read the second will that belong to Stella Louise Hayden. He felt a little rested since that awful encounter with Willie a while back. He was up late last night trying to write the letter to Judge Patrick Dickerson the overseer of Probate Court in Tapasalle County. Baylor Tyner knew the Hayden men were not going to give up without a fight, and since he is the power of attorney, it was up to him to secure the houses, land and the money for at least five more years. He knew he could use his power of attorney to file for an extension under certain circumstances. He thought it was wise to file for as much time as necessary. He decided to use Rachel and her daughters' unknown whereabouts, and the many efforts it would take to locate them and yes, the time it would take to present his case.

He also knew because of the present age of the girls, the oldest girl would need to be at least eighteen years old to satisfy the requirements of owning the estate and the money left to them.

Six to seven years should do it, he thought to himself. He was not in this alone however, the bank's vice president, Mr. Fenton Steed has to agree to the extension, and Baylor knew that would not be a problem because he handled the bank's mortgage, and Mr. Steed was the first cousin of Stella Hayden.

I guess Mrs. Hayden wanted to keep the bank business in the family, he thought chuckling to himself. He was feeling quite pleased with himself this fine morning. He had found away to prevent the Hayden boys from challenging and trying to void their grandmother's will, at least for a while. Now…all he has to do, is come up with some proof Rachel and her daughters are alive.

Willie more than verified the girls are alive. Now what about the mama, he pondered. Well, he drew in a deep breath and sighed, first things first. I had better file these papers first and tackle the other problem later. After all, he was still thinking, I owe that to Mrs. Hayden. A promise is a promise. Hell! What she does with her money is her own business, even though she is dead and gone, she is still paying me to carry out her last will and testament.

Baylor leaned back in his old comfortable chair in the kitchen. Shit! He laughed aloud, "I am probably the only wealthy attorney in North Carolina with an office chair sitting directly in his kitchen!" He folded his arms and leaned his head back slowly, still reminiscing about Mrs. Hayden, especially the night before she died. He would never forget that night as long as he lives, why… it is as clear in his mind, as if it had happened yesterday.

Mrs. Hayden had called the office, said she wanted to talk to me. When I arrived, there was her cousin Fenton Steed the bank's vice president, standing there looking like Abraham Lincoln with his black two-piece suit and a black hat in his hands. He looked as if he was ready to leave.

"Baylor, glad you could come," Mrs. Hayden announced in that all familiar raspy voice. "Fenton brought over the envelopes that I had placed in the safe a while ago. I want you to give them out after I am gone, you understand Baylor. With a quick wave of her hand, was another well-known gesture of hers that she used to dismiss you when she is through. "You can leave Fenton; I want to talk to Baylor alone." She coughed and placed a dainty handkerchief to her wrinkle lips. Fenton walked over and handed the envelopes to me, but he didn't leave the house, he merely stepped out into the hall. Fenton was Mrs. Hayden's favorite cousin and it pained him to see her like this. I looked through the envelopes. There were four and each had $5000 in them made out to the nurse, the doctor, and the two servants. I placed them inside my suit pocket. The nurse was standing beside the bed, and quickly leaned over to Mrs. Hayden and said, "If you need me for anything, just ring the bell. I will be just outside the room." She patted Mrs. Hayden's hands and walked out into the hallway with Fenton.

"Baylor, come a little closer." She patted the bed. "Here, sit next to me." Her voice sounded weak. "I want you to carry out my wishes to the best of your ability." She paused to catch her breath. "Baylor, I don't understand why Willie is not married by now, at least Clemmons has a family. I may not like it, but what's done is done. I can't change it, but I can make it better for the mother and the girls." She was smiling as if she saw something or someone come into the room. She continued, "I guess I am trying to make peace with God Baylor, before I die, and to makeup for the hatred I held in my heart for so long."

Baylor knew she was referring to Rachel even though she didn't speak her name. The lady has a heart thought Baylor. I can see it in her face as she speaks. Struggling to speak louder and her voice getting weaker by the hour…she continued to talk. "Baylor, I will never see my great-grandchildren. I blame myself for Clemmons mistakes, and Willie …well…Willie is different. He would not let anyone get close to him. He was always a loner, you know in a different world or place. You know Baylor, Willie couldn't wait to move out on his own. Clemmons on the other hand wanted to stay…he was in no hurry, and he wanted to run the family business. Fenton helped him get started…he…he was doing fine…until Clemmons met the girl…Rachel," she paused to catch her breath.

"My world fell apart Baylor, and then that fateful morning when his mother was killed, my only daughter and child, I blamed everyone and everybody. I wanted that colored girl and her half-white children out of Clemmons life. I am sorry now...but it won't change anything. I left the money to Rachel and the girls, not to say I am sorry or for their forgiveness--but to give them the chances, I took from Clemmons. You see Baylor, Clemmons is weak and he would never have taken care of them. I don't want to die with that on my conscious. Before my husband died, we took pride in the business and we worked hard to get to the point where we were financially well off. I guess some people would say we are quite wealthy..." she trailed off the sentence. The strange smile appeared on her face again. "Baylor...I am tired, please take care of everything," were her last words. I remember Mrs. Hayden grabbing my hand and she held on to it until she went to sleep.

It was quiet in the room; I don't know how long I sat there before I noticed the nurse, Fenton and her doctor were standing in the room. The doctor came over and listened to her chest. He wrapped the stethoscope around his hands and said, "she may not make it through the night, I'm sorry!"

Mrs. Hayden lived through the night and passed quietly in the wee hours of the morning. We were still in her room when she died. The doctor pronounced Mrs. Hayden's death and the nurse arranged for the funeral home to pick up the body. Fenton and I took care of everything else. Clemmons was in prison at the time of her passing and we did not know where Willie was. However, a week later after locating Willie I broke the news to him.

Mmm...Baylor's mind was now on the present...he was thinking it seems I am always breaking some kind of news to Willie. Well, I can't waste anymore time, I've got to get back to these papers and get to the courthouse to file them.

Baylor put the papers in his briefcase and was just about to leave when he heard a tapping sound at his front door. Tap! Tap! There it is again. Baylor tiptoed very carefully to look out the side window. Willie was standing there! He's got some nerve popping up to my home! Well, Baylor thought to himself, he would just have to stand out there. I am not going to have a confrontation with him. He watched Willie walk off the porch and down the steps to his truck. He waited patiently until he pulled off.

Chapter 34

Members of the family…

Mr. Leon woke up the girls up very early. It was Monday, and they had to be in the courthouse by nine 'o' clock this morning. He had spent the weekend trying to find a ride. Mr. Harvey was taking them this morning because he had to pick up some things for Mr. Reynolds.

The girls were wiping their eyes, "what time is it Uncle Leon? Is it still dark outside?" They asked. "No, it's not dark outside. Anyway, y'all come on in here with me, and your grandma. Ms. Emma and I got to talk you about something important," he said. "Are we going somewhere," Myrtle asked. "Yes, but listen to Mr. Leon," said Grandma. "Your grandma has to go to court this morning to get custody of you two girls. It's not a bad thing… it's a good thing that is happening. You see Ms. Ruth was trying to get custody to keep you from your grandma. Your grandma filed papers a few months ago to keep you and take care of you, you understand?"

Mr. Leon tried to read the expressions on their faces. "I know about the papers Uncle Leon," said Myrtle. "We understand. Let's go! I am supposed to be in school this morning, I guess it is okay to miss one morning," Myrtle said nonchalantly and smiled at Mr. Leon. Mr. Leon looked at Ms. Emma and she shook her head from side to side and laughed. "You heard them Mr. Leon, let's go!" Ms. Emma and Mr. Leon waited for the girls to get dressed. Mr. Harvey was outside waiting for them in the truck.

Mr. Leon handed each of them a little bag. He had packed sandwiches and a piece of fruit incase they got hungry. He loved those girls as if they were his own.

Ms. Emma was very quiet, and Mr. Leon knew she was afraid she wouldn't be able to talk to the judge. Mr.

Leon patted her hand and whispered, "don't worry everything will be fine."

They arrived to the County Court House at eight-fifteen a.m. The corridors were full of people were standing against the walls and the wooden benches were full. Mr. Leon asked the clerk who was walking towards them, "Excuse me, where is Room 1A?" The clerk said, "You are standing in front of it." Mr. Leon looked up at the tall dark shinny wooden door with the gold handles, and right above the top of the door was a wooden plaque with **Courtroom 1A** in gold letters.

Mr. Leon opened the door and saw a large courtroom full of people, children and nowhere to sit. They managed to get through the crowd and stood in a corner as close to the wall as possible. The same clerk that had helped Mr. Leon came forward and asked everyone to settle down, he had an announcement, and 'they' had to be very quiet and listen for their names.

"When you hear your name called, please stand. I will take you to the Judge who is hearing your case." Suddenly it became quiet, and the clerk started calling names. After a few minutes, he called "Emma Jackson!" Mr. Leon walked over to where the clerk was standing and Ms. Emma, Myrtle and Sugar Pudding followed him.

The clerk led them down a very long hall to **Courtroom 3A**. The clerk opened the door, and stepped back so they could walk in. "Mr. Leon could not believe his eyes. They were the only ones in the courtroom. The clerk asked them to walk to the front and stand. They walked up to the large table and stood before the judge. The clerk walked up to the judge's bench and handed him some papers and a folder. The judge spoke.

"Good morning, folks! I am Judge Lester Collins. Since the courts are awful crowded today, I will be needed in more than one courtroom. I will hear your request and rule on it today. You will not have to come back unless you are asked to do so. Now, when I call your name just answer yes or present. "Ms. Emma Jackson!" "Yes," she answered. "Myrtle Jackson!" Yes," she answered. Sugar Pudding Jackson" "I am right here, standing in front of you," she said with a giggle. "That's fine said the judge," and gave a little laugh. "Ms. Emma Jackson I have read your request for custody of the two girls. All the papers are in order. I must say you seem to be doing a splendid job taking care of the girls. I see where they have lived with you for two years, and you are their next of kin, is that correct!" Without any hesitation, she answered "yes." Ms. Emma looked toward Mr. Leon and then at the girls. "All I need you to do Ms. Jackson is sign the paper the clerk is bringing to you, and I will grant you permanent custody."

The clerk handed the papers to Emma Jackson, she took them and went over to the table and sat down. Her hands were shaking. She was thinking I can't sign the papers. All of a sudden, Myrtle spoke up, "Sir can we sign too? Please," she begged. "Well, I see nothing wrong with that request, yes you can!" Myrtle signed for her grandma, and she printed her own name next to it and Sugar Pudding printed her name at the bottom. When they were finished, Mr. Leon gave the clerk the papers. "This is fine. Ms. Emma Jackson. I award you full custody of the girls, and if you need any assistance, the clerk will help you. Have a nice Morning!"

Ms. Emma could not believe what had just happened. "Can we go now Mr. Leon?" she asked. "Yes, we can go, I hope Mr. Harvey didn't leave us," he said jokingly as he grabbed the girls by the hand. "Let's go, you don't want to be late for school, do you?" "Do we have to go to school whined Sugar Pudding?" "Well, grandma…? What do you think?" asked Mr. Leon halfway joking with her. "I think they should go to school, and when they get back I'll have a nice dinner waiting for them," she said, and without warning, she reached up and pulled Myrtle's ribbon loose, and laughed. Myrtle gave her a hug without thinking and thought to herself, it felt real good.

Mr. Harvey was waiting outside in the truck. He helped the girls get comfortable in the back of the truck and they drove off. Sugar Pudding turned to Myrtle and asked, "Is grandma our grandma forever?" "Yes, Sugar Pudding, we don't have to worry about anyone taking us away."

Chapter 35

A date with destiny…

Baylor Tyner was running up the courthouse steps. He was supposed to be here by ten 'o' clock am. Waiting a while before leaving his house made him late. However, he wanted to make sure Willie had gone and not made a turn to come back. He still felt good this morning, and once the papers are filed, he will feel even better. He walked up to the third floor to Judge Patrick Dickerson's courtroom. Damn! It's Monday, and I know the courts are crowded. Maybe I can convince the clerk it's a matter of life and death, and I would be most appreciative if he could get me in to see the judge. A fifty-dollar bill should do it! Baylor walked up to the door and carefully opened it.

A few people were sitting in the courtroom. Baylor walked up to one of the clerks standing in a circle talking. "Excuse me, Good Morning," he said pleasantly. "Could I speak with you? I am looking for Judge Dickerson's chambers." "I'll take you there, but you may have to wait. Today is Monday and we are very crowded today. What did you say your name was?" The clerk asked as Baylor slipped him the fifty-dollar bill.

"Judge Dickerson, a Mr. Baylor Tyner wishes to speak to you," the clerk announced. "Good Morning, I remember you Mr. Tyner," said the judge. "You are on the board of the Bridgefield Bank of North Carolina. What can I do for you today?" He asked shaking Baylor Tyner's hand. "Well thank you sir! I am the power of attorney for Stella Louise Hayden. She passed a few years ago. I am having a little problem locating three of the heirs to her estate. I need to file an extension for five years until the third party is located." "Let me see what you have there, Mr. Tyner." Baylor handed the letter he had stayed up all night to write and the special prepared folder with information about the heirs to Judge Dickerson. A few minutes maybe twenty had pass by, and the judge was still reading and looking through the folder. Judge Dickerson raised his head and looked toward Baylor Tyner. "Are you sure you can find the mother, Mr. Tyner?" he asked with obvious concern in his voice.

"Well, I've got some pretty good leads, and I am working on them now," he lied. "I see, well I can grant you the time or an extension. Nevertheless, according to laws of probate you know the 'will' can still be challenged by the grandsons even though they were not included in the will. I am going to grant you the extension because minor children are involved. The extension will begin today. By the way, the name 'Stella Louise Hayden' sounds familiar. Is this the same Hayden's that own the saw mills in Tapsalle County, right next to Bridgefield County?" The judge asked rubbing his chin. "Yes, that is the same Hayden family," Baylor Tyner answered quickly. "I also remember something about one of the sons killing their mother…a horrible shooting accident I believe." "That's also correct Judge Dickerson," replied Baylor Tyner. "Well…one moment Mr. Tyner, let me get one of the clerks. I will be right back." Baylor was too scared to feel too good. This cannot be happening to me, he was thinking. No sooner had he finish his thought, the judge was back and with a clerk. The same one he gave the fifty dollars to. "Clifton, please take Mr. Tyner down to Wills and Probate and file the extension on his case not to exceed seven years. The extension begins today. Mr. Tyner, it was nice to have seen you again. If I can be of further help, let me know. Have a good day!" He shook Baylor's hand on the way out.

Baylor was happy for now. However, the Judge's words echoed in his mind. "The will can still be challenged." Yes Judge Dickerson, Baylor Tyner remarked quietly to himself; "but only if the challengers have proof the grandmother was subjected to the undue influence of another person or the executer of the will lacked the mental capacity to sign the document." Whether the grandson's know it or not, their grandmother was a very smart woman and thanks to her generosity, I can take a very long and much needed vacation while I am still in my mental capacity to enjoy it, he laughed somewhat amused with his thoughts.

As a police car cruised by him, Baylor thought wise to reduce his speed. He did not want anything to prevent him from leaving Tapasalle County this afternoon, nothing!

He finally pulled up in his driveway next to his well-kept lawn, opened his door and grabbed the suitcase sitting by the spiraling stairs. He had packed it a few days ago. He looked around, patted his suit coat for the airline tickets. Satisfied everything was fine, he closed the door and left.

Chapter 36

You ain't fooling no one…

Clemmons looked at his watch. Shit! It's eleven 'o' clock in the morning. Where did all the time go? He had been driving around trying to figure out his next move. He knew he had to find the girls. He didn't know exactly where to start, but he knew Willie had some ideas and he had to talk to him. He realized Willie blamed him for every goddamn thing that has happen with the houses, land and the money left to Rachel.

Clemmons pulled his new truck up in the yard. Well, he could see Willie wasn't back yet. Well, he thought to himself, I'd just go inside and wait for him. We gotta talk and no hollering, no breaking up things…just talk. He opened the door and right away, the stench of rotten food made him nauseated. Damn! The trash must have been in here for a few days. He started cleaning up the stinking mess. Clemmons was going over in head, how he would approach the subject of the wills with Willie, his hopes of finding the girls, and at the same time, do this without upsetting him. He was almost finish cleaning up the stinking mess, when he heard Willie's truck. Not wanting a confrontation, he stayed in the kitchen and continued putting things away. He had the mop in his hand when Willie walked into the kitchen.

"Hey! Willie how's it going? I just thought I would clean up a little," Clemmons greeted him trying to sound cheerful. "Is everything okay?" Clemmons asked cautiously. Willie stood there for a brief moment and finally walked over to the table and pulled out a chair. "Clemmons…he swallowed, we got to talk. I got something to tell you, something that happened this morning. It's not so good. Look put down that mop and come over here and sit down will ya," he pleaded. Clemmons put the mop back in the pail and came over to the table. He had a feeling of what Willie was going to tell him, and he thought he had better go along with the news and act surprise. "Yeah, Willie we can talk, you want some coffee or something?" Clemmons asked. "No...I'm okay, for now," Willie answered.

"You know I told you your kids were living with Ms. Ruth, the colored woman who ran the boarding house in town, right. Well this morning the house caught fire and burned up with Ms. Ruth inside. Now...wait the kids were not inside or the old colored man Mr. Leon," Willie added quickly. He did not want Clemmons to explode until he had finished. "She was the only one in the house at the time. I heard the firefighter telling some of the people standing out there; maybe she was smoking a cigarette or cooking on the stove and fell asleep." Clemmons was quiet for a minute and then he said, "Damn Willie, how'd that happen? Does anybody know where the kids are?" he asked trying to sound very concerned as he pressed for some more information. "How we gonna find the kids...uh, my girls?" He asked Willie. This time he was not pretending. Clemmons needed to know right now, where they are, if he is still going to try, and get custody of them. "I'm gonna do some checking around okay, just be calm. We gonna find them girls," Willie offered the words as some comfort to Clemmons.

He needed his brother to cooperate with him, because he had plans too, and this is not the right time for them to be hollering and yelling at each other. "Now for starters, I went to Mr. Tyner's house this morning after I left the fire, but he wasn't home. Clemmons, we need to get copies of the wills, maybe we can challenge both of them," and he went on sounding quite enthusiastic and full of energy.

Willie felt his strength coming back. "Tell me Clemmons, what are you thinking?" he asked trying to get

Clemmons to feel the same way or at least agree with him about the wills. "Well, I was thinking the same thing Willie, only contesting the wills may not work," he answered very carefully. "For one thing we will need a lawyer... that would cost a lot of money Willie...something you and I ain't got a lot of right now. What if granny was not in her right mind at the time she wrote the 'wills?' How would we know about her health? Man, I was in prison and you were out of town when granny died. Do you know who was with her when she passed? You see Willie, we would lose the case, cause ain't no one gonna say granny was crazy! You think the nurse, the doctor, Mr. Tyner or whoever was with her, gonna testify against granny?" Too late, he felt his anger slowly crawling up from the back of his neck to his jaws. He knew he had to calm down quick, or Willie will get up and leave. "Look, Willie I say we find the girls first and then we take it from there. We can figure out this mess then," Clemmons pleaded.

    Willie looked at his brother, and rubbed his chin like he was in deep thought. Shit, he must think I'm a goddamn stupid jackass, if he thinks for one moment I would go for that crock of shit he just handed me. Okay, I'll go along with his shit, and see what's on his mind. By the expression on his face, he was trying too hard to convince me that he does not have a plan. He's got a plan, I just have to find out what it is and very soon, Willie thought. "Okay, Clemmons, maybe you got a point. We'll try to find the girls, okay." Clemmons liked his own plan the best, but he had to be very careful.

Chapter 37

Trust and sadness...

Mr. Leon knew he was very late getting to the hardware store. He had told Mr. Fletcher on Saturday he had some business to take care of today. He looked at his watch. It was one-thirty already. Most of the afternoon was over. Sending the girls off to school and taking Ms. Emma to the store and back to her house took awhile. Well he thought, I'm here now, and he walked into the store.

"Good afternoon Mr. Fletcher," said Mr. Leon cheerfully, throwing up his hand and waving to Mr. Fletcher. "I know I'm late, my business took a little longer than I had thought," he explained. "That's okay Leon, come on we got a lot of supplies to put on the shelves," Mr. Fletcher said as he continued to open the boxes. "By the way, Leon, I may have to leave a little early some evenings. My wife is ailing and don't like to be home alone when she feels bad. You gonna have to lock up on those nights, okay. Don't worry Leon I'll show how to lock up. Now, bring me that ladder in the front of the store," he said without stopping his flow of words.

Mr. Leon was still standing in the exact same spot when he walked in. He could not believe his ears! When he finally came to his senses, he asked Mr. Fletcher, "You sure you want me to lock up sir...uh, Mr. Fletcher?" He asked, rubbing his neck and face with his hands." "Yes, Leon, now come on get to work!" Mr. Leon had never worked so hard before. He wanted Mr. Fletcher to trust him more than ever, after all that is why he served time in prison, for stealing. He wiped that thought away immediately and starting thinking about how he was going to spend the extra money. He was so deep in thought he had not realized it was almost six 'o' clock, and time to close the store. Mr. Fletcher called his name and that brought him back to the present. "Leon, hurry up and finish and come on back here. Let me show you how to lock the backdoor!"

Mr. Leon watched Mr. Fletcher as he locked the pad locks and slid the long black iron pipe threw the hooks that were attached to the door and the wooden frame. As they moved on up to the front of the store, Mr. Fletcher took out a keychain with two silver keys on it attached to a smaller chain with many keys dangling from it. "Leave the light on in the middle of the store Leon. Don't forget now! Good night, I'll see you tomorrow, bright and early you hear!" Mr. Fletcher walked to his truck and got in. Just as Mr. Fletcher called Mr. Leon's name again, Mr. Harvey suddenly drove up in front of him. "You need a ride Mr. Leon?" Mr. Harvey called out. Upon hearing Mr. Harvey's offer of a ride to Mr. Leon, Mr. Fletcher waved at them and drove on off.

Mr. Leon noticed Mr. Harvey was almost out of breath. "Hurry up Mr. Leon, get in! Get in now!" he said excitedly. "What's going on? Why you in such a hurry?" asked Mr. Leon as he quickly climbed up into the truck. "Ain't you heard the awful news?" asked Mr. Harvey. "No, I been working all afternoon, and I ain't seen hardly no one. Man, why don't you calm down and tell me what happened before you have a heart attack or something!" cautioned Mr. Leon.

"Ms. Ruth's boarding house caught fire and burned to the ground!" he answered still out of breath and shaking his head in disbelief. "She was in the house at the time and got burned up is what the fireman said. He said they brought out her body still smoking. The right side of her head and face was burned to the table and the back of her body was attached to the burning kitchen chair. It took them another hour and half to put the fire out and removed her burned body from that chair!"

Mr. Harvey had settled down somewhat and was wiping his forehead with his handkerchief. Mr. Leon looked at Mr. Harvey as if he didn't believe him. "You sure it was Ms. Ruth's house?" Mr. Leon spoke slowly, as if he could not believe what he had just heard. "Yeah, it was her house all right," Mr. Harvey, answered shaking his head up and down like a little child. "Mr. Reynolds told me about it this morning when he came up to check the houses. He got the news from Ms. Evelyn, John Raye's sister, when she came to pickup his dirty laundry this morning. That's an awful way for someone to die, ain't it Mr. Leon," he muttered sadly. "Do they know how the house caught on fire?" Mr. Leon asked. "Mr. Reynolds said he heard she was probably cooking or smoking a cigarette and went to sleep because the fireman found a liquor bottle lying on the table near her burned body. Ms. Ruth's head and face was badly burned and stuck to the table," he repeated the gruesome scene again.

"Mr. Harvey, please, I don't want to hear no more. Thanks for telling me. I don't know much about her kin, maybe Ms. Emma do. They were friends a long time, before I started living there. Well, I had better go. I've got to tell Ms. Emma what happened, and I guess it's better she heard it from me," Mr. Leon replied sadly. "Come on Mr. Leon, I'll take you home and go in with you while you tell her." "You know Mr. Harvey I was just thinking, what about Mr. Raye's club? Who gonna open and close it now that Ms. Ruth is dead?" "I'm not sure Mr. Leon, but Mr. Raye can't walk that good since he had that stroke, and I don't think Mr. Reynolds gonna let Evelyn, Raye's sister open and close, because he don't like her," he laughed.

"You know Mr. Harvey I used to work for Mr. Reynolds years ago. He don't care nothing for colored people. He is one nasty old bastard. Why I remember once when one of the colored field hands' was working on Mr. Reynolds porch. A small piece of the rotting wood fell and hit one of the little colored boys who were playing near by. That old-piece-of-shit-of-a-man, walked right pass the little boy… kept on walking. He didn't even offer to help him up or look down to see if the boy was all right. You know I heard that he was one of them men that have them secret meetings and wear them white sheets and funny looking hats with three holes in the front. I remember all too clear, my mama and her sister Aunt Edna would tell us little kids stories about them killing coloreds and hanging their bodies from trees. My daddy told me a story I will never forget. He said, his best friend Clarence Wilson disappeared one night, and was never seen, or heard of ever again. Story has it; he was snatched off the road one dark night walking home from picking and tying tobacco all day. All they found was his boots and a piece of his old bootstrap."

Mr. Leon was still reminiscing, he wasn't aware the truck had come to a stop. They climbed out of the truck and walked up the steps to Ms. Emma's door. As he was sticking the key in the lock, Ms. Emma called from behind the door in a frightened voice, "Is that you Mr. Leon?" "Yes, it's me Ms. Emma. It's okay to open the door," he reassured her. She opened the door. "Oh, I didn't know Mr. Harvey was with you. Come on in," she said and pushed open the old raggedy screen door. Mr. Leon made a mental note to fix that door tomorrow when he gets off from work.

Ms. Emma walked back to the kitchen where the girls were putting away the dishes and cleaning up. "Ms. Emma you wanna come on back in here, I have something to tell you that's important," said Mr. Leon. Sugar Pudding and Myrtle were right behind their grandma. Sugar Pudding walked over to Mr. Leon. "What did you bring us from the store?" she asked playfully walking around Mr. Leon trying to see if he had something behind his back. "I will have to bring you and Myrtle something tomorrow. Is that okay?" he asked smiling at them. Myrtle spoke up, "Yes, we can wait until tomorrow." "Me too," echoed Sugar Pudding.

Ms. Emma noticed Mr. Leon and Mr. Harvey were still standing. "Well, what ya'll got to tell me that's so important?" asked Ms. Emma staring at the two of them. Mr. Harvey hung his head and he began to speak slowly. "Well, Ms. Emma I was working on Mr. Reynolds farm this morning and he told me Ms. Ruth's…uh…house caught fire and burned up. Ms. Ruth was the only one inside." Mr. Harvey finished that last sentence quickly. "What in heaven's name happened Mr. Leon? Was she cooking or something? She left a pan on the stove?" She questioned as she step back to sit in the chair Mr. Leon was offering her. "We not sure Ms. Emma," answered Mr. Harvey. "I'm so sorry to hear of her terrible death!" mumbled Ms. Emma as she looked over at the girls. They were very quiet. "Well, she won't hit and yell at nobody anymore," announced Sugar Pudding waving her little finger in the air as she walked back to the kitchen. Myrtle was close behind her.

"Ms. Emma I…" "No, Mr. Leon you don't have to say nothing. I know the way she treated the girls, was not your fault. Ms. Ruth has always had one mean ass streak in her. I just never thought she would treat the girls like that. I knew the day you brought them to see me…you see I saw it in their eyes Mr. Leon…that far away look…like they weren't even here. It's over now, they is safe now thanks to you Mr. Leon. Thank you Mr. Harvey for telling me." She walked back in the kitchen with the girls…with a strange smile across her lips.

Mr. Harvey walked to his truck and got in. He sat there for a few moments. He did not want to go to work tonight. He wanted to go home. He was tired of watching those two houses for Mr. Reynolds and that other white man, ol' Willie. Maybe Mr. Leon is right, something is going on and it ain't right. Strange things went on in that big house, and he was sick of turning his head away and pretending like he didn't see or hear the arguing and the women coming in and out that big house all hours of the night.

Some nights he had to clean up behind whoever left the mess. He remembered one morning in particular. There was blood all over the floors and some was on the furniture in the sitting room. It took him two days to clean up that mess. He shuttered to think what might have happened that night. I'm gonna make this my last night coming up here, and he can have his old truck back too he thought, as he drove in and parked the truck on the side of the house. He carefully opened the tall Iron Gate and placed the latch between the handles.

As he started out making his nightly rounds, he thought he heard voices. He was afraid to go any further until he could recognize the voices. He stood there for ten minutes or so and heard the familiar voice of ol' Willie. "I tell you Mr. Reynolds, Clemmons got a plan, but he ain't talking. When I find out what it is, I will meet you back here. We don't have to worry about Clemmons coming here. He thinks the gates are locked and Mr. Tyner is watching over the estate. He don't know nothing about you and the arrangements you made with Mr. Harvey. Just keep your eye on that Harvey fellow. All them coloreds, don't do nothing but steal," he snickered.

Mr. Harvey waited for them to leave. He was afraid if he made a move, even a tiny move, they would kill him. He strained his ears hard…waiting to hear them pull off in the truck. Yes, Mr. Harvey thought to himself, this is the last night I'm coming up here. Mr. Leon was right, they is up to no good.

Chapter 38
No holiday spirit…

Clemmons got up early. It was cold and getting close to the holidays. Damn, time has sure gone by quick, he was thinking since he came home from prison. He walked over to the dresser and reached in the top drawer to retrieve the large envelope Mr. Sheldon gave him at the courthouse a while back.

When he finds his girls, he can finish filling out the papers, so he can file for custody of them and then he is going to protest the wills. He don't want Willie to know nothing. He ain't getting no part of this…he thought angrily to himself. They are my kids, I am their legal next of kin, and anything coming to them, is coming to me first. Once I get custody and prove I'm their daddy, I will take them out of Tapasalle County and put them in one of those colored homes for kids. Shit, I can't do business with the people in Tapsalle County if they really find out that the girls' mama is colored.

First, I got to get rid of Willie, maybe an accident or something. I don't want to kill him, just mess him up enough to get him out of my life. I will keep quiet until it is time for me to make my move. Maybe I will wait until after thanksgiving, he thought. I'll find a job somewhere very soon. The money I had saved up before I went to prison will be gone soon, and I will need money to pay a lawyer, and to keep him quiet! He took the papers out the envelope and stuffed them in his jacket pocket. He listened for Willie. Satisfied he wasn't up yet, Clemmons started for the front door. He quietly opened the door to his truck and got in. He pulled the papers out of his pocket and slid them under the driver' seat.

Trying not to look suspicious, he came back in the house and walked in the kitchen. "Going somewhere this morning?" Willie asked pretending he was fixing to put on a pot of coffee. "Well… as a matter of fact, I am going into town, I need a few things. You know most of my old clothes don't fit, since I came home. I thought I would pick up a few shirts and some pants," Clemmons answered, pretending he was having a hard time stuffing his shirt down in his pants. He was trying to make normal conversation, hoping he could get Willie to talk about the girls and what he thinks might have happened to them.

"You know Clemmons, I need some things too, I need to pick up some nails and a roll of screen to fix that door you rammed your fist through, and I guess after that I will stop by Ms. Emma's house. I heard she came home, at least that what Mr. Reynolds told me."

"You know Willie, the girls maybe staying there. Maybe that colored woman killed in that fire gave them back to Ms. Emma to keep. If they are there Willie, where do we go from here?" he asked.

Willie had grown tired of Clemmons plans to find the girls. "Look, Clemmons, what you don't know is that Ms. Emma is really your kids' aunt. You see Rachel's mother Ilene is Ms. Emma's younger sister. They have not had any contact in many years. Ms. Emma don't know if her sister is dead or alive. I knew it and Ms. Ruth did too. I found out later Ms. Ruth was trying to get custody of the girls awhile back, when Ms. Emma took sick. The sneaky old bitch got what she deserved. She wanted the measly old twenty-five dollars a month she would have received if she got custody. Now, I don't know why she never filed, maybe it's because Ms. Emma didn't die! Hell who knows what was on that woman's mind. It's not like she needed the money. Shit, she was running Mr. Raye's club and she was paid for that! Ms. Ruth made more than a few dollars from the two colored whores that work for her in the back room of the club. Shit Clemmons, she even made a few dollars herself on occasion if one of the girls was late. Often, she was seen taking home a few men at night to her boarding house. She lost her boarders because people started gossiping about her."

"Now, That Mr. Leon is another story," Willie continued. "You see he used to work for Mr. Reynolds and quit his job after about six months. He earned his keep doing odd jobs for Ms. Ruth around the house, helping out at the club and a few jobs for some of the white people in Bridgefield building fences. I am keeping an eye on him, because I think he knows more then he lets on. So, you see Clemmons, I don't know whether or not Rachel knew who Ms. Emma is. You see… on the note she pinned on the youngest girl, just said, 'whoever finds them, take them to Ms. Emma Jackson in Tapsalle County.' Rachel is not the only girls' next of kin!" He deliberately looked straight at Clemmons to get his reaction.

Clemmons just sit there in silence. Clemmons was angry. More goddamn information kept from him. He could recall Rachel telling him years ago, her mama left her with an uncle and never came back for her. She was living alone when he met her. Damn, he thought, I will find out where the girls are and still file for custody. He will tell the judge he is their daddy and the mother is dead. "Willie, you don't think Ms. Emma knows they are kin…do you? After all, they got the same last name," he said trying to keep the anger out of his voice. "No, Clemmons, I don't think Ms. Emma made the connection about the girls' names being the same as hers. After all, how could Ms. Emma know? I don't think she does, but I guess we need to find out huh?"

Chapter 39

Memories long gone...

  Sugar Pudding was standing patiently waiting for Myrtle to give her the rest of the dishes to dry and put away. "Myrtle do you think we will ever see our mama again?" she asked stacking the dried plates on the corner of the wood stove. Myrtle saw that all too familiar look on her face. She knew Sugar Pudding thought about their mama often. She just did not know how to answer her question without stirring up hope and later leading to disappointment.
  "I don't know if we will ever see her again, maybe we will just have to wait and see okay." Myrtle tried to change the subject. "Do you know what holiday is coming up?" "Yes I do Myrtle. It's thanksgiving and I am going to ask Uncle Leon to get us a big turkey!" she answered excitedly.
  Ms. Emma pretended not to hear the girls talking about the holidays. Holidays to her were nothing but sad times, and mostly arguments with her only sister Ilene, who was the smartest one in the family, and got a lot of the attention. There was a huge difference in their ages thought Ms. Emma. Ilene came eleven years after mama was told she couldn't have any more children! I was in the fifth grade when my sister was born. Thinking back on those days we lived all right. We were not poor. We had food, clothes and a clean house to live in.
  Daddy worked all day in the tobacco fields and we seldom saw him unless it was on the weekends, and that was for a short period. She tried hard to pin point exactly when the family went down hill. It was a little too hard to figure out, she was thinking to herself. I remember mama favoring Ilene more, extra helpings of food, better hand-me-downs. Everything Ilene did brought a smile to my

mama's lips, everything I did was always wrong or I didn't try hard enough. Ilene was pretty and had brown wavy hair the color of a hen's chest feathers. I realized years later Ilene and I didn't have the same daddy.

One morning my mama took me to an older relative's house to live. I was simply told the old woman I had never met before, needed someone to help her around the house. Ilene stayed with mama and daddy. When I saw my sister again she was eighteen years old and had plans to go up north to find a job and live. I never finished school. I managed to get to the fifth grade. After I turned twenty-five years old, my father died of pneumonia and my mother died shortly after that from what some said look like an animal had bit her. I always thought a snake bit her, because them woods and fields were full of snakes.

I remember moving back home to live in our house. I didn't get along with Ilene. She was ashamed of me and did not want me home when her men came by to see her. Finally, two weeks before Christmas she decided she was leaving. She said she didn't like staying here and was going up north with some friends of hers. That was the last time I saw her. I moved out the house a year or two later. The house had bad memories and had fallen apart over the years.

The roof leaked all over the little house. It needed a new roof. The ceiling was cracked in so many places, plaster was falling onto the floor and on the few pieces of furniture that was in the house. I didn't have the money to have the roof and ceiling fixed, and the white family I worked for was kind enough to let me stay in their servants' quarters. Then one year around Christmas, they told me they were leaving and would try to find a home for me.

All I remember is how I got this here house, it belonged to that old lady I had taken care of when I was younger. It sat on a patch of land that belonged to the Reynolds family. The white family that moved up north told Mr. Reynolds about me and that I had lived in one of the old shanties on their property and did not have a place to stay. Mr. Reynolds and his wife said I could live here and buy the old house for a thousand dollars. To pay for the house I had to work for them and anyone else that needed someone to clean, cook and do their laundry. It wasn't much of a house then and it ain't much of a house now. I never made enough money to fix the old house. I got a lot of handouts and little help from the county.

I never married because I thought no man would want a woman that could barely read and could only print her name. Years of not printing my name made me forget until Mr. Leon brought them papers to me in that nursing home. He helped me make the letters and I felt good. Thanks to Sugar Pudding and Myrtle, I learned how to write numbers and other words just watching them when they does their homework.

Holidays were just another day for me, except my birthday. It was the same day my mama was born and the same month my mama sent me to live with someone else. She jumped from the past to the present, when she heard her named called! "Grandma, Grandma are you tired?" asked Sugar Pudding softly. "Why are you just sitting there all quiet and not saying anything to us? Myrtle asked if we were having a turkey or a chicken for thanksgiving," Sugar Pudding said with a puzzled look on her face.

"Oh, I am sorry Sugar Pudding, Myrtle. I was just wool gathering… maybe we will have a turkey, we'll see all right." Ms. Emma went back to her own little world of reminiscing. She didn't have a longing for her sister, just wanted to be sure she was still alive.

Chapter 40
A few weeks later...

Ol' Willie took in a few deep breaths of the fresh cold air; a sure sign winter is on its way. The air is so very still. I can stand out in the yard and smell the wood burning from my grandmother's sawmills in Tapsalle County. It's a damn shame we don't have control over our family business. Hell, we can work for them and that's the only time we are even allowed on the premises anymore. Nolen, Bates and Edwards, the overseers' grandmother put in place when she first became ill, runs the mills and Mr. Tyner keeps track of their operations. I wish I knew who else was in on this.

Everyone is making some money except Clemmons and me he thought, shaving his face with such force, he nicked himself twice under his chin. Unaware he was bleeding until he saw small red drops on the edge of the sink. Damn! I've got to get myself together or I will bleed to death. Throwing some witch hazel in the palms of his hands and slapping it on his face, brought him back to the present.

Willie thought he had waited long enough to pay Ms. Emma a visit. He would do that today as soon as he stops by Fletchers' hardware store. If I find out the girls are living with Ms. Emma, I can put my plans in order. I got to make sure she is by herself. The kids ought to be in school. If they are there, I won't say anything to Ms. Emma. I'll just tell her I heard she was home and stop by to see if she needed a ride or something. I'll leave quickly he thought to himself. My plan should be easy to carry out. All I have to do is wait for the girls to leave for school, and take them before they arrive or before they get home. Shit, either one will work. He buttoned up his shirt, grabbed his old work jacket, and started out the door. It was very early and he wanted to be finished by late afternoon. Just incase he had to change his plans.

Getting out the house before Clemmons woke up was beginning to be a chore in itself thought Willie. Hell, he had been planning this for the last two weeks and Clemmons stuck around trying to find something to do. Clemmons gotta find a job, mused Willie cause he will run out of money soon.

Willie walked over to the truck and got in, stuck his key in the ignition. Nothing! "Shit! I don't need this happening to me this morning," Willie exclaimed loudly! He jumped out and lifted the hood. Damn, everything looked all right he said, as he touch one wire after another.

He didn't know a damn thing about engines. Sometimes when the truck would stall or make a noise, he took it to a colored fellow that stayed up the road to fix it for a few dollars, and it would work for another two or three months. He waited a few minutes and started it up again…it cranked and finally the engine turned over. Well, that's another thing I have to take care of this morning. I better take the truck and get it look at.

Chapter 41
Mind in motion…

Turning the papers over and over in his hand did not change the writing on them. Clemmons was reading the same line repeatedly. He can't file for custody unless he has the girls' addresses. He filled out the section asking for the mother's information and wrote 'Deceased' in large letters, and next to, the section asking for the father's information, he wrote, 'Clemmons Darvis Hayden,' and used Willie's address. He hope to God this works. He laid the pen down. His hands were sweaty. He wiped them on his pant leg and put the papers back in his pocket. He didn't want to leave them out where Willie may happen to come across them. He looked around, listening for Willie. He must have left early this morning he thought as he walked from window to window to make sure he had not parked that raggedly truck somewhere else in the yard. Satisfied he was alone in the house he fixed him a sandwich and started out the door. He had plans to go back to the house that had burned up a few months ago, and ask around for the whereabouts of his two girls. He started the truck and drove down the road, woofing down the sandwich in seconds.

As he approached the street that led to the burned down house, he wind down the window and drove slowly, every now and then stopping to ask if anyone had heard of or seen two little girls, that looked white. He even told a few they used to live in the burned down house, hoping that would jar someone's memory of them. His last stop was in front of few colored men standing around a large oilcan with fire coming out of the top obviously trying to keep warm until the bus comes. A few asked him which way was he going, and never bothered to answer his question about the two girls. His questions and descriptions of the girls generated a few laughs and some angry looks.

It was obvious he was getting nowhere so he turned the truck around and headed back to the house.

Chapter 42

Paying their respects…

"Mr. Fletcher is it okay if I get some screen and a few pieces of some of that old linoleum you got laying in the back corner of the store room?" asked Mr. Leon. "What you need it for Leon? It ain't big enough to cover a floor," answered Mr. Fletcher. "I want to cover a hole in the floor with it," said Mr. Leon feeling a little uncomfortable. "How much you want for it sir?" he asked again. "Leon you can have the piece of linoleum. I don't need it for nothing and look back in the back room there should be some old pieces of screen in fairly, good condition. You can have that too," Mr. Fletcher gave a little laugh. "Thank you Mr. Fletcher, thank you! You sure I don't owe you nothing?" he asked a little suspicion in his voice. "No, Leon everything is all right," he said as he extended his hand in good faith. "Okay, Mr. Fletcher." Mr. Leon reached out and eagerly shook the old white man's hand.

He carefully gathered the screen and the piece of linoleum and tied a string around them to take home later. He wanted to repair Ms. Emma's kitchen floor and replace the screen on that old wooden door. Even though it is getting cold, he figured the door still needed fixing.

As he finished stocking the shelves, he couldn't stop thinking about Ms. Ruth's house burning down, and thought to himself maybe if he were there, he might have saved her. She didn't have many friends, and the ones that came to the funeral were mostly customers from Mr. Raye's club. Neither Mr. Reynolds nor his brother came to the wake or funeral, but they sent a small vase of flowers. The card read from the "Reynolds Family." A few people in the neighborhood where she had lived for almost fifty years and a few club customers pitched in and bought her a wooden casket. Most of them did not have much, and the church donated the rest of the money. It was a very short funeral. In the poorly kept colored section of The Rising Savior Cemetery in Southend, just a few miles from Tapasalle County, is where Ms. Ruth was buried. The cemetery is rumored to be an old slave burial ground used as far back as the late 1800's.

Someone in the crowd passed around a poorly taken picture of Ms. Ruth in her younger days. Some of them didn't even look at the picture. They just passed it on around quickly, like the picture was hot or burning their fingers. I guess she had her share of enemies as well.

Mr. Leon remembered she was not well liked, especially by the women. He figured out most of them came to the funeral out of curiosity and not to mourn her as a friend but to make sure she met her master! Humph, he thought… it wouldn't be a funeral if someone didn't have something unpleasant to say about the woman. He remembered hearing one woman accused Mr. Ruth of fucking every man in Tapsalle County and a couple of them said she had went to bed with their husbands. One woman, actually said, she hope the bitch burn in hell!" Now, this sparked a few laughs. He laughed to himself as he remembered the incident.

Ms. Emma and the girls stayed home. He didn't share all of what happened at the funeral to Ms. Emma or the girls. They weren't that interested anyway. Mr. Leon thought about going back to the burned up house to see if he could find anything worth having, but he thought maybe he better not, because stories were getting around that the house was deliberately sat on fire, and he did not want to be seen in the area. He was thinking he didn't get along too well with her before she died, but he had no reason to harm her.

He stopped thinking for a moment; he thought he heard Mr. Harvey in the front of the store. He walked very fast to see if that was his friend, and it was. "Mr. Fletcher you want me to help Mr. Harvey?" "Yes, Leon, I've got two customers orders to get ready," he yelled back! Mr. Leon felt good working for Mr. Fletcher. His store was the only one in Tapsalle County that sold to coloreds, and he thought probably the only one that had a colored man working for him.

"What can I help you with Mr. Harvey?" Mr. Leon asked, happy to see his friend. "Well, Mr. Reynolds sent me here to pick up some heavy chains and two padlocks for the iron gates," he answered sort of, like he was distracted. Mr. Leon looked around for Mr. Fetcher and didn't see him and quickly ask Mr. Harvey was he all right. "I need to talk to you later Mr. Leon, I'll pick you up this evening okay," he whispered. Mr. Leon nodded his head and sent Mr. Harvey up the front of the store with his items.

Chapter 43
A revealing visit…

Willie pulled up in Ms. Emma's yard. He looked around before getting out. He didn't see anyone. He quickly got out of the truck and carefully walked up the steps looking for that gapping hole that Clemmons fell in the night they came to search the house. He saw instead newly replaced boards. Before he could knock on the door, it was opened quickly by Ms. Emma. He was startled. "Uh…Hello Ms. Emma, I thought I would drop by. I heard you had came home…I can't stay long," he added cheerfully. "Hello ol' Willie I'm fine, doing all right," she said in the same cheerful tone of voice. You sure you don't want to come in ol' Willie it's cold out there!" "No, I just dropped by," he answered casually looking around for signs, any signs that the girls were there, and he found one. His eyes spotted an empty sanitary napkin box that was crushed between an empty box of cornflakes and some old newspaper lying on top of the trash in the old wooden barrel. "You take care of yourself now, Ms. Emma! I'll check on you again soon."

He walked off the porch and got in his truck. The truck was moving before he had it in gear. One of Clemmons girls must have reach woman hood as the women say! Shit! It sure ain't Ms. Emma, the last time she used a sanitary napkin was before Moses parted the red sea," and he snickered loudly. Now where are the girls? I have got to act fast. I'll wait a while before I do anything. I need Mr. Reynolds help if this is going work. I won't say a word to Clemmons. If he brings up the girls whereabouts, I'll pretend I'm not interested. I don't need to argue with him. I've got to keep a clear head. I have one more thing to do before I go home. Willie turned the truck around and started toward Mr. Tyner's office. He had not been there since Mr. Tyner read his grandmother's will a week after her funeral years ago.

He was about an hour away. He turned on the radio in the truck. He needed to hear some music. He felt good and wanted to celebrate his finding the girls. He turned the knobs but all he could get was static. He took his fist and slammed the top of the dashboard. That didn't work either. He kept driving and thinking about what he would say to Mr. Tyner when he got there. He wanted his old job back at the sawmill as supervisor, and a copy of grandmother's wills. He was tired of working as a helper. He knew they were getting back at him because of what his brother did, with that colored woman.

Willie had to drive a few blocks away from the office to find a parking place. He parked beside an old building that looked liked an old warehouse. He made sure he was not blocking anyone. He got out and locked the truck. It was cold, and he should have worn something a little heavier then this jacket. He pulled the collar up close around his neck, and braced himself against the cold wind.

He saw the red brick building. Some one was coming out, he ran up to catch the door before it closed. He bumped into a woman, accidentally knocking her papers to the ground. He ignored her and continued to walk up to the desk. There was a young white clerk standing behind the desk talking on the telephone and writing something down on a writing pad. Willie stood there, getting inpatient with the young man. He wanted him to hang up the damn telephone and wait on him.

Realizing the young clerk was going to continue his call, he bangs on the desk right in front him. The young man didn't flinch or acknowledge Willie standing there. The clerk talked for a few minutes more and slowly placed the receiver on the telephone. Just as he was about to ask Willie if he could help him, the telephone rang again. As the young clerk reaches to pull the ringing telephone closer, he turned to Willie and said, "Just a moment sir," and he reached over to pick up the receiver.

The young man's fingers never touch the receiver. Suddenly Willie snatched up the ringing telephone out of the clerk's reach. "Call them back later!" he snapped at the young clerk, as he picked up the receiver and slammed it down on the telephone. "Now, Where's is Mr. Tyner's office?" Willie's eyes flashing with a display of impatience.

"Sir, Mr. Baylor Tyner is on vacation. Can I take a message for him?" The young man asked in a sarcastic tone of voice with an amusing smile that said, "Now fuck you Mister!" Willie stood there, and within minutes, a police officer appeared. He looked over at him. Willie turned around, walked toward the door and out into the cold wind. He banged his fist into his hands. Talking loudly, he asked himself, "What does that bastard mean going on vacation and not telling anyone?" He walked the three blocks back to the truck.

Willie thought it's too cold to go anywhere else, and he decided to have the truck fixed instead. He couldn't have it cutting off on him again. As he put the key in the ignition, he noticed raindrops on the window. It was too cold to be getting wet he thought. I'll just go on back home and wait until the weather lets up. The day wasn't a total waste he was thinking as he drove home. At least I know where the girls are staying. I can't make a move until I get a copy of the wills. Once the girls are gone and I get rid of Clemmons, I can see my way clear to challenge both wills, he thought with growing frustration.

As he got closer to his house, he saw Clemmons new truck. Damn! He said under his breath! He cut off the engine and got out as quickly as he could. The rain was coming down heavy and he was trying to make it to the porch without getting too wet. He opened the door and walked into the kitchen to get something hot to drink. Hell! He was cold and wet and he wanted to warm up before he gets sick. He figured Clemmons was sleep since that's all he does all day. A habit left over from when he was in prison.

He turned on the gas to warm up the coffee he had made hours before. After he changed clothes and put on something a lot warmer, he was thinking he would drive out to the Reynolds place. He needed Mr. Reynolds to help him with his plan. Hell! He'd better call him now! He don't want Mr. Reynolds to back out because things are taking too long. Willie walked over to the telephone unaware Clemmons is standing in the hallway watching and listening.

"Hello Mr. Reynolds, Yeah, I did…they are living with Ms. Emma. Yeah I'm sure. Okay, sure tonight is all right! Where's Mr. Harvey? Okay, I'll see you there!" Willie hung up, got himself a cup of coffee and a cold pancake that was leftover from breakfast and went into his bedroom.

Clemmons stood there watching Willie's every move. He didn't move or breathe. When he was sure Willie was in his bedroom, he tiptoed back to his room. He sat on the edge of the bed. He had a problem. He didn't know where Ms. Emma Lived. He had to find out and quick. He knew what he was gonna do. He had to go back to where those men were standing on the corner in front of the burned up house, and this time he felt he would get some answers.

Clemmons look at his watch…it was four 'o' clock. It will be getting dark soon, and he needed to drive around and ask questions until he finds someone who knows Ms. Emma. First he was thinking, I'd wait and see if Willie is going to mentioned he found the girls. Clemmons went down stairs and started making noises like he was getting ready to fix something to eat. After about five minutes of slinging the pots and pans, Willie walked into the kitchen. "Hey what's with all the racket?" he asked. "You getting ready to cook? Good, I'm hungry! Have something ready by the time I get back, will ya!" He gave a little laugh, and walked out the kitchen.

Chapter 44
True colors...

     Mr. Harvey was waiting outside for Mr. Leon. He had to talk to him, because he was sick and tired of working for Mr. Reynolds. His mind was made up after he overheard what they said about them coloreds don't do nothing but steal. He had worked for Mr. Reynolds for over thirty years and ain't never stolen nothing from him.

     He never liked Mr. Reynolds, but he was the only one in the area that paid his help, pretty good during harvest time and kept the ones on his payroll that stayed and took his shit! I could have left a long time ago, now I wish I had, he was thinking. Why are they watching me? Mr. Harvey asked himself over and over. They must be doing something they don't want know one else to know about.

     It must be bad. I'm gonna tell Mr. Leon, tonight is my last night cleaning them houses. I ain't going back there no more. He was sitting in the truck, heavy in thought when Mr. Leon knocked on the window. It frightened Mr. Harvey. He jumped, looked around and saw it was Mr. Leon. "Come on get in; let's get away from here!" Mr. Harvey said impatiently. Mr. Leon got up in the truck.

     "What's wrong Mr. Harvey? You look scared. Did something happen at one of them houses you watch for Mr. Reynolds?" Mr. Leon asked pulling his coat collar up around his neck. "No, not yet Mr. Leon, but they is planning on doing something. After tonight, I ain't going back up there. They talked about us colored people stealing, said that's all we do Mr. Leon," complained Mr. Harvey. "You think something is missing from one of the houses and they think you did it?" "Could be, Mr. Leon, I ain't the only one that comes to them houses! Look at all them women Mr. Reynolds brings up there! They could have stole something!

I don't like the way they was talking last night. I just wanted you to know, incase something should happened to me. I got a sister that lives in New York…he reached in his pocket and pulls out a small piece of paper. If anything happens to me, call her…let her know what happened, Mr. Leon." They pulled up in front of Ms. Emma's house. Mr. Harvey didn't get out. He said good-by and pulled off quickly.

Ms. Emma was waiting for Mr. Leon. She heard the familiar knock at the door, and got up from her chair to open the door. Mr. Leon took one look at her and knew something was on her mind. "Where the girls, Ms. Emma I got something for them." "They are in their room Mr. Leon, but can we talk a minute before I call them." "Sure we can Ms. Emma. Did something happen today?" he asked throwing a few pieces of dry wood into the old fireplace. "Ol' Willie came by but he did not come in. He said he just dropped by to see how I was. That's strange Mr. Leon; Ol' Willie always came in the house. He acted like something was wrong… you know looking around like he had lost something. I felt a little scared. I wonder what he up to now?"

"He just probably heard you had came home, or maybe he heard Ms. Ruth's house burned down and was wondering where the girls were, okay. You know Ol' Willie is strange acting anyway. Ms. Emma. I'll do some checking okay, but don't worry," he said trying to sound convincing. "Now, go get them girls." Myrtle was already coming in the front room, and Sugar Pudding was close behind with her hands out. "What did you bring us this time Uncle Leon?" she asked walking around him trying to see if he was holding the surprise behind his back. "Your grandma has it," he laughed! Ms. Emma gave them the icy pops cold as it was outside, and two packages of cookies.

She was glad Mr. Leon was there. She had a feeling… a knowing feeling down in her old bones that something wasn't quite right. She knew she wouldn't get any sleep, so she started working on some laundry she had taken in. It was so quiet, like the quietness before a storm...it's like you can smell the rain from a far and hear the soft rumblings of thunder off in the distance, before it hits home.

The girls were very quiet all afternoon, not saying much when they came home from school and she saw it on the face of Mr. Leon when he walked in the door that evening. She was worried, and could not figure out why. All she knew was...that gut feelings don't lie.

After everyone had gone to bed, she sat in front of the fireplace on an old wooden crate...deep in thought. Every now and then she would pick up a piece or two of the dried sticks that were lying in front of the fireplace and throw them in the fire. She watched the flickering of the flames and listened to the crackling of the burning wood. Her mind was a thousand miles away.

Chapter 45
Plan in motion...

Willie did not want to over sleep, so he decided not to take a nap. He would just lie here a few minutes more, than get up, change clothes and drive back out to meet Mr. Reynolds at his grandmother's estates. "Damn," he was thinking aloud. Mr. Reynolds didn't say which house! I better call him again before I leave. This ain't gonna take too long. I'll tell him what the plan is and he can take it from there. He was thinking, Mr. Reynolds owes me, and it's about time he paid up in full. Shit if it hadn't been for me he would have gone to jail instead of Clemmons.

Hell, it was him our mama was sneaking off to meet the day she got killed. He admitted to me the gun accidentally discharged and he saw mama fall to the ground. Hell, I know Clemmons would have gone to jail eventually, he always stayed in some kind of trouble anyway, but maybe he would not had to have served six years for something he didn't do. I'll wait a little longer before I leave. I don't want Clemmons to follow me and I don't want to act suspicious. Willie laid back down for a little while longer. Going over in his mind, how his plan is gonna work to kidnap the girls.

The short nap didn't help Clemmons either, and he didn't want a drink, not right now anyway...that would mess up his thinking. He may have to wait a little while longer before he can find out where Ms. Emma lives. He will just have to wait. I have to be patient, he was thinking. I have come this far. I don't want to blow everything with this temper of mine.

Clemmons laid back down, thinking and planning...seeing visions in his mind of getting those beautiful houses back and selling some of the land, and the rest he would farm out. The money, he didn't want to think about the money, besides there's a chance he would not be able to get that anyway. Well, he was contemplating, I still have all that land, and with the county wanting to build that highway, I could sell a good portion and still have enough left over to do what I want. I sure hope Willie knows what he is talking about. After I find the girls, file for custody and challenged granny's will, I will send them away… far away…! Willie and me really don't have to talk. Hell, the houses, land and money was left to Rachel and the girls. I am a part of this, not Willie! He felt that old anger easing up the back of his neck again. He was thinking why make Willie apart of the plan…he wouldn't do the same for him! No! He thought I've got to get rid of Willie.

Chapter 46
Final decision …

He had taken the last few iron poles out of the back of the truck and laid them down on the ground. Mr. Reynolds wanted the iron poles cemented into the ground in order to make another gate to the property. He didn't see anything wrong with the one that was there, but he said the people who owned the houses want another gate built.

Mr. Harvey was thinking to himself as he worked. Mr. Reynolds must have thought 'he' was a dumb and ignorant colored man. He knew them houses had something to do with ol' Willie. He just didn't know why Mr. Reynolds was paying him to watch the houses, especially at night. Why couldn't ol' Willie do it, and why don't ol' Willie pay him instead of Mr. Reynolds. There's a lot going on up here in them houses and I don't want no part of it, he said to himself. Should I make this my last night to watch them houses? Mr. Harvey has asked himself that same question since he told Mr. Leon how he felt about Mr. Reynolds and that other white man, ol' Willie. Well tonight will be the last night for me. I have made up my mind, he thought to himself. I will park the truck at the other house like I always done, and walk back home in the morning. I don't want to be on those roads at night, he mumbled to himself.

He finished the last pole and was glad it was getting dark. He would make one last check on the houses, turn the lights on and then leave. He got in the truck, drove to the smaller of the two houses, and parked the truck on the side of the house facing the road. Mr. Reynolds says he don't like backing the truck out, he like to drive on out and keep going. Mr. Harvey laughed, he ain't never seen Mr. Reynolds park the truck or the station wagon. Hell, he won't admit he can't drive or park. That's why he always sends me in town to pick up his supplies.

His thoughts were interrupted by a familiar sound, Ol' Willie's truck. Humph! He's kinda of early. Mr. Reynolds ain't even here yet, he thought to himself. He knew it was getting late, maybe five "o" clock or close to six, Mr. Harvey thought, as he gazed up at the sky. He couldn't look at his watch, because it ain't worked in years. He just wears it for show. A strange feeling suddenly came over him, urging him to stay where he is. His stomach contracted to a tight ball. His heart was beating so fast, he thought he could actually feel the beating with his hand. He stood perfectly still, feeling the drops of perspiration rolling down his forehead and the sides of his face. As quiet as he could, he slowly slid down by the back wheel of the truck waiting for ol' Willie's next move.

Mr. Harvey stared at ol' Willie's truck. He heard ol' Willie wind down the window. He didn't get out. He just sat there never opening the door. There were only a few yards between ol' Willie's truck and Mr. Reynolds truck. He felt scared and he was sweating badly. He was afraid to wipe his face, fearing any little noise maybe heard. He couldn't take the chance on ol' Willie finding him. Something deep down in his soul told him, 'ol' Willie will kill you and your body will never be found.'

He remembered what ol' Willie said about colored people, "all they do it steal." If he found me sitting next to the truck, he would think I stole something. He heard another engine; it was the old station wagon. That must be Mr. Reynolds. He remained as motionless as a statue. He heard footsteps that sounded like they were walking away and they suddenly stopped. They were standing next to Mr. Reynolds's truck. Mr. Harvey could smell the sweat from their clothing, they were so close, and he did not have to strain to hear what they were saying.

"Ol' Willie you sure them girls is staying with Ms. Emma? Did you see them?" "No, I didn't see them but I saw signs today that they were staying there with Ms.

Emma," answered ol' Willie as he flicked his cigarette lighter on and off. The flicking of the flames made ol' Willie's face look ghost like and menacing. "Okay, what do you want me to do Willie?" asked Mr. Reynolds. "We'll wait about a week. No, make it the Monday after thanksgiving when they go back to school. I want you to kidnap the girls. You can take them in the morning or in the afternoon when they get out of school. I have the address where they are supposed to go. A man will meet you and take the girls off your hands." He paused a moment, drawing in a deep breath. "That's it! I'll take care of everything else. You okay with this Mr. Reynolds?" asked Willie. "If not, let me know now…I can get someone else to do it," he sounded anxious and in a hurry to leave. "No, it…it's fine, I'm okay with it ol' Willie. But what about Ms. Emma…what if she calls the police!"

"You ain't got nothing to worry about Mr. Reynolds; they'll think they ran away from home. You know them coloreds is always running away… living with this one and that one! The police may look for a day or two and quit. They ain't gonna be that interested in looking for two colored girls! Come on, I got to get back home. I left Clemmons there. I don't trust him. He's been talking a lot about finding them girls and filing for custody of them. I think he gonna challenge grandmother's wills. Anyway I wouldn't worry about that now…just get the girls okay!" he said impatiently. "Okay ol' Willie, next Monday morning," agreed Mr. Reynolds as he walked slowly across the field to his station wagon.

Mr. Harvey waited until they had pulled off. He struggled somewhat trying to get to his feet. His legs shook uncontrollably, he felt sick, and he had a bad taste in his mouth. He's got to get to Mr. Leon. Them sweet little girls is in danger, he was thinking fast. He had not planned to drive Mr. Reynolds's old truck ever again. This was supposed to be his last night working for the old man, he thought as he climbed into the truck. He drove along the back roads. He was scared and frightened. He know if he is seen driving this time of night the police would ask questions, and he couldn't answer them. "God please help me warn Mr. Leon," he prayed as he drove. Saying the prayer over and over again, and stopping only to wipe the tears from his eyes so he can see where he is going. He saw the familiar house up ahead. He turned the engine and headlights off and let the truck coast into Ms. Emma's yard. He could see one light on in the back of the little house.

Maybe someone is still up, he wondered nervously. I can't call her name…it's late and it would scare her and the girls. I'll just wait in the truck until morning. No, I can't wait until morning, what if that bastard come tomorrow and try to take the girls. No, I'll take a chance on waking them up now! He opened the door and got out of the truck.

He walked carefully toward the porch steps. There was no light and it was so dark you could barely see where you are going. He swallowed hard and knocked at the door. He heard someone moving around, and then silence. Before he could knock, again someone had him by the neck! He could feel the hot breath in his face. "What you want here? The voice asked in a savage tone! "It's…me…Mr. Leon, Mr. Harvey!" "Why the hell you sneak up here like that?" Mr. Leon asked in a low voice. He let go of Mr. Harvey. "What's going on, Why you here this time of night? You in trouble?" "No, the girls is in danger Mr. Leon, they is gonna steal them…!" He said rubbing and turning his neck. "Take who? What you mean steal them?" Mr. Leon asked. Confused, Mr. Leon took him by the arm leading him to the truck.

"Take it easy Mr. Harvey. Come on lets sit in the truck, I don't want Ms. Emma and the girls to wake up!" They got in the truck and closed the door. "Mr. Harvey take your time and tell me who is gonna take the girls," Mr. Leon spoke in a whisper. "I was up at the house tonight, because Mr. Reynolds wanted me to put some more poles in the ground for another iron fence. I was getting ready to leave when ol' Willie drove up…he just sit in the truck for a while and then came Mr. Reynolds. I didn't let them see me. I sat down on the ground in the back of this here truck. I heard ol' Willie tell Mr. Reynolds he had been to Ms. Emma's house and found out the girls lived there." He paused to catch his breath. "They is planning to take the girls when they go to school and another man gonna take them somewhere's else," he explained nervously as he wiped his eyes. "I is afraid Mr. Leon they gonna do something bad to them sweet little girls."

Mr. Leon was fighting back tears. "Okay," Mr. Leon said in raspy voice. "We got to get the girls out of Tapsalle tonight. You got gas in this here truck?" he asked hurriedly. "Yeah, Mr. Reynolds filled it up," Mr. Harvey answered, a lot calmer than he was a few minutes ago. "Where we gonna take them Mr. Leon?" "I'm not sure, but we got to get them out tonight," he answered sadly. "This gonna break Ms. Emma's heart Mr. Harvey. They must have found out Ms. Emma is the girls' aunt. But why are they trying to take them away? I don't understand what's going on? What else you hear Mr. Harvey, think man!" Mr. Leon's voice was full of fear and panic!

"They said something about another man named Clemmons who was going to court and take the girls and they talked about some will. I was scared Mr. Leon! I'm trying to think! That's all I can remember right now!" he yelled at Mr. Leon. "Mr. Leon, I got a sister in New York. We can take the girls tonight to the Carverton Bus Station. They got buses leaving out every morning!" he said excitedly. "It's a good idea, but I don't have enough money to buy them tickets. Mr. Fletcher ain't paid me for this week. I can't let anything happened to them girls! Come on, I have to do something I said I wouldn't do ever again…take me in town to Mr. Fletcher's store. Now! Mr.

Harvey before I change my mind. We got to get there and back fast, okay!"

Mr. Harvey let the truck coast until it got a little ways from the house and he started up the engine. They knew they were taking an awful chance driving Mr. Reynolds truck in town. "You drop me off a little ways before we get to the store okay," said Mr. Leon. "Okay." Mr. Harvey said, barely above a whisper, moving his eyes rapidly back and forth, making sure no one is out there looking at them.

It seem like no one was out that time of night but them. The headlights on the truck spotted a colored man, along side the dark road, carrying a bag and walking with a cane. Any other time Mr. Harvey thought to himself, I would stop and offer a ride. His thoughts were interrupted by sounds of a dog's barking, off in the distance. Mr. Harvey drove a half mile more to make sure they were out of the seeing distance of the colored man walking on the road. Mr. Harvey parked the truck on the side of the road and Mr. Leon walked quickly to the store. If anybody see him, he'll just say he wanted to make sure them doors was locked for Mr. Fletcher.

Mr. Leon didn't bother to look around. He knew if he saw someone, he would lose his courage. He opened the front door quickly, and did not turn on any lights in front of the store. He felt around in the dark store until he found the cash register. He opened it and took everything that was in it. He had to get out of there now! He can count the money on the way back. He pulled the door shut, and took the two silver keys and locked the top and bottom lock. He looked around and didn't see anyone. He made it back to the truck and got in. "You okay Mr. Leon? I know what you did, but we got to save them girls." Mr. Harvey lightly patted Mr. Leon's shoulder. They drove in silence on the way back to Ms. Emma's house. Mr. Leon had one thing on his mind, getting those girls to Mr. Harvey sister's house in New

York. Mr. Harvey had a strange smile on his face; he knew he would not be going back to Mr. Reynolds's place.

It was four 'o' clock in the morning. The girls were still sleep when Mr. Leon went into their room to wake them. He put his finger to his lips, "Shhhhh, pack as much as you can, we got to get away from here. I'll explain when you get in the truck okay!" He whispered softly and firmly.

Sugar Pudding was crying softly and Myrtle was frightened. She knew something was wrong. She grabbed the book bags Nancy Rose mother gave them and packed them as full as she could. Sugar Pudding helped pack another bag full of their ribbons and pretty socks. They both grabbed their coats, hats and sweaters. "We got everything Uncle Leon," Myrtle said trying to hold back the tears. She kept swallowing them back. He couldn't look at them. His eyes filled to the brim with emotion. He hugged each one and told them to follow Mr. Harvey to the truck. "What about grandma?" asked Myrtle her tears were rolling down her cheeks and she tried to wipe them away, but more kept coming. "I'll tell her tomorrow, don't worry everything will be okay," he whispered softly. The girls took one last look at the fireplace, and the old wooden crate sitting in front of it. They got in the truck and left Tapsalle County, with everything they owned.

Myrtle sat quietly in the truck, feeling the hot tears drop slowly down her face and on to the hand that held tightly to all she had in this world, Sugar Pudding. Her other hand held onto the bags, her and Sugar had packed. Hurt and painful memories came back to her as if they had happened only yesterday.

When mama got sick, it was just before Christmas. When mama left us at that old cold bus station, it was before Christmas. When we were living with Ms. Ruth and Mr. Leon there was no Christmas. Again, we are being sent to God knows where, and it's almost Christmas again and we still do not have a home. Her heart was heavy with emotion, and in her mind, she sadly realized that this is probably why, Santa Claus don't come to no colored girl's house.

Chapter 47

Life changing events...

Ol' Willie woke to the smell of bacon frying and fresh coffee. He got up out of the bed and walked into to the kitchen, snatched a piece of bacon out of the frying pan and poured himself a cup of coffee. "Damn Willie, ain't you gonna wash first?" asked Clemmons trying to be cheerful. "What the hell I gotta wash for, ain't no women in here is it," Willie said jokingly to Clemmons. In a more serious voice Willie asked, "Why you up so early? You gonna look for a job? You know you can still work at the mills in Bridgefield County. Ain't nothing stopping you from going over there today is it?" "Naw, I can go over there, but later. I got a few things to do this morning," Clemmons answered rather calmly.

"What you gonna do today Willie? Any chance you going by that Ms. Emma's house today. I thought I would go with you if it's all right." He pretended to be busy fixing the rest of the eggs and bacon. "Why you want to go over there?" asked Willie, a slight tone of agitation in his voice. "I don't want to go in... I just want to see where she lives that's all," Clemmons answered placing the pan with the eggs and bacon in the middle of the table. "Well, I guess there ain't no harm, since you been there before. She lives over on Hollowcreek Road where all them coloreds live. You ought to remember Clemmons you fell through the hole where the step was missing that night we went looking for them papers. "The houses ain't got no numbers Willie," Clemmons joked. "Yeah, they got numbers, I just don't remember them that's all," he said laughing.

Willie like the idea of humoring Clemmons, that will keep him busy for a while, at least until I am sure them girls is gone. I will check back with Mr. Reynolds later on during the week. Hell! Today is just Tuesday, and Thursday is thanksgiving. I want to be home eating my dinner. Later on, I'll tell Mr. Reynolds to plan on taking the girls that Monday. My plans will be in place before Clemmons can mess things up. Shit, ain't but so much we can do until that bastard Mr. Tyner gets back from his vacation. I can't file anything because I don't even have a copy of the wills. I would go back to his office and see if the clerk can get me a copy, but he would remember me from the last time. Mmm…maybe that's what I will ask Clemmons to do this morning. Before he realized it, he had eaten all the bacon and eggs. Shit, he can cook some more he ain't got nothing but time, Willie thought to himself. He belched loudly and threw his dirty plate in the sink.

"Hey! Clemmons you going into town today? I need you do me a favor, okay!" yelled Willie from the kitchen. "What is it?" Clemmons asked walking back to the kitchen. "See if you can get copies of grandmother's wills," answered Willie. Clemmons was thinking, did he hear right? His brother is asking him to go to Mr. Tyner's office. "Okay, I'll do that. You have an address for him?" Clemmons asked. "Yeah, I'll find it and give it to you before you leave," answered Willie as he threw the frying pan in the sink.

Clemmons got dressed and went back in the kitchen to ask Willie for Mr. Tyner's office address. Willie was looking through some papers and handed a small piece of paper with the address written on it to his brother. "I'll be back later," Clemmons said as he walked out the kitchen. He was thinking, maybe Willie asked him to go to Mr. Tyner's office because he is thinking maybe we can challenge the wills and get what's rightfully ours back, or that may not be the plan at all. He stopped a few feet away from his truck…having second thoughts. Maybe he had better find out where this Ms. Emma lives and go to the courthouse and try filing for custody for the girls. Willie had no intentions of telling me, that he had found the girls.

Why would he keep that from me, and why did he call Mr. Reynolds? Clemmons felt a coldness run down his back, he shivered, must be the weather he thought.

Driving through Tapsalle County, Clemmons never thought of it as a county where mostly colored people lived. He just figured they live where they wanted to live and probably felt safe in the county. Hell, he couldn't imagine any of them living in Bridgefield even though he saw a few walking around in the daytime. He just never saw them at night. Bridgefield and Tapsalle sat on the dividing line. Strange though, you walked two steps over to Tapsalle, there's the coloreds and if you walked two steps to the west of Tapsalle, toward Bridgefield County, you saw nothing but white people.

The two counties were a lot different especially the part where the coloreds lived. The sidewalks were mostly dirt or gravel and some of the houses always looked like they were going to fall in. A lot of them had gardens planted in the back, on the side and sometimes in front of their houses. Most of the time, there is an old colored woman or old colored man sitting on a crate trying, to sell their crops to any one that happened to drive by.

Occasionally, you would see some young colored children running up to the cars or trucks yelling, "Corn! String Beans! Tomatoes!" what ever else they were trying to sell. He saw a lot of that since he had been home. Jobs were scarce for coloreds in Tapsalle County. Many of the storeowners wouldn't hire them, for fear, none of the whites wouldn't shop in their stores and they would lose their business. Shit! He laughed to himself somebody is hiring them. They are driving cars and trucks like everyone else.

He remembered when he was in prison; the colored prisoners would talk about a colored man they called their savior, who was going to fix everything for them. He was going to get them jobs, nice places to live and they could go to any school they wanted to go to. Hell, that's a tall order for this Negro miracle worker, he thought. Some of the white people ain't gonna like the changes. Hell, they are complaining now, especially in the sawmills in Bridgefield County. They only hired three coloreds that he knew of, to stack bags of sawdust in the warehouses and load up trucks. Shit, that's what I was doing before I went to prison.

Clemmons was so lost in his thoughts; he almost missed the turn off to Hollowcreek Road where Ms. Emma lives. He saw a weather beaten sign, most of the letters was missing or had faded away over time, but he saw enough to make out it was "Hollowcreek Road."

He parked the truck off the road, and got out. He decided he would just walk around and ask a few people where her house is. He looked around, and what few houses he saw were far and in between, and sitting in thick wooded areas. He started walking toward an old gray house and noticed an old colored man gathering up some dry branches that had fallen to the ground.

"Hey there, can I ask you a question?" he called to the old man. "You lost fella?" the old man answered back. "No, I'm not lost; I'm looking for Ms. Emma's house!" Clemmons called out. "Then you is lost. Everybody knows where Ms. Emma live at!"…the old colored man answered with a chuckle. The old man looked at him and kept on picking up the dried branches. After a few minutes, the old man asked, "What you be needin her fo? She got enough kids dat is livin' off her now! You got some mo' you is trying to find a home fo?" "No sir, I ain't looking for a home for no one," Clemmons said getting a little agitated with this old man. "Well, suh, you ain't the po'lice or the sheriff. Why is you here dis early in the mo'nin?" The old man asked, eyeing Clemmons with suspicion. Clemmons had to think a few seconds before answering the old colored man. "A friend of mine told me to look her up and see how she doing," he answered back a little irritated with the old man's questions. "Who's yur friend?" the old man asked, as he continued to pick up the fallen branches. "Uh, Willie!" That was all Clemmons could think of at that moment. He watched the old man's legs shaking gingerly with ever step he made, moving slowly as if he had all the time in the world. He saw the look on the man's face soften a little bit. "Ms. Emma lives two houses up da the road." The old man answered and continued picking up the fallen branches. He never looked up. "Do you know the house number?" Clemmons asked trying to sound cheerful. "I'd jus told ya; she lives two houses up da road. What you be needin' with numbers fo?" questioned the old colored man. "Thank you," Clemmons answered. Seeing as though he was not getting anywhere with the old man, he began walking back to his truck.

  He stood for a second remembering the night he and Willie went to the house to look for Ms. Emma's papers. "Oh Yeah, I fell through a gapping hole walking up the steps to the porch. "Well, I will just look for a broken step or steps missing off the porch," he muttered to himself. He had been walking for a few minutes when he saw a small grayish colored house sitting back off the gravel and dirt road. As he walked closer, he saw where someone had nailed some new boards where a step was missing.

  "This has to be the house. This is it!" he said aloud. He stumbled through the thickets of over grown weeds and trash. As he got closer, he saw a weather beaten, piece of flat wood nailed over the front door with numbers on it. It looked as if someone tried to paint over them with white paint, and the numbers were somewhat faded. He stared up at the piece of wood, walking closer to get a better look. He made out the numbers one...nine...two...and what look like a three. Shit, he was thinking, that's close enough. That's the address, I'll use this morning when I go to the courthouse. He walked back to his truck, got in and scribbled the information on the back of his court papers.

Willie will just have to wait for them copies of the wills, because this is more important. He looked at his watch, It was too early to go to the courthouse he was thinking; maybe I'll park around the corner and take a short nap.

Chapter 48
Looking for signs...

It's awfully quiet this morning, she thought slowly getting out of the bed. She had noticed a lot of stiffness in her legs lately. It seemed to take her longer to get out of bed and walk. I hope I'm okay. She was thinking I sure don't want to go back to no old hospital. She walked toward the girls little room to wake them for school. She pushed the door open to call them, and she stumble back...their names never reached her lips. The room was empty...the bed never made up, and no sign of them in the house. She stepped back and quickly looked around the house. The cot that Mr. Leon slept on was not made up and no one was in the kitchen...she would be able see or hear them.

However, this morning she didn't hear anyone. Just silence. Dead silence. Maybe Mr. Leon took them to school early...she thought. But, I didn't hear them getting ready. Sugar Pudding always runs in my room and grabs that old car mirror to look at herself and those pretty ribbons she likes so much. Strange, I never heard them this morning. She walked slowly into the kitchen, and over to the wood stove to start a fire for her coffee. Maybe Mr. Leon had to leave early and they didn't want to wake me up. She put the coffee pot on the stove and walked back to her room to get the washbasin to wash up.

The water in the bathroom sink ran cold water only and very slowly. It took forever to fill up the basin. After filling the basin, she walked over to the old wood stove, lifted the iron top on the reservoir and poured the water in very slowly. If she poured it too fast, it would splash and put the fire out. She had to wait until the water heated before she could wash. As a habit, she would fire up the stove; sit the basin and the tin cup on top of the stove for the girls first thing in the morning. The girls did not want to be late getting dress waiting for the water to get warm. Mr.

Leon usually had the corn flake cereal and milk on the table for them. She looked around, and saw no bowls in the washtub and no cereal waiting for the girls.

"Well, I don't know what's going on, so I will just get dressed and wait for them to come home," she muttered aloud. She walked back into the small room that was supposed to be a bathroom. She pulled back the old sheet that served as a door and slowly bent down, grabbed the slop bucket by the handle and started for the back door. The old out house seem farther away then yesterday, she thought. She banged on the raggedy door with a piece of dry wood just in case some small animal or snake was hiding in there. Part of the roof had fallen in; however, the door was broken and leaned open with just enough space to sit the bucket on the edge of the rotten toilet seat.

As she poured out the contents from the day before, Ms. Emma suddenly remembered why she did not want the girls to dump the slop bucket. She was afraid they would pour it down the wrong hole, or better yet splash the shit all over them. She remembered, with sadness the first morning they woke up looking for the bathroom. They were told, there was no toilet in the house and they had to use the bucket. Ms. Emma paused a moment, and smiled to herself. It took Sugar Pudding a few days to get use to peeing and doo dooing in the bucket. Myrtle often stood by her, and telling her it was okay to use it. She walked back to the house and put the slop bucket back in the bathroom. Walking over to the stove, she opened the top of the reservoir and stuck her finger in the water. "Yes," she spoke softly to herself, "the water is warm."

Chapter 49
Desperate changes…

Mr. Leon, Mr. Harvey and the girls arrived at the Carverton City bus station about fifty miles outside of Fayetteville. Mostly coloreds use this bus station. They knew no one would be suspicious seeing two old colored men with two half-white young girls in the bus station. Often the colored maids and the colored men servants would pick up members of the white family they work for or take them back and forth to the bus station. It was part of their job, and it did not raise any suspicion.

Mr. Leon counted the money he had stolen from Mr. Fletcher's store. He had three hundred and seventy five dollars and four dollars in change. Mr. Harvey went up to the window that had a sign over it reading "Coloreds Only" and asked for two tickets to New York. The old white man behind the glass never looked up. "That uh' be eleven dollars and fifty cents," and tapped his index finger on the counter for Mr. Harvey to slide the money to him through the little space under the window.

Myrtle was sitting on the bench and Sugar Pudding laid her head in Myrtle's lap. Two packages of cookies were sitting next to them. Mr. Leon didn't know quite how to explain to them why they had to go to New York. He knew he had to tell them something.

"Myrtle I don't know how to tell you this, but it's not safe for you and your sister to stay in Tapsalle. Ol' Willie is trying to take you away and maybe cause you some harm. Me, and Mr. Harvey gonna send you to New York to live with his sister. Y'all will be safe there. I will contact you as soon as I can. I am giving you two hundred and fifty dollars to give to Mr. Harvey's sister. Her name is Ms. Leola Harvey, and Mr. Harvey says she got a daughter about your age Myrtle name Julia. You take care of Sugar Pudding." He couldn't say anymore. He felt his sadness for the girls' swell up in his throat, and the sting of tears starting. He kissed each one on the forehead. Suddenly, they heard the announcement, "Bus number eight to 'New York' boarding now!" "Uncle Leon, will we ever see you again," Sugar Pudding asked, still holding on to his hand. Myrtle pulled her gently away from Mr. Leon. "Come on Sugar we will see them again, okay. We will be gone a little while. We will see grandma and Uncle Leon again," she whispered trying to choke down tears and smiling weakly at Sugar and Uncle Leon. Mr. Harvey overcome by his emotions, kept his back turned to them. Swallowing hard, the memories of when his one and only sister left for New York, to become a nurse, suddenly flashed in his mind. He missed her greatly. Regaining his composure, he turned around and walked over to them.

Mr. Leon and Mr. Harvey walked the girls to the bus and the colored baggage handler took their bags. He tied a tag around them and wrote their names real nice, and told Mr. Leon he would see that they got there safely. Mr. Leon and Mr. Harvey watched them get on the bus, and walk to the back and sit down. Sugar Pudding was near the window, and Myrtle was sitting beside her. Mr. Leon turned to Mr. Harvey, "they will make it." His lips twitched nervously as he tried to form a smile for the girls. Mr. Harvey wiped the tears from his face, and coughed a few times to clear his throat.

They stood and watch other people board the bus, and remained there until the bus pulled off. Mr. Leon thought that would be the last time he would see or hear from them. Mr. Harvey placed his hand on Mr. Leon's shoulder, "Come on Mr. Leon we did all we can do. The Lord God ain't gonna let no one hurt them, that's why they is got us. I called my sister and she is waiting for them. We'd better be starting back we got a long drive ahead of us. But we'll make it," he said solemnly. "You want me to take you to Ms. Emma's house before I drop the truck off to Mr. Reynolds?" he asked wearily. "Yeah, I guess so. I got to tell Ms. Emma what happened, and I guess the police will be looking for me too! He paused for a moment. "Mr. Harvey it was worth it," he said. His face still etched in desperation. "I would do anything to save them girls. I know I done right." "Yes, you did right Mr. Leon. We did what was right." As if he was having a second thought he said, "Look we don't have to go back Mr. Leon. I can ditch the truck and you and I can go somewhere's else to live. We can stay here in Fayetteville!" Mr. Harvey was talking fast excitement was in his voice. "No, Mr. Harvey, this is my problem, I don't want you in no trouble. You go back with the truck, leave me here"....he trailed off. "How will I contact you Mr. Leon...about the girls?" "Keep in touch with them Mr. Harvey. I still have the number you gave me. When the time is right, I'll call and see for myself. You go on now." Mr. Leon barely spoke beyond a whisper.

  They embraced and patted one another on the back. Mr. Harvey got in the truck, and he never looked back. He drove slowly down the street thinking, in deep sorrow, for his old friend and the girls...trying desperately to figure out what the hell, had happened this morning. He wiped at his eyes frantically, so he could see where he was going. Snot ran from his nose, building up on top of his thick mustache. Unconsciously, he wiped it away too.

Chapter 50

Trouble comes in colors...

"Just a minute!" Mr. Fletcher yelled through the closed door! I'm coming! I'm glad you got here! When I got to work this morning, I found my cash register empty!" He was almost out of breath trying to explain to the police the money from yesterday's sales is missing. "How many people you got working in the store Mr. Fletcher?" the first police officer asked, sounding like he had better things to do. "I got four, me and my wife when she ain't feeling poorly. Pete works a few days and he paused reluctantly...and Leon a colored fellow who lives in Southend." "Why you got a nigger working in your store for? That's why you ain't got no money! All they do is steal! What the fuck he look like? Tell me something old man!" the police officer yelled in his face.

Mr. Fletcher was so frightened he thought the police officers were going to hurt him. He made up a description of Mr. Leon and gave it to the police officer who was doing all the hollering. Now, please God, he silently prayed. He pleaded with all his heart and soul; I just want them to go. He wanted them to get the hell out of his store. He never hated anyone. He didn't care if Leon was colored or white, and it just didn't matter to him. He knew if they find him, they would beat him unmercifully, and perhaps kill him.

Hell it ain't worth getting a man beat...for a lousy three hundred dollars. He just wanted to think Leon stole the money because he needed it badly. Maybe he took it to save someone's life. He closed the door behind the police, pulled the shade down and closed the store for the rest of the day.

Chapter 51

A date with destiny...

Clemmons woke up from his nap and looked at his watch. It was nine thirty. The courthouse had been open a half an hour and he had plenty of time. He sat up straight in the truck and looked around for a place to eat where he could get a cup of coffee. He saw a diner; it looked all right. He walked across the busy street and went in. Fresh baked bread and other good smells made him hungry, but he knew he didn't have time to eat. He would just have a cup of coffee and go right to the courthouse.

He looked around for someone, and a waitress appeared next to him. "Why good morning honey! What can I get for you?" she greeted him cheerfully. Umm, she is pretty he thought to himself, now don't screw this one up like you did the other night. "Uh...Hi...Good morning to you too," he answered mirroring the tone of her voice. "I would like some coffee please." "You want to take it with you or drink it here?" she asked still looking at him and grinning. "I'll drink it here," he answered and smiled back at her. When she turned to go get his coffee, Clemmons let his eyes freely glance up and down her body. He was thinking to himself, he couldn't remember the last time he had been with a woman. The aches and inner longings of his body quickly told him, it had been a very long time.

Damn, he was thinking, I have done nothing but drink since I got home from prison, and think about granny's will and how she left all that belonged to me and Willie to Rachel and the girls. Clemmons head began to feel like a bag of lead, too much was going on in his head. He had too much on his mind.

The waitress's voice brought him back to earth. "Honey, you sure you won't have any breakfast, our hotcakes are the best in this county!" He looked up and noticed she had unfastened a few buttons and was showing two of the prettiest pearly white breast he had seen in while. "No I got a...a meeting. I don't have time for breakfast." He tried to sound disappointed, and smiled up at her. The waitress smiled at his response. She leaned toward Clemmons, and handed him a piece of paper and walked off. He opened it.

"No, Breakfast, come back at five 'o' clock for dinner, Virginia."

He folded the note and placed it in his jacket pocket. Well, so far today has been good, he was thinking. He finished his coffee, placed a dollar on the counter and rushed down the street to the courthouse.

He had been standing a few minutes at the desk before anyone stopped to ask if he needed some help. The building was full of people, carrying things, dropping them and bumping into each other. Finally, a clerk looking thin as a broomstick asked if he could help him. "Yes, I'm here to see Mr. Sheldon, he told me to come back when I had more information to file for custody for my two kids...uh girls," he answered nervously. "Do you have the papers with you, Mr.?" "Oh the name is Clemmons Hayden," he answered quickly. "Will I have to wait long?" "No, not that long sir, but you have to go before a judge after the papers are processed. You can wait here or have a seat in court room 1A, right down the hall and I will be right back," said the scrawny little clerk.

Clemmons handed the young clerk his wrinkled papers, and watched him disappear among the people that were walking up and down the hall. He walked down the hall and found courtroom 1A. He pushed open the door, and noticed a few people sitting quietly waiting for the judge. He sat in the back of the courtroom next to the door so he could see the clerk when he came back. He looked up at the huge room, remembering he was sentence to six years in prison in a courtroom that looked similar.

The American flag and several North Carolina flags stood tall behind the judge's bench. Two large chairs covered in dark red velvet sat directly in front of two long wooden tables polished so smooth, you could see your face in them. A sign on each side of the courtroom walls read, '*NO EATING.*'

Clemmons Hayden! He heard his name called, and looked toward the door. It was Mr. Sheldon. He got up and rushed over to him. "Good morning Mr. Sheldon. I brought the rest of the information you said I needed." Mr. Sheldon immediately interrupted him. "Mr. Hayden, come with me, we need to talk," he said firmly, exchanging questioning glances with the young clerk.

Mr. Sheldon led Clemmons to an office, much like the one he was in previously. The clerk closed the door as he walked out. "Mr. Hayden, I have some disturbing news for you... here have a seat please," said Mr. Sheldon, pointing to the overstuffed red velvet chair just like the ones in the courtroom. Clemmons felt his body stiffening in apprehension. Sweat began to ooze through the pores of his skin. His mouth felt dry. "I'll stand if you don't mind Mr. Sheldon," he spoke nervously. "Mr. Hayden the information you have given us...uh...it has to be a mistake." Mr. Sheldon spoke with a lot of seriousness in his voice and continued to look at the papers in his hand to avoid looking straight at the man. Clemmons was feeling his good day go straight to hell! "What you mean a mistake!" Clemmons asked abruptly. "Well...the two girls you are filing custody for... are in the custody of someone else," his voice was strained and cracking. "Are you sure you are their next of kin, Mr. Hayden?"

Clemmons stood there staring at the man in disbelief. He couldn't believe what he had just heard. "Mr. Hayden, the judge awarded permanent custody to another person a few months ago. I'm sorry. There's nothing the court can do for you," Mr. Sheldon said as he handed the papers back to Clemmons. "I'm their next of kin! He yelled! Who's the person that got my kids?" "Settle down Mr. Hayden, or I will have you thrown out!" As if by fate and right in the nick of time, the door opened quickly. "Is everything alright Mr. Sheldon?" the scrawny little clerk inquired, looking very displeased at Mr. Hayden. "Yes, everything is under control. Thank you for asking," said Mr. Sheldon quite calmly. "Mr. Hayden, the courts cannot give you that information unless you can prove you are in someway related to the two girls and I doubt very seriously if you can do anything to change the judge's decision," he said with concern in his voice. "Do you have any more questions Mr. Hayden? I have a few minutes before court starts," he said. "No, that's all." Clemmons, answered slowly. Mr. Sheldon gave him back the papers and called for the clerk to come in. "Edward, please show Mr. Hayden out. Thank you and have a good morning, sir."

    Clemmons, walked slowly back to his truck. The bad news he had just received, bounced back and forth in his head like a ping-pong ball. He shook his head from side to side trying to figure out who could have possibly filed for custody of his girls. He knew it wasn't Willie. Could it be Mr. Tyner? No, only one other person, and that's got to be Ms. Emma. He over heard Willie telling Mr. Reynolds they were living with Ms. Emma. Things were not making any sense…he was getting confused. He asked himself why Ms. Emma would want custody of two girls she don't know anything about…and she don't know nothing about the wills. Hell, she doesn't know the girls are kin to her…Unless, Willie told her, but he wouldn't do that. It would mess up everything! I need a drink! Just one drink, he kept saying over and over again. He opened the door to his truck and got in.

    He threw the papers on the floor of the truck. They ain't no damn good to me now, he was thinking. He was angry. The back of his neck felt like he had a fever. He pulled out onto the street, looking for a store. He had to get a drink. He drove a few minutes and saw a sign that read, *"Triple Ace Bar and Grill."* He backed onto the gravel lot and parked the truck facing the highway.

He got out and walked in. The place is dimly lit and the bar was crowded. He walked quickly to the back of the grill and sat in one of the smaller booths, alone. He looked around and noticed the walls were made of light pinewood with playing cards plastered all over the walls. They were yellow with age, grease and stained with years of cigarette smoke. Large red and black ace's are printed on the cards.

A waitress came over to take his order. She was tall, with black hair and a lot of make-up on her face. She would probably look all right if it were not for all that red shit on her cheeks. "Yeah, just give me a bottle and a glass!" he snapped at the waitress. His hands were in his lap, balled into fist. She just smiled and asked cheerfully, "What kind of liquor would you like sir?" "Any kind, the cheapest you got, okay! Hurry up will ya!" She left and came back with a pint of *"Rolling River Rock"* whiskey and sat it on the table in front of him. "That will be a dollar and fifty-cents," she said in a friendly voice. He handed her a five-dollar bill and told her to keep the change. He tried listening to the music on the jukebox. All he could hear were the words...*you ah never miss your woman, till she walks out on you...!* A few people were singing to the tune, and others were just talking.

He poured himself another drink. It burned his throat and made him cough a few times. He felt around in his pockets for his cigarettes, and pulled out the pack, took one out and laid the pack on the table. He sat there drawing heavily on his cigarette, trying to figure out what the hell had happened in Mr. Sheldon's office this morning.

He was beyond angry. He was numb with madness. His temper had gotten worse when he went to prison. He remembered being locked up all day, sometimes too hot and sometimes too cold. Getting sick and waiting for days before you could see a doctor. He felt the same way now, hot, cold, sick and angry! He was a man when he had Rachel, and he's not a man now!

He gave up all pretense of using the shot glass the waitress had left. He roughly picked up the bottle, took a couple of gulps from it and put it down on the table. Why did he listen to his grandmother? Why didn't he have the guts to say, "This is my life and I will live it the way I see fit!" He should have taken Rachel and the kids and left Tapsalle County. His grandmother had ruined his life, and threatened to leave him out of her will. "Leave that nigger woman alone!" That's all he could hear…he was tired of hearing it! He should not have gone hunting that morning. He knew he didn't have a license. He knew the rifle was not his…! Pow! Pow! Pow! It was not his rifle that went off.…He tried in desperation to tell them that!

He did not want to go to jail. No one would listen, not even his own brother. Too many awful things were going around in his head, too many memories and too many voices! He slowly got up from the booth and grabbed the bottle of whiskey and his pack of cigarettes. Clemmons stumbled out to his truck. He leaned on the side of the door trying to steady himself. He finally opened the door and crawled in. Straightening his body in an up right position, he placed the bottle between his legs and laid the cigarette pack on the dashboard. He waited a few minutes, stuck the key in the ignition. Before pulling off, he looked down at the floor of his truck where he had thrown the court papers.

He grabbed the bottle from between his legs and took a long swig. His body trembled a little at the searing sensation of the whiskey running down his throat. He wiped the trickles of the liquid from his mouth and chin, with the back of his hand, and place the bottle back between his legs.

He sat for a few moments trying to clear his head, trying to figure out, which way he wanted to go. Should I go to Mr. Tyner's office and tell that old rotten stinking bastard what I think of him! Or, go back to that colored woman's house? Uh, What's her name? He asked himself…uh…yeah…Ms. Emma. He started the truck and pulled out into the street, he reached for his cigarettes. He never heard or saw the eighteen-wheeler….

Chapter 52

Home sweet home...

Mr. Harvey parked the truck at Mr. Reynolds house and walked back to his home. He has his alibi ready if Mr. Reynolds asks where he's been all morning. He'll say he spent the night at the big house and just got in. He didn't worry too much about going home late, he was thinking to himself. Anna Mae knew he worked for Mr. Reynolds, and it ain't no tellin' what time he's gonna be home.

He and Anna Mae had been living together for fifteen years since her husband died. He remembered they met at her husband's funeral. Mr. Harvey thought of all the men in Tapasalle, he was the only one who would drive the hearse for Wiley Johnston Funeral Home. He was surprised so many colored men were afraid of the dead. It was the only colored funeral home in Tapsalle County. When Mr. Johnston died, he went to work for Mr. Reynolds as a field hand. Right now he thought, he don't want to remember nothing about Mr. Reynolds. He turned his thoughts to his wife, Anna Mae. Anna Mae and three of her sisters shared a house down by Stallman's creek and he later moved in to help out. Years passed, her sisters did not care whether they were married or not. It didn't matter to them.

After hours of walking, he finally arrived home. He went straight to their room. He paused a moment, looking at Anna Mae's large hump under the sheet. He was so glad they never had any children. He knew he would love them too much to let them out of his sight. He sat down slowly on the edge of the bed. He didn't want to wake her. He just wanted to be beside her. He lost a friend this morning, and he did not want to go to sleep.

Chapter 53

A change of space...

Mr. Leon was sitting on the bench in the Carverton bus station. He was new to this area of North Carolina, and was trying to figure out where he could go and get some rest.

Even though he had a little money left, he didn't want to spend it all on a hotel room. He saw the colored baggage handler, and called to him. "Good morning, I'm new here and I need..." "Someplace to stay"...the baggage handler finished it for him. "I know a place not too far from here. Mr. Eddie runs a boarding house just for men...he charges twenty dollars a month and you got cooking rights. Now, if you can wait awhile, I'll take you there. Now what your name be?" the baggage handler asked, as he extended his hand for a shake. Mr. Leon was so relieved. "My name is Leon Thomas," he answered shaking his hand. "Mine is James Lee. I been working here for a long time. I suppose you gonna be needin a job. They is hiring down at Morgan's Factory...where they make tables, chairs and other furniture. It don't pay a whole lot, but it's probably more than you got in your pockets right now," and they both laughed.

Chapter 54

Quiet and revealing moments...

Ms. Emma stood on the porch, one hand on her hip, and the other drawing the collar of her sweater up around her neck as she stared up and down the road looking for the girls. School was out a while ago, they should have been here by now she was thinking. She stood a little longer; as the wind got cold; she turned and went back inside. She walked over to the fireplace and threw some more wood on the smothering fire, trying to get it warm for the girls when they came home.

She sat and sat. Ever so often, she would get up and go to the door to look down the road. It would be dark soon...they ain't never been this late. Maybe Mr. Leon picked them up. He spoils them something awful, she thought to herself; always buying them cookies and what they call that stuff in a green bottle...oh yes...icy pops.

She went to the kitchen and warmed up some food. She had not eaten all day. She was wondering why she was not hungry. She felt fine, just not hungry. Her thoughts wandered off to when the girls first got there. After they had been with her for a while, she had this feeling she had met them before. She thought, they kind-of reminded me of my sister Ilene, especially Sugar Pudding. She knows how to bat them eyes and Mr. Leon would melt. She never had kids of her own, but somehow she was always taking care of someone else's.

Touching the small piece of chicken with her fingers, to see if it was warm, she sat down to eat. Ever so often, she would strain her ears to hear voices...familiar voices. It was getting late and still, no sign of Mr. Leon or the girls.

She finished a portion of the chicken, not wanting anymore; she got up from the table and placed the small bowl in the washtub. As she started toward the bathroom, she looked down. There was one of Sugar Pudding's ribbons on the floor. Its lace caught between the cracks in the wooden floor. She bent down to pick it up, fingering the delicate material she started to walk toward the little room they shared. As she pulled open the drawer to drop the ribbon in…she saw it was empty. Slowly she pulled out each drawer. All of them were empty. There was no closet in the little room. Mr. Leon had put some shelves up on the walls, so they would have more room to sit their things. They were also bare. A small shinny black shoe lay turned over on its side in the corner of the small room. Her body movements were stiff and awkward as she slowly bent over and picked up the shoe. A yellow piece of lacy ribbon and a shinny small black shoe was all that was left of her family.

    She felt tired, very tired and lonely for the first time in her life. Now, she understood why they were late, but why did they pack everything and leave without telling her.

    Was I such an awful person, that they didn't want to live with me anymore? She asked herself, overcome with emotions, tears trickled slowly down her shriveled brown colored cheeks and onto her hands. Tears of sadness, and of helplessness fell upon the two most precious things she held in her hands, Sugar's shoe and Myrtle's piece of ribbon. She turned to walk into the front room. Her arms felt cold; she had to get to the fireplace.

    Her gait slow and unsteady, her shoulders drooped not from old age but from the devastation of suddenly being alone again. Forcing her steps one by one, she eased her tired body down onto the wooden crate. She carefully placed the pretty, lacy ribbon and the small shoe in her lap. She watched the flames dance around and about the dried branches. Slowly, she reached down to the floor, and picked up a few more branches and with precision, she threw them onto the smothering fire.

Chapter 55

Strange faces, strange places, in a strange home...

    Myrtle woke from a short nap and looked over at Sugar Pudding who was staring out the window of the bus. Myrtle leaned back against the itchy blue plaid cloth on the back of her seat. Where do we go from here she was thinking. We have never stayed any place more than a few months or a few years since mama left them in a cold bus station years ago.
    She wondered what this person 'Ms. Leola Harvey' is like. She hoped with all her heart she wasn't like Ms. Ruth. She will talk to Sugar Pudding and remind her to be nice. Say, "yes thank you," and "no thank you," and most of all don't beg for nothing.
    She looked at the buildings and streets as the bus rode by. There were tall buildings, with colorful storefronts and people walking all around, almost as if they are in an awful hurry. She had never seen and heard so many car horns before, and decided New York is a very noisy city. She hoped Mr. Harvey told his sister where to pick them up. She was not sure where they were, but the bus driver was telling everyone to get their things together, we are fifteen minutes from the Grey Hound bus station in Brooklyn New York.
    Myrtle shook Sugar Pudding. "Wake up. We are almost there," she spoke very low. Sugar Pudding rubbed her eyes and looked at Myrtle and smile weakly. Good sign, thought Myrtle at least there were no tears.
    They waited their turn to get off the bus. They held their smaller bags tightly and looked around for someone to reach the bags placed up over their seats. The bus driver handed them their bags and told them to wait over by the benches inside the station. "Is someone coming to pick ya'll up?" ask the white baggage handler. "Yes our aunt is

picking us up," Myrtle answered firmly. They walked over to the benches, dragging their heaviest bag behind them.

They had been sitting for about twenty minutes, when they saw a colored woman wearing a pretty, green dress and a white purse in her hand, walking back and forth, as if she was looking for someone. Myrtle knew it was Mr. Harvey's sister. "Sit here Sugar Pudding and don't move." Myrtle walked over to the pleasant looking woman and asked, "Are you Ms. Harvey?" The woman looked at Myrtle, and grabbed her hand. "Yes I am," she said laughing and giving her a hug. "Where is your sister…Oh there she is…it's Sugar something? Come here honey…! I am Ms. Leola Harvey," and she gave Sugar Pudding a hug as well. "I am so glad you all made it here safe and sound. Come on, I got a taxi waiting, and they are not the cheapest ride in the city," she said in a friendly tone of voice.

She picked up both of the heavy bags and carried them to the taxi. "Come on get in, it's okay. Everything's gonna be fine," she said patting their heads.

Myrtle liked her and Sugar Pudding seems to like her as well. She had a nice voice, almost musical Myrtle thought. Finally, the taxi pulled in front of a tall building. Ms. Harvey gave the driver some money. He got out the cab, grabbed the bags from the trunk, and sat them on the sidewalk. Ms. Harvey thanked him and she picked up the bags.

"Girls follow me," she seemed to sing. They walked close behind, watching Ms. Harvey as she walked to the tall grey building. She looked up at the large door and sat the bags down. "My, they are heavy;" she said catching her breath, as she rearranged the bags and picked them up again. "I live on the second floor of this apartment building with my daughter Julia. We don't have too much further to go." Myrtle looked at the walls of the building, they were light brown and the floors were dark brown. A few colored people passed them as they waited for the elevator. Some of them spoke others just looked and kept walking. This was the first time they had ever been in an elevator. Sugar wouldn't move, and Ms. Harvey sensed something was wrong. "Have you ever ridden in an elevator?" she asked them. "No Ms. Harvey, but I'm not scared," Myrtle answered. "Come on Sugar Pudding hold my hand and step in," Myrtle said, coaching Sugar into the elevator. Sugar looked from one to the other, swallowed and stepped into the small area. "See it's not that bad," Ms. Harvey laughed. "You will get used to it, okay."

They reached Ms. Harvey's apartment, and waited until she took her key out of her purse and opened the door. "Come on in…this is where you live now, make yourself at home," she beckoned them to come in. Myrtle looked around. It was a nice place. She saw a television sitting over by a table. She had seen them in magazines and Nancy Rose had one in her big pretty house, but she had never seen it on. Ms. Harvey guessed as much, and walked over and turned the knob. At first, there was a fuzzy picture and then some faces appeared. She turned the knob again and there were those strange faces that did not look real. Ms. Harvey called them cartoons, and told them to sit down and watch for a while. She was going to take their things to their room.

Myrtle and Sugar sat down and watch the antics of the cartoons for a while. Ms. Harvey returned a short while later and told them they could wash their faces and hands and get ready to eat. "I know you are hungry and that was a very long bus ride," she said, making them some sandwiches and pouring them some milk. "Myrtle and Sugar come over to the table and eat. We can talk later, okay."

Myrtle picked up the neatly cut sandwich and began to bite into it. It tasted like ham, but only smoother, she thought. Sugar had woofed hers down without stopping. She was really hungry. Myrtle noticed a small white clock sitting on the counter, the hands indicating it was five 'o' clock. She couldn't believe they had been on the bus since six 'o' clock that morning.

Myrtle got up and removed the plates carefully from the table, and sat them in the sink. Just as she was getting ready to wash them, Ms. Harvey walked in. "Myrtle, I'll do those later honey, come over here. Come on Sugar and sat by me. I need to get some information so I can enroll you two in school." Myrtle answered all her questions, and asked how far they would have to walk to school.

"Well, we are blessed. There are two schools in this area. I will show them to you Monday okay. My daughter will be home in a while, and I am sure she will tell you a lot about the schools and the kids in this area, and by the way, please call me Aunt Leola, is that all right? Ms. Harvey makes me sound old," and she wrinkle up her face. Sugar thought that was funny and started laughing. So far, myrtle thought... everything is okay.

She watched with curiosity as Aunt Leola went back to the kitchen and started washing the few plates in the sink. She opened the refrigerator and took out the small turkey to thaw out for tomorrow's thanksgiving dinner. So much had, happen to them over the past few hours, she had forgotten about thanksgiving, and she may as well forget about Christmas.

Aunt Leola looked over at the girls and thought these girls need someone to love and take care of them. I hope I am doing the right thing. They will have a hard time as it is fitting in. Even when her brother described them over the telephone, she had no idea they looked white. She knew she had to help him. If it had not been for her brother, she would not have made it this far. He sent money to her every month to help pay for her nursing degree. She owed him that and much more. She missed her brother, but he wouldn't move to New York. Therefore, they keep in touch with one another by telephone and sometimes she sends him a letter or a greeting card, and a gift for Christmas and his birthday.

She stood in the kitchen, and prayed softly, "Lord Jesus, please help me to take care of these girls and keep them safe. Amen."

As Myrtle was walking to the kitchen, she heard her praying. Myrtle turned and went back to the living room. She stayed there until Julia; Aunt Leola's daughter came home.

Julia was just like her mama, happy and loved to talk. She walked in asking in a loud but playful voice, "Where are my sisters, mama?" Myrtle didn't know what to say. She stood there and smiled at Julia. "I'm Myrtle and this is my sister Sugar".... she tried to sound happy but the look on Julia's face had said enough. Okay, here we go again with the stares and horrible name-calling, Myrtle thought angrily. "Mama, these girls are white." She sounded disappointed, but not angry thought Myrtle. Julia walked over and reluctantly gave each of them a big hug.

Aunt Leola was standing there waiting for the right time to say something. She deliberately did not tell Julia they were "light skinned." She raised her daughter to love everyone regardless of their race. After all, that is what Martin Luther King expects of us. She kept up with the civil rights leader and admired what he was trying to do for the Negros. She watched Julia get over the initial shock of seeing the girls, and left it alone. They will work it out she thought to herself and sent up another silent prayer.

Later that night as they were getting ready for bed, Julia showed them where to put their toothbrush and other things they had brought with them. She even asked Myrtle for one of her pretty, lacey ribbons, and Sugar handed her a handful and said, "Here Julia, pick one!" She looked at Julia with those big brown eyes and that smile was a charmer. Julia gave her a hug and thanked her. Myrtle was at ease again, however, she wasn't sure if Julia was going to be like the other kids they had gone to school with, always talking about their hair, the color of their skin or how they sound when they talk. She will have to wait and see.

Their room is large and very neat. Pictures of baby animals hung on the walls and lined up around the wallboard were a few small rag dolls and stuffed animals.

Aunt Leola noticing the strange look on Myrtle's face explained her aunt had lived with them for a while and when she became sick, she sort of acted and thought like a small child. "We put up the pictures and got her some dolls to make her comfortable until she was placed in the old folk's home. I turned the den into an extra bedroom for my daughter Julia. The largest bedroom, the one you and your sister are sharing was my aunt's bedroom. Please feel at home and decorate it anyway you like, it's okay.   Now girls, don't stay up too late, we've got to get up early tomorrow and cook, it's thanksgiving," she said as if she getting ready to break out in a song. "Mama, Myrtle will probably go to my school, and sugar will go to Lil' Kenny's school." Julia had worked it all out. "Thank you Jesus!" Aunt Leola sent up a silent prayer. "Who's Lil' Kenny, Sugar asked?" "Oh, he's Miss Jean's little boy, they live down stairs, you'll meet him," answered Julia. "Good night, see you tomorrow morning," said Aunt Leola.

"Myrtle, are we gonna be all right?" "Shhhhh...Go to sleep Sugar," answered Myrtle, and she playfully threw a pillow at her.

Chapter 56

Thanksgiving morning...

Willie wasn't surprised when Clemmons didn't come home last night. He was probably out drinking and slept in his truck again. He was pouring a cup of coffee, when the telephone rang. "Hello, yes, this is the Hayden's residence. What did you say...an accident! Where is he now? Okay I'll be there right away...thanks for calling!"

Ol' Willie forgot the coffee, grabbed his jacket and ran to this truck, hoping it would start right up. How in the hell did he have an accident? The Doctor said he was badly injured, and to come right away! Damn! I hope he makes it! "Don't you die Clemmons! You had better wait until I get there!" he yelled frantically as he started up the truck. He had a long ways to go. I wonder why they took him to a hospital in Bridgefield. Why was he in Bridgefield? He asked himself. Maybe he was looking for a job after all. The Hayden's Saw Mills and factories are there. He was trying hard to think of a reason for the accident. He turned on the old radio to hear some music. He had to be calm when he walked into the hospital, because he has no idea what to expect.

He had to park his truck in the back of the hospital. All the parking places were full. He walked around until he had reached the front entrance of the hospital. He pushed open the large glass door and ran up to the desk. "Good Morning, my brother was brought here...he had been in an accident!" "What's your brother's name sir?" the middle age nurse asked in a soft voice. "His name is Clemmons Hayden," he answered quickly. "Just a minute, let's me see. Oh, yes he's in intensive care. Take the elevators on the left side of the hallway and ride up to the third floor, and make a right. Stop at the desk and ask for the nurse sir."

He left the desk and followed her instructions. When he got off the elevator, he saw the sign *"INTENSIVE CARE FLOOR."* There was another sign that read, *"VISITORS ARE PERMITTED FIVE MINUTES ONLY!"* He stopped at the desk and asked for Clemmons room. The nurse stepped from around the desk and led him to his brother's room. She carefully opened the door, and asked Willie to step in. He was not ready for this...his legs were shaking and he felt weak. Clemmons head and face was bandage, and you could barely see his eyes. Only his nose was more visible and he had a tube in it. His head was in some kind of harness with braces, and tubes in each arm. Thank God! He was sleep!

He couldn't take anymore; he left the room and leaned up against the wall. He felt his stomach churning. He quickly put his hand to his mouth. "Sir, it's always like this when a family member first see their love one, in a condition like this. Here sit down a moment, until you feel like you can stand on your own. The men's bathroom is directly across the hall. Can I get you some water sir?" she asked softly. Willie sat down in the chair. He held his head in his hands. "Is he gonna die?" he asked weakly. "He has a fifty-fifty chance is what his doctors said this morning. He has some very bad injuries. You see he was pinned under the eighteen-wheeler. He was lucky neither of the trucks caught fire with all that gas leaking on the ground. The other truck driver got a few cuts, scratches and some bruises," she added.

"There is nothing you can do right now, why don't you go home and get some rest. I'll call you if there are any changes Mr. Hayden." "Thank you, I'll come back later." He walked away from the nurse, and from his brother.

He made it to his truck, and sat for a few minutes. I'd better call Mr. Reynolds, and tell him what happened. He drove back to Tapsalle County slowly. He had a lot of thinking and planning to do.

He decided at the last minute to stop by the Reynolds farm instead. He saw Mr. Reynolds, walking around the truck and looking like he was angry at the world. "Hey! Mr. Reynolds, you all right?" He waved at him. "I got to find some help! Mr. Harvey ain't coming back to work for me. Shit! He ain't gonna find another job like the one he had here. What other white man go let a colored man keep and drive his truck back and forth? Now I ask you ol' Willie, who the hell gonna do that?" "Look I know you are angry, but something has happened! Clemmons been in an accident and he may not make it. He's over in the Bridgefield County Hospital on the intensive care floor. He is all messed up." Ol' Willie shook his head back and forth slowly.

"Well, sorry to hear that, now, what you gonna do about them girls? Today is thanksgiving. You forgot about that. Ain't no more school until next Monday! You want to go on with our plans," asked Mr. Reynolds as if he did not hear what Willie told him about his brother. "Yeah, might as well. Mr. Tyner is on vacation. That will give me a chance to file papers to challenge grandmother's will.

Hell, the houses got to be kept up and Mr. Tyner said granny had made provisions to pay the taxes for three years after her death or until Rachel and the girls take over. Hell, Mr. Reynolds it's been longer than that! Come this spring. I intend to fight for what is rightfully mine. If I can convinced the judge there ain't no other living kin, then they ain't got no choice but to give us the houses and the land. Do you really think a white judge and jury is gonna let some Negros take our estate? Hell no Mr. Reynolds…you be ready next Monday and tell your friends not to do a sloppy job you hear!" He turned on his heels and left the farm. Mr. Reynolds went back to cleaning up the truck.

Chapter 57

Palm Trees in winter...

Baylor Tyner was enjoying his vacation. He had not seen his niece Olivia and his sister Alease in three years. They invited him out, said he needed a vacation because he worked all the time and never took anytime off for himself. He thought, his sister was right, what a wonderful way to spend a vacation. He had been in Jacksonville Florida for more then a few months. He had opened up a new office here, and was not going back to Tapsalle County, thanks to Stella Louise Hayden.

He told his clerk Calvin to send everything to him. It's no law saying I got to live where I practice. I have taken care of the Hayden's estate for the next six years and neither Clemmons nor his brother Willie can challenge that will. Judge Patrick Dickerson has all the necessary papers, stating the girls exist as well as the mama. It's a waste of time for them to file anything or challenged their grandmother's wills. After the holidays, he decided...he will put some ideas together with a private detective to try to find Rachel. He knows where the girls are. His law clerk Calvin, sent him a letter letting him know, Ms. Emma Jackson has permanent custody of the girls. That should knock the shit out of them Hayden brothers, he laughed to himself.

Thank God, I have copies of the girls' birth certificates. I had to wait three months for Rachel's birth certificate, but they found it and sent that also. The hospital where Rachel was born, incorrectly spelled Rachel's mother's name with two 'L's in stead of one for the name 'Ilene.' If I don't find Rachel, I will have to make contact with Ms. Emma, the girls' real aunt, and let her know about the wills. I just hope the old woman lives that long, he was thinking. I am doing my part keeping the estate in good shape and their money is drawing interest, as well as mine.

Nevertheless, I have one last thing to do…and that is to fence off the entire estate as soon as possible to keep Willie from trying to move in or perhaps damaged the estate. Mmm… he drank the last drop of his ice tea…on second thought, I better take care of that now! When he finds out I'm away on vacation, he may take advantage of that fact and file some worthless challenge, hell anything to keep me tied up in court!

He walked back inside the house, and picked up the telephone receiver. He asked the operator to put a call in to Tapsalle County Court House in North Carolina. He wanted to speak to Calvin Turner. He looked out his beautiful bay window, watching the palm trees as they swayed back and forth, dancing with the gentle breeze. He noticed it was late evening and it would be getting dark soon.

Chapter 58

When the Spirit moves you…

Ms. Emma was digging deep in her old trunk, looking for something nice to wear this Sunday. She wanted to go to church. She had not been in a long time, and felt she should go this Sunday. She found a navy blue dress with the collar a bit yellow, but she could press it with the hot iron, and she found the shoes they gave her at the nursing home when she was sick. They were old, but they would have to do.

It was almost eight 'o' clock am before she got dressed. She went in her room and got the pretty yellow ribbon with the lace around it and tied it in a bow and pinned it to what little hair she had manage to gather and plait. She looked at herself in the old car mirror. She quickly put it back down on the old dresser. She put on her warmest coat and scarf. She didn't have any gloves, but she had a nice purse Mrs. Tompkins gave her for taking care of her when she was so sick.

She walked to the door, and thought if I can make it to the bus stop in time; I might meet up with Ms. Ella. She reached for the walking cane in the corner by the kitchen door. The nurse gave it to her when Mr. Leon came to pick her up from the nursing home. She had better take it she was thinking; her legs were a little stiff this morning.

She walked gingerly out to the porch and locked the door behind her. She was more than half way to the bus stop, and she recognized Ms. Ella standing there waiting for the bus. "Good morning Ms. Ella! Are you going to church too?" shouted Ms. Emma. "Why yes I am Ms. Emma, it's so good to see you again. I have been standing here for an hour or more. Come on I think I see the bus coming." Ms. Emma stepped up on to the bus, took the dime out of her coat pocket, and put it in the change box.

The bus is crowded with colored people standing in the narrow isle, and the only empty seats were midway to the front. She was afraid to sit there. Memories of what happen to that other colored lady who sat in the front of the bus still haunted her. She and Ms. Ella stood in the back of the bus until they reached their stop. They had to wait until the other white people got off, and then the bus driver told them to hurry up and move it along. Ms. Emma didn't say a word, she moved as quickly as she could, and stepped off the bus very carefully. They walked the rest of the way bringing each other up to date on the latest gossip.

As they approached the white and brown church with the wooden cross nailed over the door, Ms. Ella ask Ms. Emma if she would sit next to her this morning. Ms. Emma felt so good; she knew people would look at her and wonder why she took so long to come back to church. They sat as close up front as they could get. It was warmer and the Bibles were in better condition. Even though she couldn't read, she liked holding it in her hands. After they had said the Lord's Prayer, the preacher talked about sharing and loving one another. Before he ended his sermon, he asked the congregation to turn to one another, and say, "God wants me to share my friendship with you and love you as God loves me." The choir sang, *"Jesus is Just a Prayer Away,* and *Lord Let Me Stay a Little Longer with Thee."* They were Ms. Emma's favorite hymns.

She knew in her heart, she had made the best decision, coming to church this morning. She lingered after service talking to some of her friends and old neighbors she had not seen for years, and promised them she would be coming back. Ms. Ella called to her, "Ms. Emma we better be going we don't want to miss the bus to go back home."

They waved to the other members and started the long walk back to the bus stop. The weather had turned chilly and the wind was beginning to pick up. Ms. Emma pulled her coat collar up around her neck and wished she had grabbed a hat or scarf to put on her head.

"Ms. Emma, can I ask you a question?" "Yes you can. What is it Ms. Ella?" "You know I live with Ms. Sarah in her boarding house over on Carver Street. I just can't stay there too much longer because someone in that boarding house is stealing my clothes and even my money. Ms. Emma you know the stealing didn't start until Ms. Sarah starting renting to them young women. I know one of the women used to work at night in Mr. Raye's club before it close down a few years ago. Here lately, all kinds of men and other strange people done begin to hang out on Ms. Sarah's porch, especially on Friday nights. You know Ms. Emma, if I didn't know any better, I would think them women is bringing them men up to their rooms, and Ms. Sarah is looking the other way. I...I was wondering if I could stay with you for a while," Ms. Emma. "Yes, you can stay with me, but it's a small house, you can have the girls room, is that okay?" asked Ms. Emma.

Ms. Ella almost knock Ms. Emma to the ground, she hugged her so tight. "Thank you, Thank you Ms. Emma!" Ms. Emma saw tears in Ms. Ella's eyes, and knew right away, a weight had been lifted off her shoulders. "No one wants anyone to steal from them," agreed Ms. Emma. "Ms. Ella or... should I call you Ella? You can move in today if you like. Do you have someone to help you with your things?" "No., but I can use all the help I can get. You feel up to it Ms. Emma? I have a few bags," she said. "Come on we'll go back to your boarding house and get your things," said Ms. Emma sensing a tide of joy washing over her entire body, and thinking, 'I will not be lonely anymore, because I will have someone to talk too.'

Later that afternoon, they managed to walk down to the bus stop. Stopping frequently to rearrange the bags and rest a few minutes. There was an old man sleeping on the bench. As they got closer, he rose up to let them sat down with their bags.

The bus finally pulled up. Stepping up onto the bus proved to be a tiring feat for Ms. Emma, and Ms. Ella. Later they both made fun of themselves and how they looked carrying all those bags with them. Ms. Emma was happy she would have someone to talk to. She didn't feel lonely, desperate to have someone to talk to, or share a meal, until the girls and Mr. Leon left. They were the closest to her having a family in a very long time. She wondered, maybe one of these days she will find out why they left in a hurry without telling her good bye.

Chapter 59
The Plan...

The two men had been standing for a while on Carver Street waiting for the girls to walk by. A few boys ran by playing in the road, throwing rocks at each other. One dropped his books and when he bent, down to retrieve them, another boy pushed him down and they began to wrestle.

They saw few girls going home from school, but none of them fit the descriptions that Mr. Reynolds gave them. They made up their minds to wait a little longer, maybe the girls are running late. "This is the easiest fifty dollars I ever made," remarked Neil. "Yeah Eddie, all we got to do is grab them and put them in the back of the station wagon and drive them to Southend and drop them off at the address on this piece of paper, and go back and tell Mr. Reynolds we finished the job." "Yeah, but don't forget, he said to take something from them and bring it back to show we did the job. He gonna pay us when we get back," said Neil moving around his hands up and down his arms, trying to keep warm. The heater in Mr. Reynolds old station wagon did not work.

Neil and Eddie kept their eyes peeled for the two girls' fitting the description of looking, 'just like white people.' Two hours had gone by and they talked about leaving. "Maybe Mr. Reynolds got the days mixed up," Eddie suggested. "Well, today is Monday, and he said be here the Monday after thanksgiving, and we is here," Neil explained in a tired voice. We have been out here since six 'o' clock this morning, and it's almost four-thirty and we ain't seen nobody that look like them girls." "Come on Neil, it looks like it's getting ready to rain. We'll tell Mr. Reynolds nobody came by here looking like what he said," said Eddie. They got in the station wagon and left.

Willie pulls up beside Mr. Reynolds truck. "Hey, you heard anything yet?" "No, but I am going to stay here for a while and wait. It shouldn't have taken this long," Mr. Reynolds said worriedly. "I hope they didn't do anything stupid," said Willie, leaning against his truck and plucking the crumbs off his jacket, tell tale signs that he had just eaten. "Willie have you been up to the estate this morning?" Mr. Reynolds asked curiously, not taking his eyes off Willie. "No, I hadn't planned on going up there today, why you ask?" answered Willie. "Well, yesterday when I rode out there to turn the lights on, I saw some men working on the iron fences, and they had the entire place blocked off. I couldn't get on the property. I thought you knew about it," he said, scraping the dirt from under his fingernails with the tip of his pocketknife.

"Blocked off...what do you mean blocked off? I don't know anything about anyone working up there!" He yelled at Mr. Reynolds. "Why are you just telling me this? Come on we are going up there to see what's going on!" "Willie, I can't leave right this minute! You forget I'm waiting for them to get back! Don't you want to know if they got the girls and delivered them at the address?" asked Mr. Reynolds, his facial muscles twitching nervously.

The two men hired to kidnap the girls pulled up in Mr. Reynolds station wagon. They quickly jump out of the car and ran up to him. "Mr. Reynolds! Mr. Reynolds! We couldn't do it...ain't no girls showed up sir! We waited for eleven hours!" Eddie explained nervously. "What you want us to do now?" asked Neil. "Nothing, that's all," mumbled Mr. Reynolds as he got back in his truck. "Ya'll go on home! I'll talk with you later!" Mr. Reynolds and Willie drove off toward the Hayden estates. Neil and Eddie looked at one another, shook their heads and started walking back down the road. It was beginning to rain.

"Stop the truck right here, don't let them see us!" snapped Willie. "Damn! It looks like they've been working all night!" exclaimed Mr. Reynolds." "I'm going up there and talk to whoever is responsible for blocking off the entrance," Willie called back, as he ran up to a few men standing by the tall iron gate. "Hey who are you and why you got this damn place blocked off!" he yelled. "What goddamn business is it of yours?" They yelled down to Willie. "We got orders to block the entire estate and we are doing as we were instructed. You don't like what you see, then call Mr. Tyner!" They turned around and went back to what they were doing.

    Mr. Reynolds grabbed Willie by the arm. "It's too many of them, and it's only one of you. Come on, don't start no shit with them…you are out numbered Willie," he pleaded. "Mr. Reynolds I have been keeping a watch on those houses, and the land since my grandmother died. Why is Mr. Tyner preventing me from going on the property? Has that bastard gone crazy? This is mine…all of it…you here! It's mine goddamn it!" The rain was coming down in a fine, but cold drizzle.

    Willie ignored the rain and began to pick up rocks and stones, throwing them at the men. They just kept on working as if he was not there. Mr. Reynolds walked and ran most of the way back down the hill to his truck. He thought to himself, Willie has a bad temper, and he ain't going to jail for Willie's shit! He got in the truck and pulled off onto the road, leaving Willie still throwing things, getting soaking wet and cursing at the men.

    Mr. Reynolds was thinking, this maybe it…closing time for them Hayden boys. He never knew much about their grandmother. He had only met her once or twice. Hell, he met her daughter Elizabeth at one of their horse auctions one summer. He helped her pick out a horse for riding, and they were friends after that. She said she was divorced and her husband, the boys' father lived in France. The boys didn't know I was seeing their mama, until one night Willie was sneaking a young girl in through the servant's quarters and saw me leaving. He didn't say anything and I didn't say anything.

He had problems reliving the past, especially when Elizabeth Hayden was killed in the woods. He could never reach the point, where he shot and killed the Hayden boy's mama. When he thought about it, it made him very sad and angry! Why did she have to come out there that morning? He remembers holding the rifle to aim at what he thought was a deer, and as he moved to get in closer his foot trip on some under brush and his rifle discharged accidentally. He heard other rifle shots rang out as his rifle went off. He told Willie they were all shooting at the deer; it could have been anyone's shot that struck his mama.

It was strange the way he took his mama's death. He couldn't remember Willie grieving. Clemmons took it rather bad, but he too was all right in a few days. I always thought it was my fault, and deep down I tried to be of help to Willie because he knew I was seeing his mama, and I didn't want him to hold it against me. I helped him watch their grandmother's estate, spending my hard, earned money securing the houses and the land. I felt I owed them boys something. I felt bad for them when the grandmother did not leave them the estate, the business or the money.

Deep in thought, Mr. Reynolds asked himself, what kind of woman would do that to her own kin, unless something was awful wrong? Hell, the old woman knew Clemmons was seeing that colored girl. Everybody in Tapsalle County knew it. He didn't try to hide it. Their mother knew it and Willie knew it....wait a minute...he suddenly stopped the truck. How did the grandmother find out about the colored girl and the kids....now it's beginning to make some sense! "Willie! That's it!" He said aloud. Willie told the grandmother hoping she would leave her estate to him....shit! "Well, the jokes on both of them," he laughed as he started the truck up. He drove the rest of the way home in silence, listening to the old windshield wipers swishing and scratching against the truck's window glass.

Ol' Willie was tired, wet, confused, and angry as hell! How could Mr. Tyner do this? Had he planned this all along? First, Clemmons has an accident with a truck, and now barred from his grandmother's estate, what else can happen to him today? He asked himself as he drove back to his house. I am not giving up without a fight! I am going to court and try to get back what belongs to me!

He was thinking how much he stayed out of everyone's way, look the other way when he saw things he should not have seen. He never gave his grandmother or his mother cause to worry. He finished school. He didn't want to go to college, he had plans to work for his family, and perhaps one day run their sawmill business. Clemmons was always her favorite. He did what he damn well pleased. Fucked up often and nothing was ever said. He got what he wanted by giving grandmother and yes, our mama, that smile and they would give in to him.

Clemmons had the choice to work or go to college. He choose college for a while playing around with the girls, and then he decided he wanted to come back home. Grandmother sent the car for him, "no grandchild of mine will ride on any bus or train with them niggers!" It was clear he was the 'apple' of 'granny's eye' as Clemmons called her.

One night he remembered, there was a terrible storm, and Ben one of the colored servants had to stay over night. Ben was afraid of lightening, and grandmother told him he could sleep in the one of the rooms, and he could go back to the servant's quarters early the next day. Well, it's evident that suggestion didn't sit too well with Ben because he decided to try and make it to the servant's quarters before the storm hit. The servant's rooms were in the smaller house quite a distance from the main house. The servants were not allowed to come or leave through the front or side entrance of the houses. Ben thought because it was getting ready to storm, he would take that chance, and leave out the side entrance just this once, hoping no one would see him.

Well, no one saw him, but he did see Clemmons sneaking a colored girl through the side entrance of the home. Ben ducked down behind one of the massive oak trees on the lawn, and waited until they were inside and he made a break for it. The next day, Willie remembered, Ben told him, "Mr. Willie, I don't won't to git nobody in any trouble, Lord knows I don't, but that young'en done bring home a colored girl last yesta' day evenin' when the storm was acoming! Now, if'en Mother Hayden finds out, she gonna kill us all!" "Why are you telling me this? Ben, go tell Mother Hayden as you call her!" Willie snapped at the old servant.

Clemmons had really fucked up this time. Hell, sneaking a colored girl in the house was like committing a damn crime. Willie thought at the time, Ben is his witness, and this was my chance to show grandmother, Clemmons ain't perfect! I never got the chance to tell grandmother because someone else had told her first. He remembered, she called him into her room one evening, and just asked right out… "Why didn't you tell me Clemmons was seeing a colored girl? Why if Elizabeth hadn't seen them this morning…in his truck together, I would never have known about it! I told Elizabeth to take care of it immediately! No grandson of mine is going bring such disrespect to the Hayden's family and name! So, if you got the same idea Willie, I suggest you forget about it! You can leave now!" She dismissed me as if I was nothing! I got blamed because I didn't tell her…! Now ain't that some shit!

He was still confused and he asked himself that same question over and over. Why did she leave all she owned to Rachel and her kids, and cut us out all together?

Willie was getting angrier and angrier the more he thought about the wills.

Now, that bastard Mr. Tyner has blocked me from the estate. I'm going over to his office and find out what's going on. Then he had a bad thought, maybe the county is trying to take the land after all, no one is living in the houses and all that land is just sitting there waiting to be developed. Yeah...he was thinking back, Mr. Tyner said we had a little time left before the county and state would take over. He even suggested we try to find Rachel and talk to her, and maybe we could reach an agreement about the houses and land, and yes, he had forgotten about the mills.

Damn! Rachel will have part of the business as well! But...wait, he thought he was on to something. Mr. Tyner didn't mention the Hayden's Mills, so who is really operating them and why weren't they mentioned in grandmother's will? He had to find some answers and soon.

Later that afternoon he placed a call to Mr. Tyner's office. "I am sorry Mr. Hayden, I can't give you copies of your grandmother's will without written permission from Mr. Tyner, and Mr. Baylor Tyner is on vacation, and we do not expect him back before the first of the New Year. Can I help you with anything else?" asked Calvin.

Chapter 60

My nose is itching for a man...

Ms. Emma and Ms. Ella were walking toward the house when they saw a truck pull up directly in front of the house. A few more feet and it would have been sitting in Ms. Emma front room, thought Ms. Ella. The truck was directly in the front of the porch steps. Ms. Emma knew something was wrong, that was ol' Willie's truck. "I wonder why he's here," Ms. Emma said to Ella as she leaned on her cane for extra support. Ms. Emma got a little closer and saw ol' Willie coming from the side of her house. He was stumbling and fumbling with the zipper on his pants. A large wet spot trailed down his pant leg. It looks like he had peed on himself she thought and made a disgusting frown on her face and watched as he fumbled with the zipper. Giving up on the zipper, he started walking toward the house. Part of his shirttail was sticking through the opening of his pants.

"My, Lord Ella, He looks like he's been drinking." They stopped a little ways from the porch and from ol' Willie. "Oh, there you are," he called out to Ms. Emma, as he stumbled, trying to hold on to the door of the truck. "I came by to see them girls. Where are they?" he asked fishing around the pockets of his jacket for a cigarette. "The girls are no longer here ol' Willie," she answered nervously. She didn't want to lie, but she didn't want this White man to come back to her house ever again. "Their mama came and got'em before thanksgiving! Ain't that right Ella?" She looked over at Ella, hoping she would go along and say 'yes.' "Yes, they were so happy to go with their mama," Ella said with strained laughter.

"Ol' Willie we are just getting home, and we are some tired old ladies. Can you move the truck so it won't block the porch steps?" Ms. Emma asked in a firm but I'm not taking 'no' shit from you today, kinda voice. Ignoring her, and trying to hold in the urge to belch, he asked in a slurred voice, "Where's uh...Mr. Leon?" Ms. Emma looked directly at ol' Willie. "I don't know. He don't live here ol' Willie!" They both stood their ground. They were not gonna let no drunk ol' white man scare them. Before they could say anything else, and quite a surprise to all, Mr. Harvey appeared from nowhere and walked up behind the two women. "Evenin' ya'll, How you Ms. Emma, Ms. Ella. How much ya'll owe Mr. Willie for the ride home?" He reached in his pocket and pulled out a dollar. "Is this okay Mr. Willie?" he asked handing him the crumble up dollar bill!

Ol' Willie got back in his truck, and backed it up and out of the way of the porch steps and drove out of the yard. He threw an empty whiskey bottle out the window as he drove away.

"Ms. Emma I have a message for you from Mr. Leon, can we go inside." "Sure we can Mr. Harvey. Ella this is Mr. Harvey, Mr. Leon's friend." She looked at Mr. Harvey hoping it was good news. She locked the door incase ol' Willie may try to come back. "Tell me what you got to tell me Mr. Harvey. I know the girls and Mr. Leon is gone. I just don't know why they left and didn't tell me good-bye." Her voice was quivering and she knew she was going to cry, and she didn't want to cry. Mr. Harvey walked over to Ms. Emma and told her she had better sit down.

"Ms. Emma you want me to hear this?" asked Ella. "Yes, it's okay Ella, you stay in here." "Ms. Emma the girls' is fine. They is all right and so is Mr. Leon. Mr. Leon and I found out a while back, ol' Willie and Mr. Reynolds were planning to kidnap the girls that Monday after thanksgiving while they was gonna to school and take them away to another place. We couldn't let anything happened to the girls so we sent them to another city to save them."

"They were in danger, and we don't know why Ms. Emma," he was shaking his head from side to side. He continued, "So Mr. Leon did the best thing. We couldn't tell you because we had to do something fast. I don't know much about what happened, but them girls got something to do with ol' Willie's plans. That's all I know. Mr. Leon told me to stop by ever so often and check on you, see if you be needing anything Ms. Emma." He sat there waiting patiently for a response from Ms. Emma. She sat quietly for a few moments.

"Mr. Harvey, I had custody of them girls. Mr. Leon helped me fill out the papers. He told me to sign I was the girls' next of kin. I did that, and the judge a month later gave me custody. Why did ol' Willie want to kidnap them?" she was crying softly. "Ms. Emma, Mr. Leon told me to tell you…you is the girls' great aunt." He waited for Ms. Emma to say something. She was crying and coughing at the same time. Ella rushed over to comfort her friend, and Mr. Harvey went in the kitchen to get her some water.

He continued to explain as he handed her the cup of water. "Ms. Emma… Mr. Leon told me the girls' mama is Rachel Jackson, your sister Ilene's daughter. He found out about them from Ms. Ruth." "You mean to tell me, Ms. Ruth knew the girls were my nieces and she kept that from me, but why! I don't understand Mr. Harvey. How she know and I didn't know about the girls?" "I can't answer your questions Ms. Emma, because Mr. Leon and I didn't have much time to talk. He told me to tell you not to worry, and that he is sorry you had to find out this way. Ms. Emma, Ms. Ella, ya'll can't tell a soul what I just told you, cause ya'll could be in danger if ol' Willie thinks you know where the girls are!" he warned. "What did ol' Willie want Ms. Emma?" "He asked where the girls were, and I told him their mama came and got'em." "Good, you told him that! Maybe he will stop bothering you and Ms. Ella." "It's getting late Mr. Harvey; you got a long ways to go?" asked

Ms. Ella. "Yes, but I will be okay. I'll walk through the back woods, and be careful." "No, you can stay here until tomorrow morning," suggested Ms. Emma. "At least you can see if someone is following you, okay. You can sleep on Mr. Leon's cot. Mr. Harvey thank you for telling me about my…my nieces, and if you see or hear from Mr. Leon again tell him I said thank you for taking care of us." "Mr. Harvey, you didn't tell me where the girls are?" He paused a few moments. "Ms. Emma don't worry no one can get to them, they is okay." He walked silently out the door.

Chapter 61

Time and life moves on...New York, middle 60's

"You have class tonight too?" Sugar asked Myrtle. "Yes I do, what about your homework? You finish yet?" "No, but I am working on it." "Come on Sugar, you are what? Thirteen years old or fourteen years old?" she asked teasing Sugar. "Don't no men want a dumb woman; remember what Aunt Leola told us, and speaking of Aunt Leola, she is going to drop by this evening. I am so glad she helped me get this apartment, and that job at Brooklyn County General." "Yeah, and my check helps out too," echoed Sugar. "That little itty bitty check," laughed Myrtle. "Look, we have come a long way, and we are still alive and making it. If it had not been for Mr. Harvey, Mr. Leon's friend, and especially Aunt Leola, we may not have lived to see today. Those bad men wanted to take us away, to where I don't know. However, we are here in New York. This is where we live now. I want to forget all the bad and hurtful things that happened to us, okay." She smiled at Sugar.

"Now, about this home work... what's the problem Sugar?" "Well the teacher asked the class what we plan to do when we finish high school, and write a paper about it...and I can't think of anything, she shrugged her shoulders, except I like to draw and paint," she said rolling around on the bed. "Okay, you can be an artist, or an art teacher. What do you think about those ideas?" Myrtle asked. "Great! I know what to write now, thanks!" Myrtle picked up her books for class, and reminded Sugar not to open the door for anyone, but Aunt Leola.

She loved going to class in the evening and it fits in well with her job during the day. Aunt Leola told her she should study to be a nurse because she likes taking care of people and she has done a fine job taking care of her sister, and watching the neighbor's children once and awhile.

So far, her classes are coming along great, and working as a nurse's aid, she can use the experience for her internship, she was thinking. Anyway, she thought to herself, there is one other thing I would like to have…a car! Most of her school friends have a car or something to drive back and forth to school and to work. Nevertheless, she could wait. She promised Sugar she would wait to get a car after she graduated from high school, and that's a few more years away.

Every now and then, she would think about grandma and wonder if she is still alive. She remembered she was born in 1896 and this is 1964, she should be at least sixty-eight years old. However, she was thinking, "I always thought grandma was much older than that." One day I will try to find out if she is still alive. Maybe…no we can't do that…she thought…those men may still be looking for us. She put her mind on her class, and walked through the front entrance of the Allen T. Wilson School of Nursing.

A quiet peace had settled around Sugar Pudding as she wrote of her desire to become an art teacher. She thought back to the first time the teacher gave her a box of crayons, and the first picture she colored was a turkey. She remembered Ms. Foster her kindergarten teacher. She was so nice to us, always bringing us cookies and cupcakes, she had baked, to surprise us. The rest of her teachers treated her okay. She just remembered some were just not as friendly as the others were. It was a shock to most of the teachers as well as the students when she walked in the class the first day school began. However, after awhile they all got used to the white looking girl who often said the first thing out of her mouth, without thinking.

She sized up her friends and concluded, she had more friends in elementary school then she had in junior high. The older students she surmised…wondered more about her parentage and showed it when they would sometimes go off and leave her standing there by herself, or they did not include her in many of their conversations. Well, the boys like her, and sometimes went out of their way to help her, especially if one of the girls gave her a hard time. Most of the teachers liked her because she stayed to herself, and never cause any problems. Aunt Leola told her and Myrtle shortly after they had come to live with her, "if anybody bothers you, you had better let me and Julia know about!" She said it as a warning. Sugar Pudding thought, I know exactly what aunt Leola mean; if anyone gives you a hard time about the color of your skin, or your hair, we need to talk about it.

Sugar got used to the stares and comments. It was very little to put up with compared to where they had live, and how badly some of the people treated them in Tapsalle County. Now, they are living in a nice place, and are very happy, thanks to Aunt Leola and her daughter Julia who had taken care of her and her sister until they moved to another apartment. They live in the same building, and it's good that she can see them anytime and have talks with Aunt Leola.

Sugar was thinking I wish things could stay like this. She got up off the sofa and walked over to the record player Aunt Leola had given them as a gift for their apartment. She watched her aunt very carefully as she showed her how to put the record on, so she would not scratch or crack the record. She liked one record in particular and kept the record on the turntable, so she could listen to it when she ever she wants. She waited for the arm on the record player to ease down ever so gently and touch the dinner plate size black record. Sugar listened for the song to start, "Candy, why I call my sugar candy"…

Chapter 62

The past and present, in retrospect...

Rachel had felt at one time, she was at the height of her career and her life. She was 39years old, had her own apartment and a pretty, good paying job and living in Brooklyn New York. However, she was not happy. I have given up much of my life...yes a great portion of my life was without my girls. After years of trying to make enough money to go back to North Carolina and find them, I gave up, she thought to herself. She did not want to see the hate in their eyes. How could she tell them, she didn't try to find them because she was not making enough money to take care of herself, let alone two little girls! What could she say to them? How would she explain her actions that she had to go back to school and get some training to make enough money to keep a roof over her head? Hell, she couldn't even explain it to herself.

She had thought of them constantly wondering how they look, and who is taking care of them. Myrtle is a least nineteen years old and Sugar Pudding is fourteen. I know I will have to face them eventually, but I don't know where to start. Quite a lot of years have past, and I really don't know if they would want to see me. I left them...no I abandoned them. I was sick and not thinking right at that time. All I want is a chance to explain to them why I had to leave them. If they can't find it in their hearts to forgive me, I'll understand. I know I need to think about this a little longer, but I have to find them soon, since I have recently, been diagnosed that my cancer has came back, and the doctors are only giving me a year or maybe a shorter time to live. It is so strange, she was thinking, you go to the doctor complaining about one thing and they find something else.

I knew something was wrong a year ago. I felt the swelling and pain under my left arm. I thought maybe it was a boil of some kind or maybe from too much shaving under my arms or the deodorant I put on every morning. My right arm would hurt so badly, and then other times just like the pain came, it went away, sometimes for days at a time. I felt relieved, until I saw that the lump had gotten larger under my arm.

A year ago, the doctors removed most of it and my left breast. Now I take at least six pills a day, now that the radiation treatments have stopped. Maybe my hair will grow back eventually. I still have a lot to do before I die. She often wondered if that old white woman, Clemmons grandmother, had not force her and her daughters out of Southend, if her life would have been better. She remembered how she faced constant accusations of being a colored woman who betrayed her race because she fell in love with a white boy and had two beautiful girls.

The civil rights movement was not new to her, she thought, but even the cause we are fighting for, is understandable and we all should be treated equally, and be given the same rights as white people. My girls and I were not given that right, but I don't blame the white bigots for their hatred of Negros, I blame them for having the audacity to think we could not ever measure up to them.

She didn't like to relive the past, she thought to herself. Yet, I wonder what went through Clemmons mind when we were not together. Did he think of me as just a colored girl he wanted to go out with simply because he had never been out with a colored girl before. Damn! Why did I wait until I am almost forty years old to figure out whether he loved me or not and for what reason? I guess I should know the answer to that question in the event I find my daughters.

The girls have probably looked at the color of their skin and figured out their father is white. I can only imagine the hell they went through being different. I am afraid….no… I won't think like that. They are okay. I have to believe that. At least I am going to try to find my girls' that's more than my own mama did for me. It's like she disappeared off the face of the earth. So many years have gone by, if I saw my mama I would probably not recognize her, and I do not want to experience that with my own daughters. I would know my daughters anywhere especially Myrtle; she has a reddish heart shaped birthmark on her right arm. I often wondered if it got any bigger, and Sugar Pudding has a brownish colored freckle the size of a nail's head on the bottom of her left foot. Being her mother, even I didn't know it was there at first. One of the nurses pointed it out to me, when Sugar Pudding got pneumonia and had to stay in the hospital. She slowly rose from her chair, rubbing the middle of her chest, trying to make the nagging pain go away. She walked into the kitchen to take another round of pills to keep her alive, and keep her thinking.

Chapter 63

Here we go again...

Baylor Tyner, glanced at the clock on the wall, I should be leaving here shortly if I plan to be in North Carolina by this evening. He was angry to hear, after all these years, Willie Hayden had not given up the fight for his grandmother's estate and got a lawyer to look into his Grandmother's wills again. After being told there was nothing he or any family member could do to change the wills, he thought Willie might have given up. He probably wants to talk about a deal. There is no deal Willie, no deal period.

He concluded, Willie probably found out the State of North Carolina decided not to extend the new highway through Bridgefield and Tapsalle County. It is still a waste of time and it did not make much sense for Willie to find me and request a meeting. I'll go, but I have the last say in as much as the estate is concern.

Hell, the girls are old enough; at least Myrtle can take over and assume some of responsibilities as the legal heir and owner of such a vast portion of land. Until she gets the hang of it, she will need legal advice and help in sorting everything out. Legal terminology, he thought to himself, can be a pain-in-the-ass. I hope they understand and keep me on as their lawyer. The detective I hired found them living in Brooklyn New York. However, he still has not located the whereabouts of the mother. Well, at least I have all their papers in order. However, getting to them and explaining 'who' I am is another story. I cannot forget I am the one who asked their mother to take the money and leave Southend where they had once lived. I hope the girls find it in their hearts... if they should happen to find out about everything, to forgive me.

Baylor thought, standing here thinking about the flight back to Tapsalle County is depressing enough. This time I will make sure Willie understands there is nothing he or I can do. Of course, I won't tell him I know where the girls are. That is none of his business, he thought as he picked up his brief case and started out the door and down the pathway to a waiting car.

He will have all of what he has to say together by the time the plane arrives in North Carolina. He had made prior arrangements to stay in the Bridgefield Hotel, and have Willie meet him there. In the event Willie decides to act stupid, the place is full of police.

From what Calvin his law clerk reported a few years ago, Willie did not like the idea the houses and the land is being monitored by his office, which is why the additional guard fences went up. This is in compliance, with the extension he obtained from Judge Patrick Dickerson. If Rachel or the girls are not located during the extension, the houses, money and the land go back to the state of North Carolina. He was smart to put the money in a trust fund for the girls. At least he had their names at the time. He really did not need an address. He knew he was going to find them. He was thinking, I will have to tell Willie the same thing and try to make him understand, and after that, I need to contact those girls. What a way to spend the Christmas holidays, he sighed in exasperation.

Chapter 64

Just fairly middling...

"Ella!" Ms. Emma called from her wheelchair. "I have a feeling we maybe getting a visitor." "Why you say that Ms. Emma? Is your right eye itching again?" Ella asked slightly making fun of Ms. Emma, by rubbing her eye. "You can laugh if you want, but somebody is coming here before long," she said in serious tone of voice. "I just got a feeling it's a woman, cause I pulled a long string of brown hair off my clothes today!" Ms. Emma laughed pretending to pull a string of hair off her clothes. "That's an old wives tale with no truth in it Ms. Emma, you just probably rubbed up against someone that's all," said Ella as she poured Ms. Emma some orange juice to take her pill. "Here take this before you forget. How's the legs today?" asked Ella with much concern in her voice. "Aw...I'm okay, they feel a lot better, and maybe I can get out of this wheelchair pretty soon. I really appreciate Mr. Harvey bringing it from the church. I told him I was going to take good care of it, incase someone else may be needing it."

Ella was thinking this maybe the best time to tell Ms. Emma she may have to move soon. Ms. Emma has been so good to me. I really don't want to hurt her feelings, and I really hate to leave her alone. It's almost Christmas and I don't want to spoil the holiday for her. She was walking around giving Ms. Emma the impression she is straightening up a bit...but she notice how Ms. Emma was watching her. As if she could read her mind, Ms. Emma said, "Ella, sit down a few minutes, and what ever you was doing can wait. Is something wrong Ella?" Ms. Emma asked cautiously. "There is nothing wrong Ms. Emma. I have something to tell you, and I just been trying to figure out how to tell you without sounding like...well, like I wasn't grateful for you letting me live here with you.

I…Ms. Emma I been here for the last five years. Did you know this is the longest I ever stayed with someone," she said nervously. "I thank you so much for having me. I guess there ain't really no way of saying this Ms. Emma"…she paused a few moments.

"I got a friend…well you know the man I been seeing, well he wants me to move in with him. I…I told him I would after you got better…Ms. Emma." "Now Ella, don't wait for me, I can stand a little while on my legs, and if I have to go back to that home…then I will. I want you to be happy, understand. You are not as old as I am. You need someone Ella,"…she said sadly, as she pressed the corner of the ragged old kitchen towel she had in her hands to the corner of her lips. "Are you getting married Ella?" she asked in a cheerful voice. "I'm not sure Ms. Emma, we have to wait and see. I won't be leaving until after Christmas, okay. Now what's for dinner tonight? I have a taste for some biscuits with strawberry preserves." "That's sounds fine Ella," said Ms. Emma trying to sound as if everything is all right. Nevertheless, she could never let Ella know how she really feels. She felt happy for Ella, but sad for herself. It seems as if the ones she loves are always leaving her alone.

Chapter 65

Brooklyn General Hospital, New York...

"Good Morning Nurse Tate, I know I'm a little early, but I noticed yesterday my shift's been changed to the cancer ward," said Myrtle. "Yes, the young lady that usually work this floor had an emergency and we really needed to fill the time slot, that's okay isn't it?" she asked. "Yes, it's fine with me," said Myrtle as she removed her coat and sat her bag down behind the counter. "How many patients do we have today?" "Well, we have eight, and another emergency admission. The woman has cancer of the breast, and apparently did not seek any medical attention until a few days ago. The doctor admitted her but they have not brought her to the floor yet. You may want to set up her bed, she is not on radiation for now," said Nurse Tate. "Don't worry Myrtle this floor is easy to work. You just have to follow the doctor's instructions to the letter, and you will be fine. Besides we need you on this floor, most of the patients are colored. I know they would like to see a familiar face," laughed Nurse Tate, who is white and a lot of fun to work with. Aunt Leola had told Myrtle about Nurse Tate, and she was right. Myrtle liked her from the very beginning.

Myrtle was thinking working with the elderly was not so stressful; all they did mostly was sleep. Some had been there for a while, because they had nowhere else to go. Brooklyn City General is a state ran hospital, and many people come here for care because they have no insurance. The patients on the cancer ward are separated by gender only. The male patients were further down the hall, and the female patients are at the other end of the unit. Negros and whites were in the same ward. You cannot segregate death.

Rachel noticed, after a few days working on the cancer floor, some of the patients did not stay there too long. Frequently, the cancer ward became too crowded. Not all the patients were sick from cancer; some of them, were unfortunately, abandoned during the holiday season, because they became a burden to their families. The doctor would evaluate their conditions in two categories, patients that were able to feed and take care of themselves, the hospital transferred them to a nursing home, and the patients not expected to live much longer then a few weeks because of their terminal illness, remained on the cancer ward. The doctors and staff knew they did not have much time left, so they made them as comfortable as possible. Myrtle tried to make them as comfortable as she could.

  She was combing an elderly woman's hair when the evening shift changed. They rushed in and she rushed out not getting a chance to say good-bye to her patients as usual and tell them she would see them tomorrow. She had a class to catch, and she did not want to be late. She gave her patients' charts to Ms. Davenport, the evening nurse standing next to Dr. Adams. He was waiting to begin the evening rounds.

  "When did the pain occur?" asked the pleasant and handsome Dr. Adams. "I…had the pain for a few days. I just thought I had caught a cold or something," she winched as she answered the doctor's question. "You know Rachel the cancer may have spread. We will do some test tomorrow morning. Now get some rest." This is all I need thought Rachel. Now I have to put off my plans to go back to Tapsalle County until I can find out what is wrong with me.

  This was third time she has been back to Brooklyn City General Hospital, she thought to herself, as the nurse standing beside her bed adjusted the flow of clear liquid that ran slowly into the tube inserted in her arm. The nurses are nice, but you can smell death…a sweet lingering odor, just waiting to engulf you and all that is around you. As long as I know who I am, death will not take my identity. I have something I have to do. With that thought on her mind, she let the sedative take control.

Chapter 66

Bridgefield County Rehabilitation Hospital...

"Well, what do you think Dr. Alcott? Will he regain the use of any of his limbs, asked Willie?" in a voice that was obviously void of any concern. The doctor quickly picked up on Willie's nonchalant attitude regarding his brother's dismal condition. "No, Mr. Hayden there is nothing we can do for him except to keep him comfortable. He is aware of people around him, but he cannot communicate with anyone, at least not right now. I believe that your brother suffered mild brain damage, and perhaps from the head injury...deadly fumes from the wreck along with the lengthy time it took to get your brother out from under the truck, caused considerable swelling of the brain."

"Mr. Hayden, the best we can do here is to evaluate your brother's condition for long term care, which is to refer your brother to a facility that can take care of him twenty-four hours a day for the rest of his life. There is a possibility of transferring your brother very soon, to the state hospital and nursing home in Wellington Grove in Rocky Mount. I am sorry I do not have any promising news for you. But, I believe you knew that when you walked in," the doctor knowingly commented.

"Does he have any family other then yourself?" asked Dr. Alcott. "Well...Willie thought for a moment. "No he don't have nobody else, just me. Our folks are dead," he answered acidly. "I see I'll contact you when we are ready to transfer him. It should be in a few weeks. I have other patients to see. If you'll excuse me, have a good morning." The doctor left, not wanting to be in the same room with Willie Hayden a minute longer. The man made him uncomfortable. He couldn't explain it, but this man acted as if he didn't know his brother. "Humph," it's probably the Christmas holiday coming up and his brother's condition is not showing any signs of improving, is probably on his mind the doctor thought, and pushed elevator button to go down.

Willie went back in Clemmons room and looked at the figure lying in the bed, wrapped in bandages from head to toe; at least you could see his face and parts of his ears. Everything else seemed to be in a cast. He tried to look into his brother's eyes. Just a blank stare. Well, that leaves just me, Willie was thinking. If he had not been drinking, we probably could have sued the trucking company. However, that police officer, who called him at home, said they found a half-empty liquor bottle between his legs when the firefighter pulled him out.

Willie still could not imagine why he was drinking that early in the morning. Something must have happened to make him take a drink. He scratched his head and walked quietly out of the room. He had to get Clemmons condition off his mind and get ready to meet Mr. Tyner. He should be flying in today. This is my last chance, to find out all I can about grandmother's wills. He will have to answer my questions or I will take him to court, he was thinking to himself. He could feel the anger creeping up his neck. I want answers to everything…including the mills. That's what I am going to say to the old bastard! He was rehearsing exactly what he was going to say as he jumped up into his truck.

Chapter 67

Old familiar faces...

That was a nice flight, Baylor told himself. He was not the type to fly. He didn't like airplanes, but it beat traveling on a train. He just wanted to get this meeting over with. He only agreed to meet with Willie to tell him or better yet show him...the wills and give him a copy if that is what he wants...shit anything to make this man go away. He had left word for Calvin his law clerk, to drive out to Willie Hayden's home and leave the letter with instructions where they were going to meet. Since he was staying overnight at the Bridgefield Hotel, he thought he may as well have the meeting there.

A tap on his hotel room brought him back to the present. He opened the door and standing before him was the dumpy looking freckled face hotel clerk. He handed him a piece of paper with the room number of the small conference room he had scheduled for his meeting with Willie. Well, since the meeting isn't until two 'o' clock in the afternoon he could go down and have a drink at the bar, and see who he could bump into, he smiled to himself.

He had not been back in over five years. Things still had not changed that much. He recognized a few faces and spoke courteous to them, and shook a few hands at the bar, all the while listening to the various comments, "You are looking well! Where have you been? It's certainly nice to see you again!" He expected a few of his old clients to ask if they could stop by the office. He had to explain however, he was only seeing clients in the North Carolina office by appointment only, but he could refer them to one of his associates. Being the 'gentlemen' that he is, he paid for a round of drinks and went down to the conference room to wait for Willie.

As he expected, Willie Hayden was on time. "Good afternoon Mr. Hayden! Glad you could make it!" he extended his hand. Willie ignored the gesture. "Look Tyner, I won't pull any punches. I just came to get my copies of the wills and to ask you who is running the family saw mills in Tapsalle and Bridgefield," Willie said sarcastically. "You got some explaining to do Tyner! Why did grandmother give you so much power over the estate and why aren't the mills; the family business mentioned in the wills? I got all day! Start talking old man!" Willie barked at Mr. Tyner.

Mr. Tyner, in a deliberate show of authority and confidence, took off his suit jacket, carefully folded it across an empty chair and casually leaned back in his chair, feeling very comfortable that the police, if he needs them are in the next room. "Mr. Hayden if you would kindly have a seat, we can get down to business," he responded calmly. "First things first…you asked who is operating your grandmother or the family business? I am operating the business with three other people your grandmother chose in the event of my death or if the state wishes to gain control for one reason or another.

Since your grandmother chose not to include you or your brother, she arranged to have the business turned into a corporation. The business will continue long after you and I are gone, or until it is no longer a business. You understand so far?" Tyner asked with a slight tone of-come-uptness. "The operation or ownership of the company is not challengeable by you, me or anyone else in your family that may think the courts will rule against your grandmother's will. That is why the mills were not made apart of the estate as with the houses and the two-hundred and thirty acres, and her financial holdings. I am currently a shareholder with fifty percent ownership. The bank's vice president which you know is her cousin, Mr. Fenton Steed, has twenty-five percent and the other twenty-five percent of the business belongs to Rachel Jackson's two girls."

Baylor Tyner leaned further back into his chair, picked up his drink, sipping the liquid contentedly. He had saved the best for last. He continued the meeting with much confidence. "The estate as well as the land she left to Rachel is a life estate, to which the houses if still standing can be left to their family members as well as the land. The houses or the land, however, can be deeded out to whom ever they choose. Look, I have explained everything that is important Willie," he said almost giddy but with control. "Here's the copy of the wills." He slid them across the long table carefully watching Willie's every move. Willie just sat there. Finally, he slowly reached for the papers, giving Mr. Tyner a distrusting gaze. He looked at the wills, he was still not satisfied the mills were not mentioned, yet still curious as to why Grandmother sold the family business.

What Willie could not figure out from the story Mr. Tyner told, is that this may have been in the works a long time. There is no way I can get anything back, he angrily thought. Realizing he has to except the explanation, he asks Mr. Tyner one final question. "Mr. Tyner, did she ever tell you why my brother and I were not a part of the will?" Willie held the papers in a tight squeeze. His eyes flashed in a familiar display of impatience, as he waited for Mr. Tyner to answer his question.

"Why yes, she did speak to the reason why, but I didn't directly come out and ask her. In my opinion Willie, I believe she felt you and Clemmons had your chance but you chose different avenues to exercise your interests. I honestly believe she left the bulk of her estate to Rachel and the girls because she felt guilty for what she had done, and wanted to make peace with God. Your Grandmother assumed this move would, and in some way, make up for her mistakes. The mean and nasty way she treated the Negro people, including Rachel and her great-granddaughters." Baylor waited for the expression on his face to change, seeing none he continued.

"Willie you were not there, but your grandmother had a peaceful look on her face the night she died. We were there until the end. Look, I know it's hard to except what has happened, but you really need to move on with your life. You have spent the better part of it trying to figure a way to void the wills. You are wasting your time Willie. You would be better off trying to buy into the corporation rather than hinder its existence. It's up to you Willie," said Mr. Tyner exhaustedly throwing his hand up in the air. "I have nothing else to add."

Willie was quiet, a little quieter then usual. Now, he was thinking to himself. Did Mr. Tyner expect him to believe his explanation over the lawyer he is paying to help him? He had planned to take the papers back and let the lawyer he hired, look them over to see if maybe he has a case. Since the family mills are out of the question, all that's left is the houses, and the land. The financial holdings, stocks, and bonds, granny left to Rachel and her girls.

He would feel a lot better if he had some control…some kind of control over his family business he thought. It's as if nothing ever existed, at least the sawmills and the houses were theirs at one time and should have remained in the family. He will never understand why his grandmother took everything away. He realized he was getting a headache. He pressed his fist into his temple, trying to make the pain go away.

"Okay, Mr. Tyner," said Willie staring at him intensely. "I still believe you had an awful lot to do with grandmother changing her mind. I may not be able to prove it, but in the back of my mind, you planned this whole damn thing! What's in it for you old bastard…besides the ownership of fifty percent of the family business? It can't be the money; you have got plenty of that ripping off your clients! He suddenly pounded his fist on the table. The vibration shook the liquor in Mr. Tyner's glass. "I'm leaving but you have not heard the last of me!" he said bitterly. Willie got up and walked almost reluctantly toward the door. He paused as if he had a change of mind. He chewed fiercely on his bottom lip and walked hastily out the door.

Baylor Tyner picked up the telephone and ordered another drink. This meeting went along better than he had expected. I need to get back to Florida, he thought to himself. He was picking up his things and putting them back in his briefcase. He felt good. He had accomplished exactly what he had planned. The only other thing on his agenda was to find the girls and give them some good news. He strutted out the door and down to the lobby. As he approached the counter to pay his bill, the clerk gave him a long white envelope. "A gentleman left this for you," he said casually. Waiting for the clerk to add up his charges, he opened the envelope slowly.

"Why that dirty son-of-bitch, a subpoena!" he cursed aloud. Baylor Tyner figured Willie was quiet for a reason, and now he knows why. He couldn't risk putting his hands on me. He knew immediately, the police would arrest him. Well Willie he thought smugly to himself, "I, no… we will see you in court." He looked at the subpoena and saw that he had to appear in court in sixty days. He thought this would give him plenty of time to contact Rachel Jackson's girls and bring them in court with him. He did not feel positive about finding their mother, 'Rachel.' The detective is having a difficult time trying to find her. "There's a possibility over the years, she changed her name," the detective said. Baylor was thinking since the oldest girl, Myrtle, is of age she can take over the estate and do as she pleases. I'll be there in the event she needs some guidance and legal assistance. Moreover, I have a feeling she will need both.

Chapter 68

Curiosity killed the cat...

Maybe I ought to drive by grandmother's estate on the way back to Tapsalle County thought Willie. After all, I haven't seen the houses in a while and I need to be sure they are still standing. In their last meeting, he forgot to ask Mr. Tyner, why another fence was put up around the property. He felt an explanation of some kind is needed. Hell, if he wanted to, he could have moved into one of the houses years ago when the property was not fenced off. As he drove nearer to the road that leads to the estate, he became outraged. The workers had extended the fence to the road and chained locked it. It was impossible to see anything from where he stood. There were signs reading, *"Private Property Do Not Enter"* nailed up all over the place!

That old bastard must be up to something. Willie quickly concluded, if the lawyer he hired doesn't come up with anything that could help him challenge his grandmother's will, he's finished. The only hope he had was his lawyer. The detective he hired to find Rachel took the last of the money he gave him and skipped town. The dirty bastard, he cursed silently as he drove back to his house. He had to find something in the will he could challenge. He didn't have any luck with the doctor or the nurse that was with his grandmother the night she died. They did not want to have anything to do with it. They were very adamant about their decision...they just did not want to get involved. The doctor even went as far as to say, "Grandmother was in her right mind, and was in full control of everything around her until the day she died," and suggested that he just except what has happen and move on.

"I don't have to except shit!" He said aloud. Damn it! I will find out why Clemmons and I were left out of everything, and to make sure grandmother was not made to do this; I want an investigation to be sure she was in her right mind. It just does not make any sense! The judge, if he has any sense, will probably want the wills challenged as well…just to make sure they are legal. Who knows when he finds out the heirs are colored; he may award the total estate to him.

Chapter 69

Letting go of life...

      She was alive and she was alone again. Ella was still living with her, but she seldom saw her because she spent most of her time with her boyfriend. It had been a few days since Ella or anyone had dropped in to see her. She could walk a lot better and on her good days, she managed to walk down to the bus stop and ride into town to pick up the free food from the church. Most of the time she was lucky and got a ride back home with the bags, or one of the church members would drop off a bag to her every once and a while. She didn't worry too much about running out of food. Most of the time she was the only one eating and there was always some left over. She didn't eat much; here lately she was seldom hungry. She had gotten accustom to Ella sharing whatever stories or gossip she had heard, as they ate. There are no extra crumbs to brush off the table, and no extra dishes to wash.

      The deep and engulfing silence bothers her the most. She thought of her last two visitors. It was a year ago Mr. Harvey came by to tell her he was moving, and bought her a Christmas present, a new coffee pot, because the other one caught fire and the handled burned off. Mr. Tompkins stopped by a few days ago and asked if she could come to the house and take care of his wife. She told him, she was so sorry to hear his wife was ailing, but she could barely take care of herself.

      She often thought of Mr. Leon and the girls. She wondered if she would ever see them again.

      Days had past, and she finally received a letter from Ella. She could make out some of the words...enough to tell her they had gotten married, and she would get her things later. Ella had placed a folded ten-dollar bill in the letter. There was more to read, but she couldn't make out the words because her eyesight was failing her and she could barely see the words on the paper. She placed the letter on her dresser with the checks she had received from the state. She thought, Ella always cashed the check for her and bought the things they would need with the money. Ella was not there anymore. Everyone seem to have left the county, leaving her all alone with nothing but her memories and thoughts of what it was like when she was surrounded by them. She napped often to keep from remembering. She thought memories should be of good things, and thought about the girls again, and how she would love to see them again. She remembered how happy she was, to find out they were really her nieces.

I wish I had a picture of them, she thought sadly and she looked at the calendar on the wall. As if seeing it for the first time, she suddenly realized someone had changed the month to April and circled the fourteenth. She had not noticed the change until now. She swallowed the sad feeling down deeply, and realized that was Myrtle's way of tell her good-bye, because they had to leave in a hurry that awful night. Myrtle said her good-bye, using the calendar on the wall. She knew I would see the message and understand.

She was crying softly and thinking to herself, convincing herself... I know in my heart they could not have forgotten about me. Tears slowly ran down her wrinkled cheeks and on to her trembling hands, which were holding the yellow lacy ribbon she often fingered until it had become too fragile to touch and the one small shinny black shoe that was rubbed and smooth so much, it had become dull. The shine was gone like many things in her life. Yet, these precious things were a part of the girls' life that was left behind years ago in their haste to leave. These she thought as she sadly looked down in her lap, is all that is left of my family and memories of good and bad times gone by. She sat the small black shoe and yellow lacy ribbon on the table beside her bed.

Chapter 70

Holding on to life...

Rachel felt a sudden coolness about her face and arms. A faint smell of honey suckles and lilac whispered gently passed her nose. She struggled hard to open her eyes. She finally focused them upon the face of a white nurse. The face looked familiar. The nurse smiled at her and said, "Good morning, how do you feel today?" "How long have I been asleep?" she asked still in a stupor, moving her head back and forth to shake off the strong urge to go back to sleep. "You have been sleep on and off for a day or two Ms. Jackson. You were transferred from the emergency room to the floor a week ago," she answered pleasantly. "I am Nurse Tate. You will probably see my face a lot and the nursing assistant Ms. Jackson," she continued as she gently wiped the cool washcloth across her face again. "You are running a pretty high fever, and I am trying to get your temperature down. So bare with me, and let me know if you are feeling uncomfortable, okay. It would also help if you can swallow some ice water or perhaps suck on some ice chips." Before she finished the sponge bath, Rachel had gone back to sleep.

"Mmm...Maybe her fever will break sometime today," Nurse Tate commented to Doctor Adams who had just walked in the room. "Still no change Nurse Tate?" he asked in a concerned voice. "Well, it's gone down somewhat, it's 103 at the moment, she responded." "She has an infection in the old surgical site. I have no idea why she waited so long to come in for treatment. The wound will have to be opened and drained," he said as he pulled back Rachel's gown and looked at the wound. "As soon as possible, schedule the procedure for ten o' clock tomorrow morning. Nurse Tate, I'll check on her a little later." "I'll call you if there is a change she said," walking out the room with the doctor.

Chapter 71
Messages...

"Aunt Leola do you think it's okay to write a letter to grandma in Tapsalle County," Sugar asked as she carefully drew little flowers around the border of the writing paper. "I was thinking about her today. I wonder if she had a nice Christmas. I feel sad because we couldn't send her anything. I didn't mean to forget her. It's just everything happened so fast. And, Myrtle thought it was best not to write her because the men who were going to kidnap us may still be looking for us." She continued to draw never raising her head up, from what she was doing. "Well, Sugar Pudding, I would have to talk to Myrtle and see what she has to say. When she comes to pick you up tonight, we'll talk. Is that okay," she asked. "Okay, I can wait, Aunt Leola," said Sugar Pudding as she folded the piece of writing paper in half.

Aunt Leola was remembering how the girls came to live with her and Julia. Like Sugar said, things happened so fast and time went by so quickly. She remembered the last time she spoke with her brother Earl before he died. Everyday she struggles with the realization of not being able to attend his funeral in North Carolina, solely because of her promise to him to take care of the girls, and keep them safe. All she knew is that he died of natural causes, and she received the letter from his wife detailing the girls' relationship to Ms. Emma Jackson.

She has kept the information for years. Now, maybe this is the time to tell them now, however, a lot of information is still missing, she thought to herself. Why did Willie Hayden plot to kidnap the girls? Why was Ms. Emma led to believe she was no kin to them until her brother revealed the kidnapping plot?

Well, no time to play detective, she had to meet with the girls sometime tonight and tell them what has happened. How do you explain years of not knowing absolutely nothing about yourself, and suddenly you are made aware, the person you lived with and called grandma is really some kin to you? Myrtle will probably take it fine, and analyze the information and perhaps go forward with her plans. However, Sugar Pudding will probably ask a lot of questions and the most important question of all, why were they abandoned and left to the cruel harsh treatment of the many people they came in contact with, and some who hurt and frightened them? I hope I will be able to give them all the support they will need. Hell! Excuse me Lord, but I am curious too!

Her quick assessment and gathering of the facts were interrupted by the hollering voices. "I'm home mama! Where are you Aunt Leola?" "Hey there, I am in the kitchen fixing us a late meal!" She made every effort to sound like her cheerful self. Sugar Pudding bouncing and bubbly had some exciting news! She was clapping her hands together and bumping Julia with her small hips to get her attention as well! "I have some great news! Aunt Leola where's Myrtle? Is she on her way home? Can I call up stairs to our apartment to see if she is home?" Sugar Pudding as always asked many questions and never stopping long enough to let anyone answer them. "Okay, okay! Sugar Pudding, give us your news we can hardly wait!" "My career paper was chosen to be printed in our school newspaper. Wow!" she exclaimed, loudly clapped for herself.

I was almost in tears, my news could never make her or Julia smile and laugh as they are doing now! "Sugar Pudding, can we read your paper? Do you have a copy with you?" Aunt Leola asked trying to sound just as excited as they are! "Yes, I have copy Aunt Leola, but I want to wait until Myrtle gets home," she answered waving the copy in the air.

Myrtle was quickly copying notes from the lecture and thinking about getting home before it gets late. She did not want to miss her ride with Maria who lived a few blocks from her apartment building and had offered to take her home on the nights they had class together. Myrtle was thinking, Maria reminded her of her first best friend, Anna. She wore similar thick glasses and had thick brown hair she often wore in a ponytail with a ribbon tied around it. She showed Myrtle the shortest way to class and told her whom she should and should not associate with. Maria gave respect and received it as well. The difference between Maria and Anna is that Maria had a few friends. However, if the truth were told some of them made fun of her glasses and that awful ponytail, she smiled to herself.

She often wondered what happened to Anna, and remembered she still had the letter Anna wrote to her over six years ago. Mmm, maybe I will sit down very soon, and write her and let her know where Sugar Pudding and I are living. Won't she be surprise to find out we are living in New York! Her thoughts slowly turned back to grandma. She wanted so much to write her a letter and send her something nice. She feared the men were probably still trying to find them. I need to talk to Aunt Leola and find out what she thinks about the idea. She felt Sugar Pudding missed her as well, but kept her feelings and thoughts to herself.

She returned to the present, packed up her things and went down stairs to meet Maria and go home. "Go home," sounded so nice she was thinking. Maria was waiting for Myrtle. She blew the horn, so Myrtle could see where she had parked. Myrtle waved and walked over to the car and got in. "Thanks Maria, I really appreciate the ride." "Well, you better enjoy it while you can. I maybe transferring in a few months to New York University," she teased. I was offered a position at Sainte Margaret's General hospital as a counselor, and it's a few blocks from the job," she sounded very, happy. "Don't worry Myrtle; I will let you know when I make that move. Tell me what's on your agenda for tonight?"

The tone in Maria's voice suggested to Myrtle she had some plans and wanted to know if Myrtle wanted to join her and her friends. "Hell, Maria, any other time I would love to hang out with you, but tonight I have to talk to Aunt Leola about some family business," she tried to sound like she was disappointed. "That's okay, Myrtle, we can do it another time. You know maybe I should go straight home and try to get in some extra studying to prepare for my midterms. Thanks for the refusal Myrtle," and she laughed a little. "Well, you are home! See you tomorrow, take care."

Maria slowly drove off into the night. Myrtle suddenly turned her head around, a chill went down her spine. She could have sworn someone was watching her. She thought she heard a quick step or some kind of movement. She quickly ran up to the apartment building and pushed the elevator buttons to go up to the third floor. There were quite a few people standing in front of the elevator doors with packages, carts and all the while greeting one another as they waited patiently for the doors to open. She felt safe when she reached the third floor.

Quickly, she stepped off the elevator and ran toward their apartment. She could hear the telephone ringing, and tried frantically to get the key in the lock. She was the only one standing in the long corridors. Once in, she locked the door and sit down to catch her breath. The phone had stopped ringing before she opened the door. Whoever it was, she thought, they will call back! Ring! Ring! There it is, ringing again. She jumped up and snatched up the receiver, and said a quick hello! "Sugar, okay, I'll be down there in a minute, okay! Yeah, I can tell by all the laughter and giggling in the background. You have something to tell me too. Yes, okay, okay! Sugar here I come," and she hung up the telephone.

Walking toward Aunt Leola's apartment, she could smell the aroma of fried chicken, her favorite. I hope she made some potato salad too! Myrtle's mouth was watering and she could hardly keep her mind on what Sugar Pudding has to tell her. She knocked at the door, and it flew open just as fast! There stood all three of them, rushing her in. "Come on before the food gets cold," commented Julia.

"Sugar has something to..." "No, don't tell her Julia," Sugar exclaimed excitedly waving her hands in the air! Let me do it she begged." All of a sudden, and to Aunt Leola's surprise, Sugar Pudding pulls out a dining chair and jumps up on the seat! Aunt Leola said playfully shaking her finger at her, "Girl! You better make this a good one," and she laughed. "This is the only way I can your attention," Sugar said, putting her hands to her mouth laughing. Finally getting herself together, she started. "Myrtle you remember the paper I had to write for my career assignment? Well, thanks to you, my paper will be printed in the school's newspaper next month!" She didn't have to clap again. They all did it for her, and commended her on a job well done. For her *"kitchen chair finish,"* Julia handed Sugar the paper she wrote, and Sugar read it aloud while Aunt Leola fixed their plates.

Aunt Leola tried to avoid their faces, because she had tears in her eyes. She was so happy and yet sad, because she had to talk to the girls tonight, all the "girls" she thought solemnly. She listened to the quick chatter and soft hum of their conversation as they ate their dinner. She rose from the table, so engrossed were the girls in their talking, they never noticed she had left the table and gone into the kitchen. They never heard the splashing of water and glasses tinkling and silverware hitting the bottom of the sink. Aunt Leola thought to herself, I really don't want to have this meeting with them tonight. What I have to tell them can wait until tomorrow she decided. "Anyone want anymore chicken before I put the rest in the refrigerator?" She called out, above the laughter and squeals. Julia was acting the fool and had Myrtle and Sugar howling with laughter!" One of the girls had turned the record player on, and Julia was showing them a new dance. She heard Julia yelling over the music, "Come on Sugar you have to shake your behind a little harder then that!"

Chapter 72

The finishing act...

"Dr. Adams, this is Nurse Benton. Yes, how are you? No, I am on the night shift tonight. I am calling you because I have a patient, Ms. Rachel Jackson on the cancer ward, and it looks as if she is taking a turn for the worse. We are trying desperately to get her temperature down and there is some bleeding from the surgical site. I have cleaned the wound, and administered her medicine as ordered. I saw where you left the message if there were any changes to contact you as soon as possible. Yes, I see... in an hour, sure I will see you then, good-bye."

Nurse Benton continued to sponge bath Rachel. She took her temperature again and logged it in her chart. She saw where the doctor had scheduled her for an exploratory incision of the wound and several tests to see if the cancer had spread to other parts of her body. Nurse Benton looked through her chart to see who the next of kin is. Nothing. There was no family names were mentioned. She made a mental note of her findings. She would talk to the doctor when he gets here. Making funeral arrangements as well as taking care of the patients were apart of their duties as well. It was especially sad when there are no relatives to talk to and to turn over their personal effects. Most of the clothes are given to charity and the patient's jewelry is placed in a small manila, colored envelope, and put in the hospital safe. The city usually sends a representative to pick up the things about once a month. What happens after that, she hasn't the slightest idea.

Chapter 73

The connection...

"Mr. Tyner, I found the apartment where the girls are living," the detective spoke assuredly into the receiver. "I was almost seen, but everything is fine. Sure, I'll pick up the money tomorrow when I get the other assignment. You are welcome sir! Sure, it's nice doing business with you too!" He hung up.

Baylor Tyner felt like the weight of the world, is lift off his shoulders. He would have to figure out a way to meet with them, now that the girls were located. There are a few weeks before the court date and he could work on that a little longer. He can't afford to make any mistakes, he was thinking. I am so glad to get this whole thing over with. I am getting old I want to enjoy the rest of my life, and perhaps get married. His mind wandered to the woman he had been seeing for a few months. He had always said he would never marry, but now he was thinking seriously about Ilene. She was colored and pretty. He never thought much about her color. He didn't know there was anything to think about other than she worked for one of his associates and is a very efficient employee.

Over the years he had never given her much thought, until a few months ago he was eating in the "South Florida Keys," a restaurant on the beach. He noticed her waiting patiently for someone to take her order. It seemed all the waitresses were busy or they did not want to wait on her because she was colored. He recognized her right away, got up from his table and walked over to her. "Good Afternoon, It's...uh, Ilene isn't it?" He asked extending his hand to shake hers. "Yes, it is! How are you? I'm sorry I forgot your name," she spoke softly. "It's Baylor, Baylor Tyner. Look, do you mind if I join you?" She looked rather strange at this friendly white man. "No, It's fine," she hesitated a brief moment. "As you can see, I am having a hard time trying to get a cup of coffee," she smiled.

He noticed she has a beautiful smile. He signaled for the waitress. A little skinny pale white girl with protruding teeth and stringy dull brown hair skittishly walked over to the table and suddenly stepped back. "Would you bring us two cups of coffee please, and we will let you know when we are ready to order," he said casually. The waitress looked at Ilene, and then back to Baylor. She tapped the pencil she held between her fingers on the plastic menus she held in her hand. With a display of insolence, she pulled her stringy hair behind her ears and finally spoke. "We are not supposed to wait on coloreds in the dining room," she said coldly. "That's a shame Miss. Please, go and bring back your manager," he asked her nicely. "Why you want him?" she asked with some agitation in her voice. Baylor didn't respond, and turn his conversation toward Ilene. "Now what would you like to eat for lunch?" He looked into her face, smiled and patted her hand lightly. Ilene was enjoying his company, and admired the way he took over.

Their relationship took off from day one and now Baylor thought I would love to spend the rest of my life with her. However, I have to finish what I started more than six years ago, and keep the promise I made to Stella Hayden.

His thoughts turned to the court date coming up, and his plans to tell the girls the truth about their fortune, and about the "Woman" Stella Louise Hayden. He has all but made up his mind to contact the girls before the court date. He has to make sure everything turns out in their favor. The whole thing could turn very ugly if Willie ever finds out he knows about the girls' whereabouts. He didn't want to imagine subjecting them to an unpleasant and perhaps dangerous situation if they should come face-to-face with Willie Hayden, their uncle. It's a shame about their father Clemmons but they will have to know about that as well. Baylor thought to himself, where would he get the courage to tell them what part he played in their mother leaving Southend. He decided long ago…to tell the truth, and he will after the court date.

Baylor Tyner never made it a habit discussing his cases with his friends or relatives. Moreover, he did not regard Ilene as just a friend. He cared a great deal for her and wanted her to know where he was going in a few weeks and that she could not go with him. He thought it would be nice to put her up at his home until he returned. He would hire some help for her. All she had to do was wait until he returns, and they could pick up where they had left off.

Chapter 74

Weeks later...

Myrtle was running late. She glanced at her watch. It's almost seven thirty am, and she had to be on the floor to review the patients' charts on the ward where she worked. They had several patients the nurses feared might not make it through the weekend. She had a feeling it maybe the little old lady, Ms. Finney. She was weak and could not eat anything, and no one ever came to visit her. She ran up to the hospital door and swung it open in a hurry to catch the elevator.

She waved bye to a few of the workers who had just gotten off from the midnight shift. Well, she had arrived just in time. The doctors were there to make the early morning rounds, and she is required to attend with the nurses. They had been in and out of the various rooms and left the newest arrivals last. Myrtle was standing in the back as Dr. Adams, walked over to the first bed. "This patient came in a few weeks ago, cancer of the breast and removal of the left breast. Now, there is a distinct possibility that the cancer has spread to other vital organs. The patient also has an open infection at the old wound site and has been running a very high temperature off and on since she arrived. Exploratory surgery showed the cancer has spread to several other sites and her right breast." They walked over to the next bed, and Dr. Adams opened the patient chart. "This patient is terminally ill, has not been able to eat any foods or hold down liquids. She came in comatose, and sadly, there is not much we can do for her, but keep her comfortable," he spoke in a lifeless monotone.

Myrtle listened as the doctor gave a report on the last patient and recorded the last of her notes. Dr. Adams, walked back toward the small colored woman lying in the second bed, and spoke with her. Myrtle was too far away to hear what he was saying to her, but he reached out and patted her hand, and walked away. Nurse Tate was running late so Myrtle decided to start without her, first giving out the medicines, changing their intravenous solutions, change their beds and gowns.

She was working on the third patient when Nurse Tate walked in. "Good morning Myrtle, Thanks for getting started. I had car trouble this morning. How's our patients' doing?" she asked cheerfully, waving to them regardless of whether they could see her or not. "I tell you what Myrtle… I'll start from the back of the ward and catch up with you, okay." "That's fine Nurse Tate," answered Myrtle, as she carefully turned the patient over so she could remove the sheet that was sticking to her open bedsores. "I may need your help over here," called Myrtle. The patient's bedsores were terrible and they had an awful smell.

Myrtle thought this is death. This is how death smells, and she wondered if the stench of death changed with the type of illness the patient was dying from. She let her mind leave the present task and wondered back to grandma. She was thinking of writing her a letter and have some pictures taken of her and Sugar Pudding. As a last thought, she would have to figure out how to tell grandma in the letter not to show them to anyone. People would still recognize them, even though it has been a long time since they left. They have changed quite a bit. Their skin color and hair are the same. It would not take much to add two and two together, and to realize they were the same half-white girls that once live with grandma.

Still reminiscing, Myrtle went back to that awful cold night when her and Sugar were abandoned. The worse of the bad times were trying to creep in on her thoughts, ganging up on her, all at one time. She shook her head roughly trying to get rid of them, and vowed she would never ever go back there again. She knew she had to try much harder to forget everything and the people who meant them no good. Nurse Tate walked up behind her and tapped her on the shoulders. "Myrtle, didn't you hear me calling you?" "I'm sorry Nurse Tate. I was away for a while. How can I help?" She asked, but there was still a lot of distance in her voice.

Nurse Tate picked up where she had left off, still eyeing Myrtle strangely. "The patient in bed two with breast cancer…her temperature has gone up again, and Dr. Adams wants to be notified if there is any change in her condition. He left a number in her chart where he can be reached. If you sponge her I'll finish the patient you are working on and call Dr. Adams okay," said Nurse Tate. "Sure, I'll do it immediately," responded Myrtle as she walked over to the counter, and started to fill a basin with cool water.

I am having a hard time trying to stay focus today, she wondered if it could be because it was time for her period. As she got closer to the patient, her hands began to shake. She gently pulled the sheet back off the patient's shoulders, picked up the chart that was lying on the end of the bed and introduced herself. "Good Morning Ms. Jackson." Myrtle never thought much about the last name, only that there must be a lot of people with the last name Jackson. "I am going to give you a sponge bath to try to get your temperature down." She spoke softly to the frail woman lying there with her head turned toward the dingy wall. Myrtle glanced at the wall and saw where someone had scrawled the words, *"Many have lay here for days, wings broken, and eventually died."*

"Myrtle!" called Nurse Tate. "Has her temperature gone down?" "I'll take it in a few minutes." Myrtle replied, never missing a stroke as she gently wiped the patient's face, neck and arms. She finished the sponge bath and took the patient's temperature, and called back to Nurse Tate. "It has gone down to 102 degrees," and she recorded it in the patient's chart along with the time. She cleaned up the mess, and started over to the next bed. "Ms. Finney," she called softly. "It's Ms. Jackson." Myrtle looked at Ms. Finney and noticed she had not moved, and her eyes were slightly open.

It suddenly occurred to Myrtle that Ms. Finney had passed. She had no idea when or what time. She hurriedly checked her pulse, neck and wrist and listened to her chest. "Nurse Tate," she called with nervousness in her voice. "I believe Ms. Finney has died." "Record your findings Myrtle, and I will be with you in a minute okay," answered the nurse. Myrtle recorded Ms. Finney's death at eleven-seventeen am. She knew the drill, call the morgue, pack-up the patient's belongings, check the patient's chart for next of kin, telephone number or address, have Nurse Tate sign off and put it in the box for processing the next day. The clerk will call the newspaper and post the death for seven days under a small section headed *"Death and No Next of Kin."* If anyone recognizes the person's name and description, and call the hospital, they can pick up the patient's belongings providing they can prove they are kin to the patient. If, not the body is buried in Waker's Cemetery for Colored People, and Mullins Sunrise and Sunset Cemetery for the white people. Myrtle thought this was a terrible way to treat a human being.

Nurse Tate and Myrtle finished the last patient before the next shift started. Myrtle walked over to where the frail colored woman lay and took her temperature again. Hmm… she thought not much change from that afternoon, and she recorded the information in her chart. She was tired, but she couldn't leave until the evening shift arrived. Myrtle got prepared to sponge off the patient with breast cancer, and deep in thought about how she would spend her evening. Sounds of hello and footsteps frequently could be heard in the hospital's corridors. Finally, the evening shift is here Myrtle thought as she put the basin away. She had to hurry and meet Nurse Maxwell who was waiting patiently for her to review the remaining patients' charts. She would usually stick around and help the evening shift for a while if she did not have an evening class. However, tonight she thought she would get some rest and listen to some of Aunt Leola's records, and see what kind of a day Sugar Pudding had.

Chapter 75

Shift and mind changes...

The room was very peaceful and quiet. A slight breeze entered, the door to the large ward opened, and a face looked in, checking to see if everything is all right. Far away, the humming and static sounds of a radio, coming from one of the rooms, penetrated the quietness like an annoying fly.

The two nurses on duty tipped around softly so as not to disturbed the patients. There is plenty time for that when it is time to take their vital signs. The evening shift was usually very quiet, nothing much to do on the cancer floor but monitor the patients and give them their medicines.

The patients sleep most of the time, too weak to move or ask for anything. Many just lay there waiting for the subsequent visit of the angel of death. The nurses on the evening shift spend most of their time knitting baby blankets and bed spreads. One of the nurses rose up as if on cue and walked into the cancer ward and over to Rachel's bed. She gently felt her forehead, and looked at her chart.

Feeling a presence of someone near, Rachel tried to open her eyes and look around. She felt like she had been sleep for a long time. She tried desperately to focus. Was it day or night? Her eyesight was blurry and her mouth was very dry. What is that smell? She wondered as her nose detected a soft light fragrance of lavender and lilacs. Who was lying beside her? The sheets are nice and white. Where did all the old white people go? "Clemmons... Am I dead? I really have to go home before your grandmother finds us," she mumbled aloud. Delirious from her fever...she closed her eyes and went back to sleep.

Nurse Beckett got the basin, filled it with cool water and went back to sponge off the patient. The other nurse called Dr. Adams. "Her temperature is very high Dr. Adams, and the patient is delirious," the old nurse spoke softly into the mouthpiece. The infected site looks bad as well. She has had three changes in the last six hours. All right Dr. Adams we will see you later. Good-bye."

Chapter 76

Getting it off your chest...

"Evening Myrtle, you got here just in time," said Aunt Leola. "Here sit down and have something to eat. Sugar Pudding went to the store with Julia. Look Myrtle, I need to talk to you and Sugar Pudding, its very important. I am not sure how to tell you this...but I have been keeping something from you and your sister for quite sometime. I didn't say anything to you because I wanted to keep you safe as I had promised my brother," she explained watching the stricken look on Myrtle's face.

Myrtle stopped chewing and looked at Aunt Leola's face. She looked worried and nervous. I hope she is not going to tell me she is dying, Myrtle thought. I just can't take another person I care so much for leaving me and Sugar Pudding. Myrtle swallowed and asked, "Are you very sick Aunt Leola?" "Oh, No sweetheart, I am not dying. It's nothing like that. I am okay. It's not about me, it's my brother Earl." "You mean Mr. Harvey?" asked Myrtle confused and somewhat relieved that she was not dying.

"Myrtle my brother died over a year ago. I could not go to his funeral because I could not risk being seen and someone find out you two were living here with me. It hurt me to my heart not to see him ever again. Nevertheless, I made a promise to Earl to keep you and Sugar Pudding safe. A few months after his death I received a letter from his wife Anna Mae. My brother wanted me to know who your grandma is, and explain some things to you and your sister. I am not sure where to begin, but I want to wait until Sugar and Julia get back. Is that okay," she asked pleadingly. "It's fine Aunt Leola. We can talk more when they return. I am glad we are having this talk. I want to write grandma and send her some pictures of where Sugar and I are living. I just felt she needs to know that we are all right and thanks to you Aunt Leola, we are doing fine."

Myrtle was quiet for a moment. Aunt Leola just sat there listening to the quietness. Finally Myrtle spoke. "Aunt Leola does the information have anything to do with our mother?" "I'm not sure Myrtle." She answered slowly, and rose from her chair and walked into the kitchen. "Do you want something else to eat Myrtle? You hardly touched the food on your plate." Aunt Leola pretended to be busy putting the food away, washing the few dishes that were left in the sink, and wiping at absolutely nothing on the immaculate white counter top.

She was trying to kill time waiting for the other girls to return. She felt her pocket and the letter was still there. She removed the letter from her bible with the intention of reading exactly what Anna Mae had written, to the girls. She hoped deep down that, some of the information would end the speculation that their mother might be back or that they would some how find her. Just the thought of the girls being abandoned so very young brought tears to her eyes. She thought I could never abandon Julia, no matter what. Why even the thought of leaving her alone was frightening and made her tremble.

The sounds of Sugar Pudding and Julia's loud chattering entered the kitchen. "Well, what's all the talking about," ask Aunt Leola, as she wiped off the top of the dining table. "Mama, Sugar Pudding wants to change her name!" shouted Julia as Sugar Pudding playfully hit at her and put her fingers up to her lips and shaking her head not to tell! "What brought this on?" asked Myrtle. Sugar paused for a moment. "Well I am almost fifteen and I really do not like my name. I want to change it," she answered defiantly. "I have picked out a name and I asked Julia what she thought of the name, Helen." "That's an old name! Find something else," Aunt Leola laughed. "Yes please," chimed in Julia and Myrtle trying not to laugh.

Aunt Leola was glad the atmosphere had changed in the room to laughter, because she had to bring all of it to a halt and discuss something very serious and important to Myrtle and Sugar Pudding. Aunt Leola walked into the living room and called the girls in to have a seat.

They looked at her with wonderment and sat down as she spoke. "Myrtle, Sugar Pudding and Julia, I have some news for you and I have a letter I need to read to you from my brother's wife Anna Mae. To begin with, my brother Earl died a year ago and I was unable to attend his funeral because I promised my brother I would look after you and keep you safe. My brother had some information concerning you Myrtle, your sister and about the woman, you lived with after you were abandoned. It turns out the woman you refer to as grandma, is really your great aunt, Emma Jackson. Ms. Emma had a sister, Ilene, who had a daughter named Rachel and the daughter had two girls, that is you Myrtle and your sister Sugar," she read from the letter.

Without looking up from the letter, she listened for a response, hearing none she continued to read. "Now the letter does not say where your mother is or what happened to her. It does not even explain why the two white men wanted to kidnap you and take you away years ago. It's confusing I know," she said sadly. "However, this is the information my brother wanted you to have. I know you girls want to write to your grandma, but do you think it's wise to do that right now?" "Aunt Leola did Grandma, uh...Aunt Emma know about us?" asked Sugar Pudding sounding a little confused. "Well, I believe she does now. In the letter Anna Mae wrote, my brother told her after you were sent to here to live with us," she answered quickly.

"That still does not explain why we were left in a cold ass building to die or some strange person may have found us and killed us!" Myrtle complained bitterly. "I don't even want to remember the hell me and my sister went through trying to survive!" She lowered her head and a sob escaped. "Why tell us now?" She said in a tired voice, wiping her eyes with the back of her hand as she tried to regain her composure. "Look I really don't want to talk about it. This is not important now. Sugar and I have a home and we are doing fine. Why drag up the past, haven't we been through enough?" She asked, her eyes and face displayed the inner pain she felt.

Sugar walked over to Myrtle and gave her a hug and clung ever so tightly, just as she did when she was a small child. It made Myrtle feel good. "I am sorry. I had a bad day at the hospital. I guess it's too many people dying around me, and it's getting to me a little," she said apologetically. "Aunt Leola is there anything else? I am a little tired and want to turn in a little early tonight." "No, I didn't mean to upset you and Sugar. I know that you wanted to write and send your grandma or your aunt some pictures and let her know how you are doing. I know the letter does not explain why the men were trying to kidnap you, but honestly, Myrtle…you could still be in danger. Wait a while before you try to contact your Aunt Emma," she pleaded. "I know you are right Aunt Leola. But now that we know she is a relative, I feel bad not telling her we know the truth" said Myrtle. "There are a lot of questions that need answering Myrtle, and I wish I had the answers," said Aunt Leola. We can talk about this another time. Get some rest."

"Come on Sugar. Now, about changing your name, did you have another name in mind?" Myrtle asked. Sugar gave her that smile that says everything is all right.

Aunt Leola had a feeling the letter was just the beginning. There's more, much more going on in Tapsalle North Carolina. She could feel it in her bones.

Chapter 77

The beginning of the end ...

"I'll give you five hundred dollars for the truck Willie," the salesperson offered. "I'll take it," answered Willie. The salesperson wrote out the check and gave it to him. "Nice doing business with you, come back again, okay." Willie walked off the car lot and got in the front seat of Mr. Reynolds truck. "Thanks for bringing me," said Willie. "Now that I have sold the truck, I have enough money to pay that lawyer to investigate grandmother's will before we go to court.

I need to find something in that last will to challenge. Maybe I can get the judge to see the houses and land belong to my family," he said with a slight tightness in his voice. "Calm down Willie, you got to be prepared in the event they don't find anything wrong with the will. At some point man, you got to call it quits!" Mr. Reynolds said with a warning. "You have been trying to dig up information for the past few years, and you have come up with nothing. You would probably be better off trying to find the girls and their mother. If you act right, they may even give you one of the houses," Mr. Reynolds said tiredly, trying to reason with him.

"Ain't no half-white nigger going to give me something that already belongs to me!" Willie yelled at Mr. Reynolds. "You know you need to stop talking about your kin, your nieces like that. Hell, Willie what's done is done! You and no one else can change that!" Mr. Reynolds snapped. "What the hell's gotten into you all of a sudden?" Willie asked, surprised at what he just heard. "You agree with my grandmother leaving our houses, land and money to those Negroes and leaving me and my brother out of her will!" He yelled again, sweat poured profusely from his forehead as he wiped his face with his handkerchief.

"Whose side you on anyway, yelled Willie?" "Look Willie, I am not on anyone's side. I think you need to look at this differently, that's all!" Mr. Reynolds knew when to give up.

Willie was not going to listen to reason. He will have to learn the hard way. Hell he thought, they go to court in a few days, maybe this will all be over soon. He did not want to be included in another one of Willie's hair-brain ideas that had anything to do with those girls and their mama. Hell, he could go to jail if anyone ever finds out he hired them colored men to kidnap them girls years back.

The realization suddenly came to Mr. Reynolds that someone else knew of their kidnapping plan. We never found out how the girls disappeared. What ever happened to that friend of Ms. Ruth's…Mr. Leon? Strange he thought no one has seen him since Ms. Ruth's house burned down years ago.

He suddenly pulled over to the side of the road. "What you stop for? You gotta pee Mr. Reynolds?" Willie asked with agitation in his voice. "No, but I just remembered something that maybe important about how those girls suddenly disappeared." "Look Willie, someone else knew about the plan to take the girls and send them away, and that same person may know where they are living today."

"What ever happened to that man that lived with Ms. Ruth?" he asked Willie. "Wasn't his name Mr. Leon?" Mr. Reynolds knowingly threw the question out there for a reaction. "Yeah, Mr. Harvey's friend," answered Willie. "I don't know...anyway what he got to do with the kidnapping plan?" Willie asked with interest. "I never talked to him and never saw him again after the fire. I remembered he stayed with Ms. Emma and the girls for a while and…wait a minute Mr. Reynolds! Are you thinking Mr. Leon hid the girls somewhere? Hey, that still don't explain how he knew about the plan…unless someone over heard us talking that night at the big house, and told him." "Well, Mr. Harvey was supposed to check the houses that night and I told him he could take his woman up there," answered Mr. Reynolds. "But I don't recollect seeing him that night, unless he came before we got there," he said, scratching the back of his head in hopes of remembering.

"Hell, Mr. Reynolds he could have hid almost anywhere on the land or in the house," said Willie. "You know it won't hurt to find out Willie. We need to find that Mr. Leon. If anything comes out that I had something to do with them girls missing I could to jail Willie, and I am too old to go to jail!" "Damn! Mr. Reynolds, the hearing is next week! You don't think we gonna come up with some answers before next week? Just forget about it, you hear! It don't matter who knew about the plan! Those girls are gone, and I have a chance on getting the houses and the land back and who knows maybe even the money," he said in sarcastic tone. "You know your problem Mr. Reynolds is that you worry too much about nothing. I have already made up my mind to tell the judge everything... that is everything except the plan to take the girls away," he said clearing his dry throat.

"Okay, you think you got this all figured out Willie. I just hope and pray that it doesn't backfire in your face," Mr. Reynolds warned. "Forget it! Let's stop by the old lady's house on the way back," suggested Willie. "What, Ms. Emma's house?" Mr. Reynolds asked in total disbelief. "Why are we going there? What ever you got planned Willie, I don't want no part of it understand!" "Well, it's been a long time, hell she may not be living there, but it's worth a try. I want to ask her some questions that's all, and then we can leave," Willie explained quickly. "I think it's a bad idea. What if someone sees us?" asked Mr. Reynolds in a strained voice. "Why we just tell them we stopped to see if she was all right," Willie tried to answer in a reassuring voice. "After six years or more, you just gonna stop by to check on her? Man you are crazier than I thought! Shit!" "I'll stay in the truck!" said Mr. Reynolds anger mounting in his voice.

A few minutes later, they found themselves on Hollowcreek Road. It looked a lot different thought Willie as he noticed the old gravel road had been paved with tar, and the house where Ms. Emma lived was still there, but seemed further back off the road, maybe the paved street made it look like that he thought. Mr. Reynolds brought the truck to stop and parked a few yards from the old house. "You sure someone is in there Willie?" asked Mr. Reynolds. It don't look like anyone has lived in that old house for a long time. You sure she is still living?" he asked again, this time getting a little agitated with Willie. "I don't know if she is in there or not...let me get out and knock on the door," Willie answered, as he jumped out the truck. He walked over to the steps and on to the porch. He knocked, once, twice and three times. No answer.

"Well it looks like she ain't home Willie!" Mr. Reynolds called out from the window of the truck. "Come on let's go! You done made your damn point!" Willie walked off the porch and got back into the truck. "Okay, Mr. Reynolds, drop me off by the house. We'll talk tomorrow."

They had driven about a mile, and noticed a small circle of colored people staring at something lying in the street. "Blow your horn Mr. Reynolds, so these nosey colored people will move on!" he snapped. Mr. Reynolds blew the horn, but the people never paid him any attention and kept standing there. Mr. Reynolds turned the truck around and went down another street, to avoid the crowd of people.

The small figure was leaning up against the bus stop pole, like an old discarded rag doll. The arms hung down, one hand curled up in the lap, and the head drooped down on the chest as if one was just taking a nap. A few people walked toward the small figure, peeking and stepping back, shaking their heads and wondering what happened, or who it is. A torn paper bag and its contents lay scattered about on the ground a few feet from the street curb. The wail of a siren heard off in the distance, becoming louder as it neared the small group of colored people milling around in the street.

A white freckled face young man jumped out of the ambulance and asked the crowd to step back. He walked slowly over to the lifeless form that was leaning up against the bus stop pole, and pulled back the scarf that was covering the face. He looked up at the people standing around. "Anybody saw anything?" The ambulance driver asked the question to no one in particular as he removed the headscarf. The mumblings of the words "don't know nothing, didn't see nothing" was echoed a few times. A second young man climbed out of the ambulance, and walked over and helped the ambulance driver put the crumbled body on the massive stretcher. They picked up the contents that was scattered on the ground, and laid it on top of the crumbled body and quickly placed the stretcher in the back of the ambulance. They closed the doors and the two white men got back into the ambulance and quickly drove off. The small crowd of people scattered quicker then ants at a picnic after you remove the food.

'*D.O.A.*' the ambulance attendant wrote on his chart; there is no identification on the body. This is a small frame colored woman age around seventy to seventy-five years old. Died possibly do to an heart attack or stroke, and under 'autopsy' he checked, 'no.' The ambulance driver listed the personal contents on the woman's body as; a white scarf, blue coat, white shoes, dress, bra, cotton drawers and a faded yellow ribbon with white lace that was tied around a small patch of gray hair. The contents of the bag had a picture of two white young women, a letter, an old calendar with the month of April missing, a child's small black leather shoe, and five-hundred and forty dollars in cash. The young ambulance driver pocketed the money, and wrote 'zero' in the column under 'valuables' and sign the ambulance report.

Chapter 78

Getting everything organized...

Now, it looks like I have everything in order Baylor Tyner was thinking to himself. I need to call Ilene and tell her when I can pick her up. I am glad she decided to stay in the house while I am gone. Just incase I have to stay over a few extra days in North Carolina. He picked up the telephone and dialed the detective. "Yes, this is Mr. Tyner. Are you ready to leave? Good! We can catch the afternoon flight to New York tomorrow and we should arrive there by evening. Thanks a lot, see you then. Good-bye!" He had to make another call, to Ilene.

"Hello, Ilene this is Baylor. Look, the car will pick you up at eight 'o' clock am tomorrow morning. Don't worry everything will be all right. I will call you when I arrive in New York. I should be gone no longer than two days. I will miss you sweetheart, okay! If you need anything just ask Mrs. Martinez the housekeeper, she will get it for you. Okay, Bye-bye!"

Baylor inhaled and slowly let the air out of his lungs, he was a little nervous. He had one last call to make. "Hello, how are you? This is Baylor Tyner; will you be there on Thursday? You sure you don't need any money? I want to thank you again for your help. If we are going to win this fight, you have to be there to answer some questions.

I have a room waiting for you at the Douglas Hotel in Tapsalle County. No, honest, it was no trouble at all. They will book rooms for coloreds. Yeah, me too, I am sorry it has to be that way as well. I will see you this Friday at the courthouse. Uh huh, that's right, at nine 'o' clock am. Have a good evening." "Well, what's next?" Baylor asked himself.

Chapter 79

Death pays another visit...

"Good morning Nurse Tate!" "Good morning Myrtle, it looks as if you and I will be the only ones on the morning shift today. Nurse Benton called in sick. We have seven patients between the two of us. You know Mrs. Finney died last Friday, and Dr. Adams said we may lose two more before this week is out and today is Wednesday," she said tiredly.

"How is the patient doing with the high fever," Myrtle asked as she filled the medicine cups and laid out the syringes. "There has been very little change in her condition. She is getting worse everyday," Nurse Tate said very quietly. She hasn't eaten much of anything since she got here, and she sleeps on and off all day, and waking up every now and then. She mumbles a few words. It's as if she is in another place or time. Always mumbling or asking about white people, old white people with umbrellas and someone named Cleveland or something that sounds like that." "Maybe she is dreaming Nurse Tate," said Myrtle. "You know at one point during her mumblings, she seemed frightened and began to cry softly. I feel so sorry for her...no one has visited her since she arrived on the floor," Myrtle commented placing the medicine cups on the trays.

"You know Myrtle, after a while taking care of very sick patients, it starts to get next to you. I think I will make this my last year and find some other type of nursing work. I am tired of seeing people die and suffer; especially colored people. You know that is why I came to this hospital. They really didn't have any nurses. Most of the white nurses did not want to work in a colored hospital. It didn't matter to me I wanted to help. I have been here fifteen years and there have only been two white nurses other than myself who stayed." Nurse Tate stopped folding the towels and was quiet for a moment, reflecting on their conversation.

"Do you think things will get any better between the white and colored people?" asked Myrtle. "Well that depends honey, people will have to want to get along, and a lot will have to change. My Aunt Jessica marched with the colored people during the bus boycotts and she sat at the counters with the coloreds when they were refused service. After a while, she got tired and couldn't take the rough treatment of being thrown to the ground and kicked by the police and other white people who thought she was a traitor to her own race. I'm not sure if I answered your question Myrtle, but I guess it boils down to everyone giving a little bit of his and her time for what is right. Oh, look there's Dr. Adams, time for him to review the patient's chart and exams. Hey, put a smile on that pretty face, we got work to do." Nurse Tate shoved her playfully and Myrtle laughed.

Myrtle walked and watched closely as Dr. Adams read the chart and examined the patients. Earlier another patient had died before he got to her. He saved the patient with the high fever to examine last, and called another doctor for some advice, on the treating the breast infection. They couldn't operate anymore on the wound, and he had given her everything possible to treat the infection, the main cause of the high fever. Myrtle heard the doctor tell someone on the telephone the patient couldn't continue this way too much longer, and wanted know if they should schedule an autopsy if the patient passes. Myrtle could tell, by the look on Dr. Adams face the answer was 'no.' "Okay, thank you for your help. Have a good morning." He hung up the telephone.

"Myrtle you want to finish sponging the patient, while I try to feed a few of the others. It's almost nine-thirty and they haven't eaten," said Nurse Tate. Myrtle walked over to the patient and gently patted the patient's neck, shoulders, and arms with the cool water. Myrtle was lost in her thoughts again. She really wanted to send another letter and some more pictures to grandma, or better yet, Aunt Emma. She knew she couldn't tell anyone what she had done. It's too late now she was thinking, she probably got the letter weeks ago.

Chapter 80

The end of the beginning...

"Flight 102 will be landing in New York in approximately three hours and thirty-minutes," the cheerful voiced announced on the airplane's public address system. It is strange sitting here trying to figure out what to say to the girls. I have to remind myself they are not little girls any more, Baylor was thinking to himself. It's going to be harder, yes harder for me to make them understand the "how and why" they were left such an enormous estate. I will have to play this all by ear. Baylor Tyner relaxed in his seat. He looked forward to this flight. Perhaps to bring an end to some very important, unfinished business or thinking maybe, the information may open up new problems for the young women.

He glanced at his briefcase. I have all of the information they need to see, he gently rubbed the black briefcase. Baylor Tyner settled back in his seat and closed his eyes for a brief moment to finish thinking, planning and try to enjoy the flight!

Chapter 81

Bargaining with the devil…

"Are you willing to tell everything?" Mr. Keys cautiously asked Willie, as he switched the stump of his cigar from one side of his mouth to the other, leaving a tiny trail of brown saliva on his bottom lip. Willie Just sat there, staring at this man and thought, "its damn right annoying watching him do that shit, and suck back the spit that had accumulated around the chewed part of that nasty cigar."

Hell, he complained to himself, as he exchange questioning glances with Mr. Keys. Shit! I ain't paying him to look ignorant. Willie could feel his neck heating up with anger! He was older, but that anger was still able to creep up on him and take over if he let it. He was trying to be patient with this man. He has given him eight hundred dollars to find something for him to use in court, to challenge his grandmother's will.

I guess you get what you pay for, Willie thought, still examining the man from head to toe. He looked like he needed a shave and he had a funny smell circling around him like something old and musty. His suit had old stains on the front of the pant leg, and he displayed signs of going bald, and teeth brownish yellow. Humph…, probably come from chewing and sucking on cigars all day Willie concluded.

"Well, what are you waiting for Mr. Hayden? You didn't answer me," said the lawyer somewhat agitated because Mr. Hayden was not paying him any attention. "Mr. Keys, I am bout as ready as I am gonna get!" Willie snapped. "That not what I asked you Mr. Hayden," Mr. Keys responded in the same tone of voice Willie used toward him. Mr. Keys kept his eye on Willie. He noticed Willie clenching and unclenching his fist as he spoke. It's evident the man is grappling with something that is making him angry, thought Mr. keys. He had better be careful talking to Mr. Hayden. Mr. Keys cleared his throat, "Mr. Hayden are you prepared to tell all in court on Friday?" "What you mean by tell all?" Willie raised one eyebrow in a questioning arch. "Everything Mr. Hayden, you know, how your brother met the girls' mother. You don't know where the girls are, and most importantly; the judge may ask you why you think the will is not valid. Are you prepared to discuss these issues and the will without getting angry?" Mr. Keys asked, steadily watching Mr. Hayden for any changes in his body language.

Feeling a little more comfortable, Mr. Keys continued with his questions. "Have you ever thought about trying to find the girls or the mother in the past few years, perhaps to tell them about their father and the family estate that was left to them? You know Mr. Hayden, these are not hard questions, but you need to think about how you will answer them, and also think about what you will do if the judge rules in favor of your grandmother's lawyer. I will go over everything again, and try to argue what I think will be a good defense. In all honesty Mr. Hayden, I can't find anything wrong with the wills," Mr. Keys continued.

"Look, witnesses to say the old lady was out-of-her-mind just don't exist because the nurse, the old lady's cousin and the physician refused to get involved. Come on Mr. Hayden, even though all of them were there the night she died, and had previously witnessed her signing the wills, not once but twice, you have got to… or we have got to find proof that she was not in her right mind at the time the wills were signed."

"You understand, Mr. Hayden. The judge don't care if they are half-white kids, or that their mama is a Negro. He is going to be looking at whether or not the wills are valid, and he will rule on that fact alone. There is really nothing much else I can do, except to cross-examine them if I get the chance. However, I doubt if there will be a slip of the tongue on their lawyer's part. The judge may find the case highly irregular. With the civil rights movement going on, I believe he will be very careful in his findings. He would not want to appear that he is prejudice against the Negroes or discriminating against the girls because they are half-white! You do understand Mr. Hayden?" Mr. Keys was putting his writing pad back in his brief case, and as he rose up out of his chair, Willie waved his finger, summoning him to sit back down.

"Look, I am paying you to come up with something! You are the lawyer, and you are supposed to find something to help me...to help me find something wrong with those wills!" he yelled. "Calm down Mr. Hayden, all I am saying is that either way it goes, you will not get the houses and the land immediately if the judge rules in your favor, or if the judge rules you get one house! Their lawyer will appeal immediately and keep appealing, and dragging this thing on for years. It can happen because your grandmother named Baylor Tyner as her power of attorney and he can do as he damn well pleases until there is a ruling!" The lawyer's voice sounded tired and exhausted.

"To tell you the truth Mr. Hayden, I have never been involved in a case like this! This is a first for me, and I am not sure what will happen in the courtroom on Friday. I am just throwing everything out there so you can see what is before us!" He wiped the sweat from his forehead with the back of his hand, and continued with mounting exasperation in his voice. "Look, Mr. Hayden if you are not satisfied with me, I can give you your money back...today!" "Okay, okay. Mr. Keys...I have sold my truck and borrowed on my house to pay you to represent me on Friday, find something please! This is my life we are talking about, my houses, my land and my money!" Mr. Keys jumped reflexively as Willie threw up his hands in despair. Mr. Keys was backing off, walking toward the open door. "I'll talk with you before Friday, okay. Have a good afternoon Mr. Hayden." He left Willie standing there, head hanging down to his chest as if he was in deep thought or maybe praying.

Mr. Keys questioned himself as he walked to his car. Why did Mr. Hayden wait so long to get help? All those years have passed and the chances on the judge ruling that the wills are not valid, just isn't there. The old lady's lawyer covered everything. He got in his car and pulled off.

Willie sat for a while trying to figure out what to do next. The lawyer didn't sound very promising and the eight-hundred dollars he paid Mr. Keys to represent him is flying out the window. I will have to stick to my original plans he was thinking. I will get my chance to tell the truth.

The ringing of the telephone startled him for a moment. He got up, walked over to the table and picked up the receiver. "Hello, Yeah Mr. Reynolds, No, heard what? What about Ms. Emma? She was found on the street corner at the bus stop?" Willie repeated what Mr. Reynolds was telling him as if he himself did not believe what he had just heard. "Yeah, the same day we stopped by her house, okay. Thanks for telling me. Uh...huh bye."

Chapter 82

Delivering the message ...

Ring! Ring! Ring! "Hello, yes this is Leola Harvey. Who is this? Oh! Hello Anna Mae! How are you! The girls are not here at the moment. Sure, we can talk... Oh, my God! Please don't tell me she is dead. How did you find out Anna Mae?... No, I don't know a Mr. Reynolds. Earl never spoke of him. Thanks for calling me Anna Mae. I don't know how to tell the girls. Tell them about what? What pictures Anna Mae! You said they were in a bag with her personal things and they gave it to you, okay please don't let anyone see those pictures Anna Mae," she begged.

"When was the funeral? Oh, there was no funeral... well where is she buried? Okay, well... that's the way they are usually buried when there is no next of kin. What about her house? You go to her house and see if there is anything worth saving for the girls, please do that for me and let me know what you found, okay. Yes, how do I get in touch with you? Where are you staying Anna Mae?" She asked, frantically looking all around for a pencil to write down Anna Mae's address and telephone number. "Okay, I've got a pencil. Yes, I have it Anna Mae! Thanks again for calling. Well, I am glad you were in the store at the time, or we would never have known of her death. Take care...I will, good-bye."

Aunt Leola was worried. Now, what do I tell them? They just found out Aunt Emma is really their aunt and now she is dead. The girls sent pictures of them anyway! Well this is one time I am glad they did not listen to me. They wanted their aunt to know how well they were doing, and I had no right to take that away from them. Anna Mae said the pictures were found in a letter and the morgue attendant asked her if she wanted the yellow lace ribbon and the small black leather shoe.

She was thinking back when the girls came to live with her and Julia. They wore ribbons tied around their ponytails with pretty lace around them. The girls said the ribbons, were a gift from a friend of theirs! Aunt Leola had tears in her eyes just thinking of the old woman carrying around what she thought was the most precious things in the world.

Well, the girls will be home soon, and I had better get ready for work she thought. I have the evening shift this week at the hospital so I will have to tell the girls the news later tonight.

Chapter 83

Brooklyn New York...

The flight came in on time. Baylor Tyner waited patiently for the plane to land. He was in a hurry to get off. Even though he had his plans in order, anything could happen to mess them up he thought. He was next to the last few passengers stepping off the plane. He looked around trying to find his ride. He did not have to pick up any luggage because he didn't pack any.

Oh! There he is, spotting his long time law clerk, Calvin. Funny he thought, Calvin hasn't changed much in the last few years, still maintains his weight and has the same comfortable disposition, and dependable as hell! Baylor thought he would not know what to do without Calvin. "Hey! I am over here," Baylor waved when he saw the black Cadillac. Calvin turned the car in his direction and pulled to a stop. He got out and opened the door for Mr. Tyner. "How was your flight, Mr. Tyner?" he asked cheerfully. "I have taken care of everything. The girls' aunt is on the evening shift this week, and Myrtle is on days at the hospital and Sugar Pudding gets out of school at two-thirty pm."

"Now," Calvin paused catching his breath..."what we have to decide Mr. Tyner is the best time to get them all together. We have to be back tomorrow by twelve 'o' clock noon. I have made reservations for six and that includes you and me." "Is there a possibility we can do it today Calvin?" asked Mr. Tyner. "Well it's close to eleven 'o' clock now, I will have to make some calls and see if Mrs. Harvey is still at home, and the rest we can safely play by ear," he responded quickly. "Do that Calvin. Let's get to a telephone and make those calls now!" Mr. Tyner said urgently. "I've got to tell them what is going on and somehow get them to come back tonight or tomorrow morning, and get ready for the most important day of their lives! Can we do it Calvin?" he asked excitedly. "We can Mr. Tyner!" They got into the car and headed for the hotel Willingham where Calvin had made reservations. It was closer to the girls apartment, and would not look suspicious if they were seen going in and out with two white men.

Calvin rushed right over to the telephone in the hotel lobby. He dialed the number for Ms. Leola Harvey. "Mmm the line is busy Mr. Tyner. I am going up to my room. I will try back in a few minutes."

Baylor was thinking he couldn't make it without Calvin. The young man is on top of everything. He reminded himself to give him a raise when he returns to North Carolina. Hell, he had been so busy in Florida; he missed the christening of Calvin's first child. Now, why would he think of that at this moment? His mind should be on the case Friday, and trying to reach the girls.

The ringing of the telephone brought him quickly back to the present. He walked over and picked up the receiver. "Baylor here," he spoke with confidence. "Okay, Calvin, I'm on my up okay." Baylor thought, this is it, we have to reach the girls or we may be in trouble. He got off the elevator. Calvin's room was directly across from the elevator, and how convenient, he was thinking. Calvin had the door wide-open waiting for Mr. Tyner. Calvin walked over and picked up the receiver. "I would like to make an outside call, yes thank you. The number is Lakewood, 12923."

The telephone is ringing...finally someone picked up. "Hello"! Calvin could hear the voice quite clearly. "Hello, May I speak with Ms. Leola Harvey, Please?" "This is Ms. Harvey, who are you?" "Hold on I have someone waiting to speak to you." He handed the receiver to Baylor Tyner. "Ms. Harvey this Baylor Tyner. I am an attorney and I represent the Hayden Estates in Tapasalle County, North Carolina. I am trying desperately to reach Myrtle and Sugar

Pudding Jackson," he said slowly to make sure she heard the names correctly. There was silence on the other end. "Ms. Harvey are you there?" he asked a little worried. "Yes, I am still here. Can you tell me what this is about sir?" Baylor could hear the caution and concern in her voice. "Ms. Harvey, I assure you I am not the bearer of bad news, but it is extremely important that I talk to you and the girls this afternoon. I am in New York and only a few minutes away," he said quickly. He did not want to take a chance on her hanging up. Silence again. "Ms. Harvey, this is indeed important," he pleaded. "Okay, did you say your name is Mr. Baylor?" she asked a little more relieved. "Yes, that's right, Baylor Tyner," he repeated it pleasantly.

"Can my law clerk and I come over to talk with you and the girls within the next hour or so?" he asked quickly not giving her the chance to hang up or say no. "Mr. Baylor Tyner, the girls are not here at the moment. I expect them back in an hour. They do not live with me, they have their own apartment, but you can come here, if that's okay," she responded with less reluctance in her voice. "That's fine Ms. Harvey. We are on our way. Thank you," he said breathlessly. "Mr. Tyner, the car has been waiting for an hour. I suggest you get a move on," urged Calvin. Baylor was nervous and he didn't want it to show.

"Okay, Calvin, let me go back down stairs and get my brief case and we can leave. I'll meet you in the lobby," he said as he walked out the door toward the elevators. He was in a hurry to get this over with. The most important thing he can do right at this moment is to be calm and try to figure out how to get the girls and Ms. Harvey to fly back with him to North Carolina.

He was worried, the confidence he had earlier had waned like a full moon. He never thought the girls might not want to talk to him, or better yet, leave New York. He entered his room and walked straight over to the table and picked up his briefcase, and walked directly out the door. He was not going to waste time thinking.

Calvin was waiting for him in the lobby and they walked outside and got into the limousine Calvin had rented. Looking at the vast automobile, he asked Calvin, "Why on earth did you get such a large car? We are not going to a funeral," and he laughed. Calvin smiled to himself. He knew Mr. Tyner's personality, and he knew he wanted to arrive in style. Baylor stared out the wide windows of the limousine and noticed how busy the city is. People were walking all over the place, and not stopping to cross at the streetlights. They seemed in a hurry to get where they are going. A colored man stood on one corner with a homemade sign scrawled with the words, *"We shall over come."* A small crowd of colored and white people stood in front of him, as he spoke about equality for all human beings. The people cheered him, but the blaring car horns blotted out much of what he was saying.

They finally arrived at the apartment building. The sidewalks littered with trash. The wind made even the smallest piece of debris dance about your head. It was March, cold and windy as the weather would have it. A few people stood outside of the building. Some stood in a huddle trying to brace themselves from the cold wind. Small children buried their heads into their mama's coats to escape the winds. The driver parked the limousine, got out an opened the door for Mr. Tyner and Calvin. The driver asked as he was getting back into the car, "what time should I come back?" "Give us about two hours, okay! If we are not out by then, just park and wait." Calvin responded a little inpatient. The driver held onto his cap and got back in the car.

Chapter 84
The last call in...

"Hello, Nurse Tate! I am fine and you! I am calling because I have some important business that just came up, and I will not be in this evening. I'm sorry, I know we are short, but this couldn't be helped. Thanks a lot, I owe you one," Aunt Leola said before she hung up.

She was not prepared for another shock! Getting a call from her dead brother's wife, notifying her that the girls real aunt was dead was enough, and now a call from a white man, saying it was important that he talk to the girls was turning this day into nothing but surprises and worry. I wonder why he wants to talk to the girls. She was a little worried, but anxious to see and hear what they have to say to Myrtle and Sugar Pudding. Mr. Tyner sounded very important, and he did say it was not bad news! I wonder what it could be. Let's see, she was trying to remember...he mentioned a name, Halley, Hudson, no it was Hayden! I don't know anyone named Hayden.

The telephone rang again! She stared at it for a few seconds, and said aloud, "Now what?" "Hello, yes Myrtle... no honey, come here first! No, right now! Look you have to be here ...yes this afternoon, and pick up Sugar Pudding from school. Look! I don't want to scare you but a lawyer is on his way over now! He said he needs to talk to us! No... he didn't say what it was...just get here as soon as you can, okay!"

She hung up the telephone and walked into the kitchen. She needed something to drink...perhaps some coffee she thought. I had better make enough for all of us. I have a feeling we are going to need it. Too much is happening. She remembered, she hasn't told the girls about their aunt's death. Maybe the lawyer coming here has something to do with Aunt Emma's death. Maybe she left something for the girls.

Trying to conjure up reasons as to why the lawyer wanted to talk to the girls, were running wild in her head. Then it struck her like a bolt of lightening. Maybe the men who were going to kidnap them years ago, are still looking for the girls! She was frightened! What I have done? Letting them come over to my home! Have I put the girls in danger? What about my Julia? I don't want anything to happen to her! Oh, my goodness, she just remembered; Julia is spending the week with her school friends in Long Island. I had better call her, and tell her to come home tonight. Long Island is not that far. She walked over to the telephone and flipped through the notepad, looking for the telephone number where Julia could be reached. She dialed so fast, it seems her fingers barely turned the telephone dial. She had to get to Julia right away! It was ringing. "Hello? Hello? May I speak with Mrs. Morris, please?" "This is Mrs. Morris, Who's calling?" "Ms. Morris this is Julia's mom. Is she there? I need to speak to her!" "Hello, Mrs. Harvey, Yes she just came in with my girls, hold on! Julia! Julia it's your mom!" She called out. A few seconds passed and Julia came to the telephone.

"Hello Mom, is anything wrong? Okay, I can leave now. You know I am about two hours away, okay! Sure, you okay? You don't sound like it! Look mama, I am leaving in the next few minutes; I'll see you then, good-bye!" Aunt Leola placed the receiver back on the hook. She stood there arms folded across her chest. She took in a long breath and exhaled. Now, I will wait until the lawyer gets here. He doesn't know it yet, but I have some questions of my own. She put on the coffee pot.

Chapter 85

Tapasalle, North Carolina, the return...

He gently placed his small bag on the floor in front of the hotel check-in-counter. An elderly white man looked to be around seventy years old or more asked him his name. "It's Leon sir, Leon Thomas," he answered nervously. He had not been back to Tapasalle County in years. Now he's back to testify at a hearing. All he knows is that with any luck he will see the girls again.

He often wondered what they looked like and how they are living. He didn't want to spend too much time in this county. He can't risk being seen or better yet, be recognized by someone. People don't forget. It has only been six years or more. He's pretty sure, Mr. Fletcher who owned the hardware store has told someone he stole money from him. He stole the money from the cash register to send the girls to New York to live with Mr. Harvey's sister. They were in danger, and he couldn't let anything happen to them. He wanted to tell Mr. Fletcher all these years what happened, but feared they would find him, beat him and put him in jail. He has saved enough money to give it back to him but he couldn't take that chance.

"Mr. Thomas here's your key to your room. Have a nice stay," said the old white man. Mr. Leon was startled momentarily. "Thank you sir, you have a nice day too," he responded, and he picked up the key from the counter.

The room was clean and smelled like flowers, even though it's a little too soon for flowers thought Mr. Leon. March is here and it's cold and windy. He remembered springtime in Tapasalle County. Ms. Ruth had an old honeysuckle bush right under the window in the kitchen. He would open that window as soon as the bush started to bloom. The honeysuckles would smell up the whole kitchen, he remembered sadly. He walked over to the bed in the spacious room, and sat down. He had to collect his thoughts, and remember he came back to help the girls. If that were the last honest thing for him to do before he dies, he would do it with out any regret. He was afraid to come back, even though that nice lawyer, Mr. Tyner said everything would be all right. He did not have anything to worry about, however, he still could not figure out how Mr. Calvin found him, and paid him a visit in Emeryville, North Carolina. He had been living there for the past few years, in the same rooming house Mr. James Lee the baggage handler from the greyhound bus station found for him. They are still good friends, and go fishing together as much as possible. Even thought Mr. Lee is his friend, he couldn't tell him where he was going and why.

He wanted to walk around and see the changes in the county. He was a little afraid to ride on the buses because of the way the coloreds were treated. It ain't right to make us sit in the back of the bus because we is colored. He sat in the back of the bus coming back to Tapasalle. He was the only colored person on the bus. However, he was not afraid. He slept most of the time. He told that white lawyer who found him living in Emeryville that he would take the bus because it was only a three-hour ride. He sent him some spending money anyway, and told him he was doing a good thing coming back to Tapasalle County.

He sat thinking for a while letting the quiet memories of the few friends he had came back to him. He often wondered what happened to Mr. Harvey. He wanted to see him and Ms. Emma. Maybe, just maybe he will go to Ms. Emma's house and visit her. He came a day ahead of time. He may have the time today to find his friends. He looked at his watch. It was eleven 'o' clock in the morning. He had packed a small lunch so he would not have to go out onto the street to find a place that would serve colored people. He didn't want to bring any attention to himself. He told Mr. Tyner, he did not want to go in the courtroom. Mr.

Tyner told him, it was a closed hearing and besides the judge and himself; the only other people in the courtroom would be him, Ms. Leola Harvey, her daughter Julia, Mr. Turner, Willie Hayden and his lawyer and of course the girls. That really didn't make him feel any better. Maybe he would feel all right if Ms. Emma were there, he thought to himself.

He suddenly got up off the bed and grabbed his small bag and the room key. He had made up his mind. He was going to visit Ms. Emma, and if he had the time, he would try to find Mr. Harvey.

The weather was very chilly. Mr. Leon pulled the collar of his coat up around his neck. He wasn't too familiar with the streets near the hotel, and he wanted to avoid asking for directions from anyone. He walked until he found something familiar. He saw a bus with the name "Carver Street Stop" written on a piece of paper propped up in the window of the bus. Feeling a little apprehensive, he walked up to the bus and asked the white bus driver, "How far does this bus go?" "You see the sign! Can't you coloreds read?" The bus driver snapped.

Chapter 86

Angels of relief...

"It looks like just you and me this evening, Nurse Tate commented to Nurse Benton. I hate to ask you to work overtime another evening, but Nurse Harvey has an emergency and won't be in this evening. So far, we have five patients. We lost two yesterday and it looks like we may lose the patient with the awful infection and high fever. Dr. Adams said there is not much we can do for her now. The infection as well as the cancer has taken over her body." Nurse Tate continued with the patient review and Nurse Benton walked from bed to bed checking the patients' vital signs and medications.

Nurse Tate walked over to Ms. Jackson's bed to take her temperature; the small woman opened her eyes. She made several attempts to speak. "I need to talk to someone about my girls she mumbled." Nurse Tate leaned over to get closer her voice was very weak. "You have a family Ms. Jackson?" she asked. "Yes, I have a family, but I have not seen them in years. I know I am not going to live much longer with this illness, sometimes I can barely open my eyes to focus," she whispered. "If I tell you their names, would you try to find them and let them know what happened to me?"

Rachel was moving around with all the strength she could find, trying to sit up. "Could you help me sit up," she begged. I don't want to leave here lying down. Nurse Tate had an idea! "Why don't I move you closer to the window Ms. Jackson, you can see the evening sunset. You are too weak to sit up. Why don't I just prop your back up with a few pillows? Nurse Benton, throw me two pillows, I believe our patient wants to sit up for a while," she called out trying to sound cheerful.

Nurse Benton playfully threw the pillows to the nurse, and asked if she needed anything else. She wanted to leave the floor for a few minutes. "No, go on! Everything here is under control. You have been here since this morning you need a break. I can manage," she called out as nurse Benton was leaving. Nurse Tate pushed the patient's bed closer to the window, and pulled back the dingy drapes that half covered the tall windows in the room. "Nurse, could I have a piece a paper and a pencil please?" I need to write a letter to my girls," she said struggling to get out the words.

This is the most she has spoken in the past two weeks, thought Nurse Tate. It always amazes me how the sickest of patients seem to rally around one more time before the final curtain call. "Here you are," she said as she handed the clipboard with paper and a pencil to Ms. Jackson. She was weak and her hands shook terribly. She made one or two attempts to grasp the clipboard, it was evident she couldn't hold it in her hands. Nurse Tate looked away, tears swelling in her eyes as she watched this woman try one more time to hold and position the board so she could write. "Ms. Jackson would you like me to write something for you," Nurse Tate asked softly. The patient looked at the nurse and mumbled the words, "yes please." "Please tell my girls, Myrtle and Sugar Pudding I love them and to please forgive me for leaving them years ago. I was sick then, and wasn't able to take care of them. I didn't mean to bring shame to them, it's not their fault their father is white."

Nurse Tate laid the pencil down slowly. "Ms. Jackson, Rachel? What did you say your girls' names were?" She asked, with a strong feeling inside of her, that something else was happening here. Nurse Tate had the urgent need to press on.... "Did you say one of your girls is named Myrtle?" The woman looked at the nurse and smiled. She answered weakly, "Yes, she has the strangest colored eyes...almost brown and then at times dark gray. She has sort of a crooked smile like her father,"....she coughed a little and squirmed lightly under the bed sheets.

Nurse Tate looked at the patient, and thought, this can't be. It's impossible, she thought as she wiped her forehead and face with her hand and ran her fingers through her hair. This cannot be. Nonetheless, the nursing assistant's first name is Myrtle and her last name is Jackson! Well, I won't get too excited. It could be a coincident, she thought. New York is full of people with the last name of Jackson. However, Myrtle does look white and she has funny colored eyes. I noticed that the first day I met her. Naw...can't be, she was thinking to herself.

"Ms. Jackson did you want to continue with your letter?" The patient turned her head toward the window. When she spoke again, everything came together. "Nurse," she whispered, "Myrtle has a birth mark, a small patch of red, kind of shaped like a heart on her right arm. It...reminds you of a strawberry, and her sister Sugar Pudding has a round brown circle, looks like a large freckle on the bottom of her left foot. I could always tell my babies from the white babies in the hospital because of their birthmarks," she gave a faint smile.

"Okay," thought Nurse Tate anxiously, I have to get myself together... even if this is the same person, I can't tell Myrtle this is her mother. When she comes in tomorrow, I will try to find out if she has a sister. I vaguely remember her mentioning a sister, but it's been awhile. "Ms. Jackson would you like to finish this letter later on, and try to get some rest?" "I just want them know I tried hard to keep them, but the people wanted me to move." Rachel was crying softly. Tears streamed down the side of her face creating a tiny puddle on the pillow where her head lay.

The mumblings Rachel made about white people, umbrellas, and horses now made sense. She was evidently remembering events that had happened to her, or reliving them. Nurse Tate removed the letter from the clipboard, folded it and put it in the pocket of her uniform. She heard the lunch cart with its squeaky wheels coming down the corridor. Nurse Benton had returned and was bringing the trays in the room. Only two trays were prepared for the room, one was for Rachel and the new patient who was admitted over night. Soup was on Rachel's tray. Nurse Benton walked over to Rachel's bed and started to pour the soup into a glass. Suddenly Nurse Tate called to her, "I'll feed her today!"

Chapter 87

Guess who's coming for dinner…

There's the unfamiliar knock. Aunt Leola hesitated before answering the door. She had to get herself together first. She has never had any white people in her apartment. She knew the neighbors would talk if they see not one, but two white men standing in front of her door. Okay, she took in a deep breath and turned the front door knob to open the door. Standing before her were two white men who did not look at all frightening. "Good afternoon Ms. Harvey. This is Mr. Baylor Tyner, and I am Calvin Turner. May we come in?" he asked as he extended his hand for a handshake." "Yes, come in," she responded nervously looking up and down the apartment's corridor making sure none of the neighbors saw the two white men. She quickly closed the front door of her apartment. "We can sit here she pointed to the recently polished dining table in the small dinning room. The girls should be here in an hour or so. Do you mind if I ask what this visit is about?" She continued in a worried tone voice. She skillfully arranged the paper napkins in the holder on the table somewhat afraid to look directly at them.

"They don't need anymore shocking news. I have not had the chance to tell them their Aunt Emma was found dead at a bus stop in North Carolina a while back. I just received the news today, and then you called. I am not sure how much of this visit will upset them even more." " Ms. Harvey, I assure you, what we have to discuss with the girls…the young ladies is not bad news but will be of extreme importance to their future, perhaps yours too, Ms. Harvey." She looked at them. She felt her heart flutter in her chest. She eased up slowly out of her chair and walked into the small kitchen to pour some coffee. She was thinking, this is going to be a long day. "Would you like some coffee or tea, while we are waiting for the girls to return?" "Yes, please, that would be fine Mrs. Harvey," answered Calvin.

As she busied herself in the kitchen, her mind returned to their conversation at the table. I wondered what he meant by the news could be important to their future? What happened in North Carolina to bring those white men here and in such a hurry? She could not figure out why, but her gut feeling is telling her their visit has nothing to do with the death of Myrtle and Sugar Pudding's Aunt Emma.

Chapter 88

Walking on familiar grounds…

A warm spring breeze touched his cheeks as he got off the bus at Carver Street. Mother Nature was playing an affectionate trick, if for only for a brief moment. Not much had changed since he had left. A few of the houses were painted and new fences put up. Something was different he thought. Then he remembered, seeing the bus stop as he stepped off the bus. He couldn't quite figure it out, but it looked as if it had fallen over, and someone tried to sit it up with an old cement block.

He started walking toward the old fork in the road that separated Ms. Emma's house from her neighbor's… about a half a mile down the road. Hell, it seem shorter Mr. Leon thought to himself. As he walked, he noticed some old houses boarded up. He recognized one house that belonged to old Mr. Teel. The weeds and tall bushes had grown up in the front yard and down the gravel path that led to his house. He walked up for a closer look, and a cat with her kittens suddenly jumped up from behind a broken wooden fence. Frightened by the sudden movement, the kittens scattered in all directions. The mama kitten stood there holding one of the kittens by the neck. The mother cat stood there, staring at the intruder.

Ignoring the cat, he kept on walking. Finally, he came up on a house that looked familiar to him. He recognized the wooden steps he had place there himself. Quickly, his heart dropped a beat…and sadness overcame him. Somehow, he knew no one had lived in the house for a while. He made his way through the overgrown weeds and trash, and stepped up on the old porch. The screen door he had repaired was lying on the porch. He wondered if maybe someone tried to break in. He walked off the porch and around to the back yard. He didn't get far. He noticed it was full of old car tires, the old bottled tree was knocked over perhaps by a storm, and scattered pieces of old dried up wood and other trash, that was not there when he lived in the house with Ms. Emma and the girls.

The back door was still intact and it looked like it had not been open. He made his way back to the front porch. He didn't try the door, it's evident the house was empty. He stood there for a brief period wondering to himself where could Ms. Emma have gone. Did she get sick and had to go back to that nursing home? He walked slowly down the old wooden steps of the porch and started walking down hill to the old bus stop. Maybe… just maybe he will see Mr. Harvey.

He pulled his jacket collar up close around his neck, and walked slowly past the houses and changed roads. He felt sad and couldn't understand why. Maybe, he thought… it was the changes around him. He really didn't recognize much of the old county. He wanted to walk around and see if Mr. Raye's club was still there, but most of all he wanted to see Mr. Fletcher, the old white man who owned the hardware store. He knew in his heart he really couldn't take that chance on running into him, perhaps being recognized, arrested and put in jail, again for stealing. After all, he was a colored man, who stole money from a white man, and he didn't care how long he had been gone from Tapasalle County, he knew they would probably never stop looking for him.

As he came upon the old bus stop, he bent down to move the old cement block closer to the pole so it would lean a little straighter. He had been standing for a while, when he saw the bus coming up the hill. Suddenly, a woman appeared next to him, seems like from nowhere and touched him on the arm. He turned; startled he was face to face with Ms. Ella, Ms. Emma's friend from church. "Hi you Mr. Leon? It is you Mr. Leon, right?" she asked looking at him rather strange. "Yes, it's me Ms. Ella," he said relieved but happily. "I am so glad to see someone I know. Where you heading Ms. Ella?" he asked as he helped her step up on the bus. "I'm going into town to pick up a few things Mr. Leon. Where you been for the last few years? You sure enough haven't been seen in these parts," she laughed.

"No, I moved Ms. Ella some time back"... he paused. "Ms. Ella where's Ms. Emma? I went to her house but it look like no one has lived there in a while. Did she have to go back to the nursing home?" "No, Mr. Leon, you ain't heard? They found Ms. Emma dead a while back at the bus stop. She was buried by the city, cause no one claimed the body. It's so sad Mr. Leon; we don't even know what she died from. I think she missed them girls. You know they left her years ago, and they ain't never been heard from or seen since."

She hung her head down and mumbled a little a prayer to herself. "You okay Mr. Leon?" she asked. "Yes, Ms. Ella I was just thinking, that's all. It was good to see you again Ms. Ella, but this is where I get off." He got up and worked his way to the door to get off the bus. He wanted to go back to the hotel and to his room. He had to hurry back and tell that fancy lawyer Ms. Emma is dead.

Chapter 89

The last supper...

"Did she eat hardly anything at all?" asked Nurse Benton. "No, she managed to swallow a little of the soup, that's all," answered Nurse Tate. "Dr. Adams looked in on her this afternoon. He didn't change any of her orders. He just wrote and underlined on the chart not to perform any life saving procedures on the patient. Maybe he expects her leave us sometime soon." "What do you think?" ask Nurse Benton as she placed the food trays on the counter for pick up. "Well, I know she can't continue living like this. Maybe we should get her things together as well. I wish there was more we could do for her," answered Nurse Tate as she folded the clean sheets that were brought up from the laundry. "You know she tried to write a letter earlier. I told her we could finish it later. My heart went out to her trying to grab hold of the clipboard so she could write the letter herself."

"I guess, as long as I work in a hospital, I will never get over patients in their last dying days. One minute they seem to come alive and the next minute they are gone. It's as if the patient was giving it one last try to keep from going to sleep. Rachel is that type of patient. She is trying to stay awake, not afraid of missing anything, but just long enough to tell you why she can't go on that journey until she is finish here on earth. That letter she was trying to write is the last of her journey, Nurse Benton. She tried to tell me all she could about her family and how sorry she was to have left them. Did you know she has two girls? Well they are probably young ladies by now," Nurse Tate said, as she continued to put the neatly folded sheets away. "I am going to start taking the patients evening vital signs Nurse Benton. I really want to finish early and take a little break." She knew she would be there all night until the midnight shift came on duty. Myrtle will not be in until tomorrow morning. At least Nurse Benton can take off until the next day she thought, taking a quick glance over at Rachel's bed.

Chapter 90

The finishing touches...

The sounds of talk and laughter interrupted their conversation. She quickly got up and almost ran to the door. She had opened the door before they knocked.

"Hi Aunt Leola" said Sugar Pudding greeting her with that questioning look on her face. Myrtle looked at Aunt Leola rather strange too. Before they could ask Aunt Leola why she was standing there looking at them...they saw the two white men sitting at the dinning room table. "Hi Aunt Leola. What is going on in here? Do we have company?" asked Myrtle still staring at the two white men, who had suddenly rose from their seats and started toward them.

"Good afternoon ladies, I know this may look a bit strange, but I assure you, just give us a little of your time and we can explain why we are here," announced Mr. Tyner. Calvin stood there nodding in agreement. "Please, can we sit down together," asked Mr. Tyner as he fumbled around for his handkerchief to wipe the sweat from his forehead.

Aunt Leola walked over to the dinning room table to remove a chair to sit in, and Calvin quickly got up and took it from her. "Here, Ms. Harvey have a seat on the sofa. I'll take the chair," he said softly. "Mr. Tyner, if you don't mind, let me introduce the young ladies. "This is Myrtle and Sugar Pudding Jackson. Girls, this is Mr. Baylor Tyner and Mr. Calvin Turner his law clerk. They have something of importance to tell you...us, and I'll just let them explain, okay." She carefully sat back down on the sofa, and looked at Myrtle. "Does this have something to do with our mother asked Myrtle?" "I don't think I want to hear any of this," Sugar said, as she got up to leave the room. "No wait Sugar, don't leave! I'm here," said Myrtle and so is Aunt

Leola. "We'll listen together. Let's hear what they have to say. Come back and sit down," Myrtle pleaded with her. "Ladies, I don't know quite where to start...he stood up to face them. "Please give me a chance to explain why we are here."

"I have never done anything like this before," Baylor Tyner explained in a nervous tone of voice. "I represent Mrs. Stella Louise Hayden and I am the executor of her estate. You see, she left a will and in the will, she left you Myrtle and you Sugar Pudding and your mother, Rachel the bulk of her estate. The shattering of glass startled them. Aunt Leola dropped the glass she was holding and it hit the table with such force it sprayed glass all over Calvin's shoes. He didn't seem to notice all the commotion. He was waiting for Mr. Tyner's next sentence, and contemplating any help to assist him if necessary.

Myrtle was stunned. "What do you mean left us the bulk of her estate? Why did she leave us her estate?" she asked waving her arms up in the air. Aunt Leola looked from one to the other, hardly believing her ears. "Is he saying what I think he is saying?" She had no idea she had asked the question aloud. She was shocked as well and thought she was talking to herself. Mr. Tyner waited for the initial shock to subside, and he continued. "You see, your mother Rachel was seeing Mrs. Hayden's grandson, your father...." "Our what!" Myrtle interrupted not letting him finish his sentence. "What are you saying, me and Sugar Pudding's father is White?" Myrtle was on her feet and walking back and forth. Sugar Pudding just sat there quietly.

Aunt Leola got up and walked over to Myrtle, "come on let's hear the rest of it. We can ask all the questions we need to ask after he is finished, okay," she said soothingly. The front door opened just as Mr. Tyner was about to continue. Julia walked through the door and stood there puzzled...looking straight at the two white men.

"Mama, what's going on in here? Is something wrong?" She ran over to her. "You all right mama?" She asked confused, a little anger in her voice. "Who are they? Why are they here?" she asked pointing to Mr. Tyner and Calvin. "It's okay Julia they are here to talk to us…and the girls about something very important that has happened. Come on sit down, you need to hear this too! Mr. Tyner, do you mind going over that last bit of information you said about the will," asked Aunt Leola, still not believing her ears. "Yes, of course I'll tell it again. Hearing it the second time was just as much a shock as the first time he told it thought Aunt Leola. "I am confused! You said my mama was seeing this white woman's son who is our father! Where is he? Why isn't he here with you," asked Myrtle struggling to stay in control. "Well, say something, don't just stand there staring at me. Tell us everything, okay," she said in a much calmer voice.

"Myrtle…I knew your great-grandmother, and this is very hard on me as well having to come here on short notice and tell you or give you some information that will change your life and your sister's forever. If you just give me a chance to tell you what I know, I'll be happy to answer any questions you and your family may have," said Mr. Tyner. "Ms. Harvey may I have a glass of water please?" His voice was raspy and dry as if he had eaten sand.

Myrtle walked over to where Sugar was seated and stood next to her. "Thank you Ms. Harvey," he said as she handed him the glass of water. "Now…where was I?" He sipped the water slowly, purposely, allowing for a grateful and well-needed interruption to get his thoughts together. "You were explaining about their father," answered Aunt Leola. "Yes, Mrs. Hayden's grandson son is Clemmons Darvis Hayden, Myrtle and Sugar Pudding's father. Mr. Hayden's grandmother was not one for hiding her feelings, and mincing her words, and let it be known, she was not pleased with her grandson and your mother's relationship because your mother is Negro, and to let him know how she felt, she left him and his brother Willie out of her will. She left two large beautiful homes, with over two hundred acres of land, and well over $500,000 in a fund for you, your sister and your mother Rachel. The estate is worth well over three million dollars."

He stopped talking, wiped his forehead and listened to the silence that had taken over. He looked from one to the other. Hands wiping their eyes, heads shaking from side to side, and that look of total disbelief. Baylor Tyner glanced over at Calvin. For once, he was not in control. Calvin seemed overcome with emotion. Baylor Tyner came out of his deep thought as he heard Calvin clear his throat. "Mr. Tyner, we don't have much time. We had better go on with the rest of the information." "Okay, yes, of course Calvin, you are right," he answered, patiently picking up where he had left off.

"Ms. Hayden's oldest son Willie Hayden, your uncle, is very upset and angry," he continued. "He has filed a challenge in probate court in North Carolina to have the will ruled invalid and is hoping the judge will rule in his favor. I am sorry to say, but you will have to return with me to North Carolina by nine o'clock this Friday. The judge has to see you in person, so he will know you two are alive and you Myrtle is of age to take over the estate and the funds. You see Mr. Willie Hayden had filed and told the judge your mother whereabouts and her children are unknown. I have the will naming you, your sister and your mother as part of her family and that she was indeed in her right mind at the time she wrote and signed the will. The will is legitimate." Before he could finish, Calvin was handing him the will. He took it and passed it to Myrtle to read. Her hands shaking, and still in disbelief, took the will and read it, and read parts of it to Sugar Pudding who was smiling and patting her chest like an old woman having a hot flash.

Calvin watched the expressions on their faces as they passed the papers from one to the other. Julia and Aunt Leola fanned and wiped their faces as they read portions of it over and over. You could hear whispers of "I can't believe it! That is so much money, and let me see it again!"

Calvin noticed however, their celebration is within their souls. He heard muffled like whispers, no loud expressions of happiness or joy was spoke aloud regarding the surprising news. He knew they were waiting for the last shoe to drop.

"Mr. Tyner, are we in any danger if we go back with you?" asked Myrtle?" with skepticism in her voice. "Myrtle I know about the attempted kidnapping of you and your sister, and I also know why and how you and your sister arrived in New York. I also have a surprise for you and some bad news as well." Not wanting to look them directly in the face with such dire news… he walked over to Aunt Leola as an act of support. "Your grandmother… the lady you called your grandmother, Ms. Emma Jackson, is no longer with us. I was informed early today, she had passed a while back. If this helps any, and brings comfort to you, Ms. Emma Jackson was your biological Aunt. Mr. Leon has told me the whole story," he said the last sentence as quickly as possible, scanning their faces for some signs of emotions.

"Is Uncle Leon here too?" asked Sugar Pudding who suddenly came to life at the mentioning of Mr. Leon's name. "No, that's the surprise, he's not here in New York, but you will see him Friday morning when we return to North Carolina," Mr. Tyner answered with much assuredness.

"Do you know where they buried Aunt Emma Mr. Tyner?" asked Myrtle as she rubbed her forehead in disbelief. She moved from where she was standing beside

Sugar and walked over to the apartment window and stared down, watching the people go and come out of their tall building.

"No, but I am pretty sure we can find out for you. I am so sorry to give you the news in this manner," Mr. Tyner answered solemnly. "I am so relieved you shared the news of Ms. Emma's death Mr. Tyner. I received the news myself, today from my brother's wife. I had planned to tell the girls when they got home," Aunt Leola, explained avoiding the girl's questioning stares.

"Well, to answer your first question Myrtle, no, you and your sister will not be in any danger if you return to North Carolina, I promise you that." He tried to sound confident. He did not want them to worry. Mr. Tyner turned to Ms. Harvey, "you will have to come with us and your daughter as well. I have made all the arrangements for you. All you need is a change of clothes," he tried to sound cheerful. "Wow! We are going too!" exclaimed Julia. She walked over to where Myrtle and Sugar Pudding were standing and they hugged each other. However, their hugs were more of support than a jubilant gesture. The hugs were not accompanied by smiles; just a tightening of the shoulders, long stares at each other, arms folded in front of their chests as if they were guarding their heart felt thoughts.

Well…thought Calvin as he watched them interact with one another, I guess they have a lot of information to digest. They haven't really asked any questions, which he found a little unnerving. However, the look in their eyes and their facial expressions told him, they had been through a lot and did not want to go back to North Carolina. The houses, the land, even the money is of no importance to them right now. It's the unknown, not knowing what is coming next, and will it be all right to relax and accept the good news. He felt sorry for them. He and Mr. Tyner did not bring them good news, just a new set of problems that will possibly bring them more heartache and worry. Hell he thought all this information is just too mind boggling, for even him to digest, Calvin smiled faintly to himself.

"What time do we leave?" asked Myrtle, breaking everyone's train of thought. She picked up her bag and started walking toward the front door. "We can leave tomorrow morning if you like around ten. The plane takes off at twelve noon, right Calvin?" "Yes, that's right! Mr. Tyner." "The car will pick you up at ten tomorrow morning. You may want to make some telephone calls to your jobs and Sugar's school. I know this is a short notice, but it is important that you all be there. Are you sure, you have no questions?" Mr. Tyner asked, bewildered and rather uncomfortable by the heavy silence that was prevalent in the small room. "No, we are fine right now," Myrtle, answered totally distracted by all the information they had just been told.

Her thoughts were a thousand miles away, wondering where their mama is and wondering what happened to their father. "Mr. Tyner before we leave… you never said what happened to our father. Is he dead as well?" she asked with no feeling. "The question caught Mr. Tyner off guard, and he looked frantically toward Calvin for an answer. "Uh…Myrtle, Ms. Jackson, there was talk in Tapasalle County, that your father may have had an unfortunate accident several years ago. I have someone checking on that now," Calvin answered calmly and confident that he has answered her question to the best of his ability.

"Thank you for coming to New York to give us the news. We will be ready by ten tomorrow morning. Come on Sugar, I am tired and need to take something for this headache." Myrtle rubbed the front of her head and briefly closed her eyes as flashes of the old bus station, a white man leaning over them….suddenly the face appeared…an old familiar face...ol' Willie! "Damn! That sorry ass white man is my uncle!" she said aloud.

Fear was beginning to takeover in Sugar Pudding's mind. She was thinking how bad it was where they had lived, and she never wanted to go back there again, never! Old feelings of hiding, going to sleep under beds, in closets, and under benches to escape the bad things that were happening or going to happen. She suddenly touched the bottom of her lip, remembering the tiny scar that has all but disappeared, and patted it for reassurance. I am happy here she thought...and safe. What if the bad men were still looking for us? She wanted to go to sleep, get out of that apartment and go down stairs to their apartment and sleep. When she wakes up, everything will be better. She got up off the sofa and walked toward the open door.

"Oh, by the way before you and Sugar Pudding leave, we will be the only ones in court. This is a closed hearing to rule on the validity of the will and the heir's entitlement to the estate. There will be no outsiders there. I have arranged for you to stay in the Wilson hotel on Pine Street in Tapasalle County. To be honest, that's one of two hotels that will welcome coloreds, and I wanted you to be comfortable..." he trailed off not finishing his sentence. "We understand Mr. Tyner, and thank you. We will be ready," Myrtle responded quickly. Oh Well, thought Myrtle living in New York for the past few years, Sugar and I are often referred to as Negros, Blacks, Coloreds, half-white, and light-skinned colored women. I wonder what we will be called, when we return to North Carolina and the news gets out Sugar and I have inherited a white woman's estate? Pondering this as she turned to leave, she stole a quick glance at Mr. Tyner.

Mr. Tyner turned toward the girls; "I wish you the best, good-evening." Aunt Leola closed the door behind the two white men. Myrtle and Sugar paused before walking out behind them. "Why did she leave her estate to us?

There is much more to this story Aunt Leola. I am glad you and Julia are coming with us. That makes me feel a lot better. I really don't want to go back there. I hated that place." She said choking back tears. "Aunt Leola I feel sad like something else is going on and I can't figure out what." Aunt Leola, grabbed both of them and gave them a hug, whispering softly, "don't worry everything will be all right."

Chapter 91

The soul is golden in the arising…

"Do you want me to record the time of her death at six o'clock pm, Nurse Tate?" "Yes, and call Dr. Adams as soon as possible, okay. Damn! Why couldn't she have held on just a little while longer to finish her letter?" "Did you say something Nurse Tate?" asked Nurse Benton. "No, I was just thinking out loud. I'll get the body ready for the orderly to pick up later tonight. You know they don't do much to the bodies, but put them in a box and bury them. I want to comb her hair and put the clothes she came in here with on her body. You know…give her the dignity she came in with." She wiped at her eyes, which had suddenly become moist with tears. She had no idea why she felt so emotional about this patient. Could it be this woman, who just died this evening, is Myrtle's mother?

The half-finished letter came back to her. She had taken it home and placed it in an envelope hoping that Rachel Jackson will find the strength to finish it. She got up slowly, and walked over to the counter to get the basin and some soap to prepare and dress Rachel's body. Nurse Benton looked over at her, and walked out of the ward, feeling Nurse Tate wanted to do this task alone.

Chapter 92

Dressing for the part...

"Willie Hayden!" Mr. Reynolds called from his truck. "Where you on your way this morning? Can I give you a ride?" "Yeah, I'm on my way into town to pick out a new suit. You know that hearing is tomorrow and I want to look nice. I'm gonna get a haircut too!" he said with a hint of tiredness in his voice. "Well, what you think Willie? Will the judge rule in your favor? You ain't gonna mentioned anything about them girls being your nieces are you Willie?" "You know Mr. Reynolds you are full of questions this morning, how about you letting me off in the next block. I ain't in the mood to be answering any questions right now. I'm saving my energy for tomorrow," he answered tightly, trying not to let Mr. Reynolds upset him. He had a lot on his mind.

"Damn," he mumbled to himself, I just don't know what to expect in court tomorrow and I am not entirely sure I should tell all the family business in front of a lot strangers. I have to save my energy for tomorrow. I will beg if I have to. That estate belongs to my brother and I. Why hell, we would look like fools if those colored girls get everything. How in the hell would I explain that to our friends, he wondered to himself. "Don't forget Willie, you and I said we weren't gonna talk about the kidnapping of them girls ever!" Mr. Reynolds yelled out as Willie jumped out of the truck.

Willie looked up and saw the bus coming, and ran for it with all his strength. It slowed down, and he got on the bus. He looked for a seat. Every seat was taken up front. A few Negroes were seated in the middle of the bus and there was one seat empty in the back. As he was making his way to the back of the bus, the bus driver yelled, "Why you going back to the back of my bus? Them politicians ain't pass no law saying you got to sit back there with the likes of them." He stopped the bus and walked down the narrow isle of the bus, and pointed to a colored man whose arm was bandaged and in a sling. "Hey you! Get your ass up and move to the back so this here man can have a sit down. You sitting too close to the front anyway!" He snickered and walked back to the driver's seat. Willie felt rather uncomfortable, and told the colored man to sit there; he didn't mind standing up. This caused some confusion. As he stood there, all at once, several people white and colored got up and offered Willie their seats. Not knowing what to do and not wanting any trouble, he got off the bus and walked the rest of the way into town.

Willie stopped at the Triple Ace Bar and Grill first. He needed a beer or something after that encounter on the bus. The place was always dark and it took a few moments for his eyes to focus as he quickly scanned the room. He didn't feel like talking and did not want anyone to bother him. He did noticed one old man, Mr. Fletcher from the hardware store. His back was half turned and he hoped the man didn't see him.

He walked over to the booth in the back near the grill and ordered a beer. He looked around the place and noticed, it had been recently painted. Wait now, something was missing in this familiar room. The old pictures of the friends and the founder of Triple Ace's Bar and Grill were hanging on a different wall; the old statute of a black faced jockey was still standing near the men's rest room with part of the right arm missing. He thought for a second, looked up and around again. It suddenly came to him the flag was not there. Old Pete, the grill's owner claimed his great-grandfather fought alongside Thomas J. Stonewall Jackson, and one of the solders who helped carry the casket to the burial grounds, took the flag off the casket and gave it to him. The flag was past down to old Pete's grandson. It was an old tradition of old Pete's when new customers came to the bar he would ask them to sign it, and if anyone asked why, old Pete would bore them to death with the story of the flag. You couldn't miss it. It was on the wall next to the door as you came into the bar. Now, in its place was a poster that advertised a new beer in town with a cowboy sitting on horse holding the brown bottle in his hand.

Hell, Willie was thinking, I should ask what happened to the old flag. When the waitress returned with his beer, he couldn't resist asking. "Hey there, pretty lady, can you tell me what happened to the flag?" He asked half heartily. "Sure can honey, it was ripped off the wall the day old Pete refused to serve a group of them Negroes who came in and wanted to be waited on. Old Pete told them he don't serve no niggers, and to kindly get the hell out of his place. A few of the Negro customers got up to leave, someone got pushed and a fight broke out among the Negroes and the White customers. Some white men chased them off with threats of hanging them; somewhere between the fighting, the flag was stolen. I wasn't working here then, that's what I was told by Ethel. You see that lady over there Mister?" She pointed to a heavyset woman with breasts the size of watermelons. "Ask her, she may know a little more about the missing flag." She took a quick glance over to the spot where it used to hang, and walked back behind the bar.

Willie forgot all about the flag as he sipped the beer, grateful for the coldness it spread through his veins. His mind was on going to court Friday. He wasn't even aware the waitress had left his booth. He had started going over in his mind exactly what he would say to the judge to persuade him to rule that grandmother's will is invalid and he and his brother should be awarded their grandmother's estate.

He thought about his brother's girls, but since they were nowhere to be found, he would play on the courts sympathy. Their father is now an invalid, and he will need some place to stay when he brings him home to take care of him. Willie knew in his heart that would never happen. He was just thinking of ways to get the houses, and land back. He was getting too old to work for anyone, and he wanted to call his own shots. Shit! He was thinking if just one person could speak on his behalf, he could probably convince the judge to rule in his favor. He sucked down more beer, avidly filling his mouth with the liquid, holding it briefly and then swallowing it down slowly. However, Clemmons is in no condition to speak on their behalf. He tried to get his brother's doctor to appear in court with him, but the doctor refused. The doctor told him he did not want to be involved. That left no one else

Willie drank the last corner of beer left in the bottle, got up and left the bar, heading for the nearest store to buy him a new suit, some new shoes, and he can't forget… a haircut. He did not want to look like he was poor. He wanted to make a good impression on the judge.

Deep in thought, he almost walked past Duncan's department store. He pushed opened the large glass door, and walked in slowly taking in all the changes. He had not been in a department store in a long time. He noticed some very pretty, potted plants sitting near the entrance of the door, a light fragrance of perfume, similar to what his grandmother used to wear, lingered softly in the air as he past the perfume counter. It felt good walking around the store. He looked up at the lights. There were large round white globes hanging from the tall ceiling on a steel chain.

Oh, here we are he said to himself, the men's department. He walked over to the where some suits were hanging, snatched off his jacket, and let it fall to the floor. He started to try on a coat when a salesman about his age walked over and ask if he could help him. "Good afternoon sir. Are you purchasing a suit today?" He inquired pleasantly. "Well, yeah I am," answered Willie, not looking up or acknowledging the sales clerk standing there. "Why don't I take your measurements Mr.?" "It's Willie Hayden…Mr. Hayden," answered Willie still occupied with looking at the suits. "Is the suit for a special occasion or perhaps a wedding or business event?" The salesman inquired diligently. "Well, I got a court appointment this Friday and I want to look good," Willie answered, as he stuck his arm in a jacket sleeve that was entirely too short. "Here sir, try this," the sales clerk said as he took the smaller suit coat from Willie, and handed another suit jacket to him to try on.

"It's a size forty-two long; the pants can be tailored for your height," the sales clerk said as he patted the suit coat in place. Willie was reluctant at first. He watched as the salesman took another charcoal colored suit coat off the rack and opened it up for Willie to put his arms through. "Here sir, let's try this style," he said pleasantly. Willie quickly slipped off the other suit coat and let it fall to the floor. He roughly put his arms in the sleeve of the suit. "It's a perfect fit sir, wouldn't you say," the patient salesman asked as he bent down to pick up the other suit coat from off the floor. He gave Willie a nod of his head pretending to agree with the satisfied look on Willie's face. "Okay, I'll take it, but I need a shirt and a tie also," he hurriedly added as the salesman ran to get the items.

The salesman hurried back with the shirt and tie attempting to show Willie that they were a perfect match…he instead watched in astonishment as Willie reached behind the counter, grabbed a bag and began stuffing the suit in it. He didn't bother to look at the shirt and tie. "Hey! Just put it in the bag with the suit. How much do I owe you?" He asked impatiently. Willie watched as the salesman rang up the items. He quickly reached in his pocket, and hoping that the bill ain't no more than what he's got, pulled out four twenty dollar bills.

"That will be fifty-nine dollars and sixty-four cents sir. The salesman announced. Willie gave him three twenty dollar bills. The salesman opened the cash register laid the sixty dollars in the till and counted out thirty-six cents. As he reached over to give the change to Willie, their hands collided and the change hit the floor. "Damn! Man you nervous or something!" Willie snapped as he bent down to pick up the change. "I'm sorry sir. Please come back again." The salesman mumbled awkwardly as Willie stormed out the door.

    Willie hurried down the sidewalk looking for a barbershop. Not really knowing where he would find one, and he forgot to ask the salesman. He spotted a barbershop across the street. It sat between a bike repair shop and a drug store. Willie walked in and noticed there were two other men ahead of him sitting next to the wall. There was an empty chair near the door. He walked over to the empty chair placed the bag under it, and made himself comfortable. He knew he had a long wait. To kill time he scanned the barbershop's walls. There were pictures of the barbers shaking hands or cutting different people's hair. Hell, he figured the people in the pictures must be important, maybe a politician or something. "Hey buddy, you next!" the slim barber called out, trying to get Willie's attention.

Chapter 93
The decision…

"All Rise! The honorable Judge Patrick Dickerson has entered the court room!" Boomed the Bailiff.

"Good Morning ladies and gentlemen you maybe seated." The Judge spoke firmly allowing his eyes to scan the courtroom. "I'm sure you are aware why you are here this morning. This is a hearing to determine the validly of one, Mrs. Stella Louise Hayden's will and its contents. Mr. Baylor Tyner are you prepared to present your findings?" "Yes, your Honor," he answered loudly. "The remaining heirs, Myrtle Jackson and Sugar Pudding Jackson are present." At the sound of their names, Myrtle and Sugar looked around the courtroom, their eyes fell on Mr. Leon, and they both gave him a smile. Sugar Pudding waved and turned back around on the bench.

"Mr. Willie Hayden are you prepared to present your proof or reasoning as to why you believe your grandmother; Mrs. Stella Louise Hayden's will is invalid?" Willie slowly stood up and looked around. He had arrived late and the clerk motioned for him to walk up front to the empty table on his left and have a seat.

He nervously looked around the courtroom. His eyes immediately fell upon Mr. Leon, and two Negro women sitting next to him. Beads of perspiration ran down his forehead, face and neck. Who the hell are all these strange people? Where the hell, is my lawyer? His eyes rested finally on the two pretty, young white women sitting next to Baylor Tyner. "No…No…" he whispered under his breath. "It can't be them." They disappeared years ago. They can't be Clemmons girls! Where have they been all this time?

"Mr. Hayden are you all right? Please answer Judge Dickerson's question!" The Bailiff said sternly. "What?

Uh…what…question?" Willie asked dumbfounded. The clerk repeated the question.

"Yes, I guess I'm ready," he mumbled. Willie couldn't take his eyes off the girls. He let his eyes leave them for a split second. Is that…Yes, that's Mr. Leon sitting behind them, but who are the other two Negro women? He asked himself. He sat down and stared at the table. The judge spoke again. "Mr. Hayden you have filed a challenge to your grandmother's will. Do you have any witnesses or affidavits to support your belief as to why your grandmother's will is not valid?" Willie looked nervously around for his lawyer and he looked over at the girls staring back at him. It seemed like every eye was on him. He could almost feel the balls of their eyes crawling all over his face, his neck, mixing with the droplets of perspiration that covered him like a nasty film. He made sudden wipes to his head and neck with the palm of his hand. He fumbled wildly in the pockets of his suit coat and pants for a handkerchief to wipe his face. I have to get a hold of myself, he thought quickly. I…got to get my thoughts together…Where the hell is Mr. Keys? He asked himself, holding onto the corner of the table until his knuckles turned white.

He swallowed loudly, "Sir, uh…your honor, Judge, I believe my grandmother intended for me and my brother Clemmons to have the land, houses and the money. The will is a fake! Both of the wills are fake! My grandmother has never had any use for Negroes!" He was yelling at the top of his voice! "Aw shit!" he said aloud…Too late, he realized he had went too far. He felt it in his bones. The courtroom was so very quiet. The ticking of the clock on the wall was all he could hear. He didn't hear the Judge when he was asked to have a seat. Instead, he felt strong hands roughly leading him to a chair. One pair of hands belonging to the court clerk, and the other pair was the court bailiff.

He heard the words that sealed his coffin. "The will is valid Mr. Hayden. I have reviewed the will and letter, and find there is nothing irregular about the contents or your grandmother's wishes, and how she wished the estate to be distributed. I am sorry Mr. Hayden. You have failed to prove the will or its intent is invalid. The will be executed as Mrs. Stella Louise Hayden has indicated. This hearing is over!" He slammed the gavel down so hard, the bench shook.

Judge Dickerson stood up to leave; he motioned to Mr. Tyner to step up to the bench. "Come closer! Mr. Tyner, do you honestly believe those two colored women will be able to live in this county in a white woman's house? A white woman who's sawmills and furniture companies employs half of Tapasalle county's white men? What do you think will happen when the town folk find out? Good God Man! What have you done?" he asked angrily.

"Look, Judge Dickerson, It was not my doing. This is what she wanted. Did you read everything I gave you? If you did sir, you would understand why she left the houses, land and yes, the money to the girls, her great granddaughters!" Baylor Tyner responded with the same anger. "They know it is not going to be a picnic. They know some danger may be involved if they attempt to move in the houses. Let's give them a few days for all of this to sink in!" "Okay, fine, Mr. Tyner, let me know if you need anything else. Good luck to you and your clients…uh…young ladies," the judge gave Mr. Tyner a troubled look as he was leaving the bench.

Baylor Tyner walked away from the bench and over to Myrtle and Sugar Pudding. Mr. Leon, Ms. Harvey and Julia were showering them with hugs. "It's not over, is it?" asked Myrtle with worry and apprehension in her voice. Baylor Tyner could see there was still evidence of shock and sadness written all over their faces. "What is going to happen now Mr. Tyner? Do we go back to New York, pack our things and move in immediately? How are we going to live in this county?" Myrtle asked angrily. "Their own kind doesn't want to have anything to do with the girls! They will run into all kinds of problems," Aunt Leola chimed in strongly as tears ran down her face. "I want to go to Aunt Emma's house!" Myrtle interrupted as she grabbed Aunt Leola's Hand and Sugar grabbed Julia's. The four of them walked out the courthouse toward the waiting limousine. Mr. Leon, Calvin and Baylor Tyner walked behind them.

Willie Hayden did not leave with the others. The Judge asked the bailiff to retain him until the courtroom was cleared. The chauffer opened the doors to the Cadillac limousine and they got in. They rode in silence. As they came to the street where Aunt Emma used to live, Sugar Pudding spoke first. "I don't want to get out. I really don't want to go in that awful old house. Please Myrtle!" She begged. "You don't have to go in Sugar. I am going in alone."

The limousine slowly came to a stop, a few feet from the house. Before the chauffer got out, Myrtle had the door open and placed her feet firmly on the ground. She stood up and looked around. The house was a few yards down the road. She recognized the hill. Even the tall weeds and trash thrown about couldn't hide the crooked road that led to the house. She carefully walked through the debris looking for the steps hidden under the overgrowth of weeds. The steps were still intact. The one Mr. Leon replaced still stuck out like a sore thumb. There were a few wooden boards missing on the floor of the porch and, the screen door was lying on the ground. Weeds had grown up and through the torn places in the screen. It only took a hard push to the door and it opened with a screeching sound.

As I stood in the old doorway, flashes of the first time I saw her and this old house, pass through me with a sudden chill, as if someone had walked on my grave. It's winter, it is bone chilling cold. Old grandma is sitting on an old wooden crate with quite a few boards missing. No need to panic or worry I thought to myself. She won't fall or tip over. She is so small and thin it will hold her leathery brown, wrinkled old body as she gingerly leans forward toward the small fireplace and throws a few more sticks, and some balled up old newspapers into the fireplace. The burning sticks and paper make crackling sounds, popping sounds, almost hypnotic to the ears.

Strange I thought standing here in this old room, remembering what it was like when I lived here. Nothing has changed. The house was still standing, old, weather beaten, damp and musty. The same cracks in the windows, and the same crackling floorboards. It was as if time had stood still embracing this old house with longevity and preservation.

Humph...probably waiting for one of us to return. I should stand here in the middle of this room and yell at the top of my voice, no...speak quietly about my past sorrows, and disappointments. Yes indeed, how much I hated this town, this old ass house, and some of the people who were a part of our lives. Did I come here to forget or did I come here to remember.

My life now is so different and defined to a certain degree. This house has a past, and I have a past I really want to forget. I want Sugar Pudding to forget as well. The damage to our souls has been done and cannot be erased. Not with large houses, more money than we will see in our lifetime, and land...yes, lots of land that I have no idea what to do with. We cannot live here in Tapasalle County. We are still not a free people.

Not all the money, houses or land in this world will make our lives any better, especially for half-white people. My eyes suddenly caught site of a yellowing and partly tattered picture on the faded and moldy covered wall, a white baby-sitting in a silver wash bucket advertising

"Bright White" washing powder. I slowly walked over and gently removed the picture from the rusty nail that was its only support. A few feet away and nailed next to it was an old outdated calendar. It was March now, I thought, but the old out-dated calendar was turned to the month of April 1955. I removed that too. Walking back to the open front door, I passed the dust covered old table. Old mail, checks that had not been cashed, old newspapers and some withered old money, one-dollar bills, five and ten-dollar bills were lying on top of the broken kitchen table next to a partly opened envelope. Lying on the floor under the three-legged table where she and Sugar Pudding had once eaten, were several five and ten-dollar bills scattered about. I gathered them up as well. I tried to remove any and everything that said or represented that we once lived here. I took one last look around the dilapidated old shack.

    I tried my best to remove all the bad memories. I walked over to the old wood stove that was still full of old dried up wood. With final fury and sadness, I threw everything I had in my arms into that stove. Suddenly Sugar Pudding appeared next to me along with Mr. Leon. Apparently, they knew what I was thinking. Mr. Leon handed me an old box of matches. I struck several of them before one actually caught fire. I stuffed old newspapers into the stove and I set fire to all the dead memories, hurt, anger, disappointments, and most of all…the memories of being cold.

    We walked back to the awaiting limousine. It suddenly occurred to me, leave this county you will never be happy. Every thing I have set on fire will eventually return and burn in my heart if I stay. I want to forget. "Mr. Tyner, we need to talk about the inheritance… tonight if possible. There is no way possible my sister and I can live here in peace." Without asking for Sugar's opinion, Myrtle announced, "I am selling everything." No one whispered a word during the drive back to the hotel. Mr. Leon smiled to himself. Aunt Leola, Julia and Sugar Pudding stared out the windows of the limousine. Calvin and Baylor Tyner's minds were a thousand miles away.

Chapter 94

Last call for alcohol...

"Sir, please sir," the waitress called to Willie. "We can't serve you another drink. You are drunk! Can I get you a ride somewhere? Is it someone we can call?" She asked with concern as she gently patted his shoulder. Willie had drunk so much liquor, he was not aware he had peed all over himself. The waitress looked at him, and recognized him from a few days ago. This man asked about the missing flag. She tried to recall his name.

Well, she thought, I guess this is my 'Do a good deed's day.' Hey! Come on fella! Let's get up now! Up on your feet! She made several attempts to get him up, but he was too heavy for her. "You need some help Della?" called the manager as he made his way over to the booth where Willie was sitting. "Yeah Floyd, help him to my truck out back, don't worry I know him. I'll be okay! Just gonna clean him up and get some coffee in him that's all," she said with a smile. Floyd half carried him to Della's truck and laid him in the back of the old pickup. "Uh, Della, how you plan to get him out of the back of the truck when you get home?" "No problem, Floyd, he will sleep it off," she laughed. After all, she thought that's how I used to do my old man before he died.

Floyd thought Della is just like a child who has found an old stray cat. Della is known for taking home the strays from the bar. He worried about her constantly. She wasn't much to look at, slightly over weight, pale woman with mousey brown colored hair. A tooth is missing from the side of her mouth. When she flashed that smile of hers, you could see the empty space. She had an old scar in the shape of a crescent moon over her left eye, where she caught a beer bottle when two customers got into a drunken brawl over who paid for the last drink.

She had never been married and had one child, a boy who died in the arms of a Negro boy he was walking home with. The way she told it, some white men in a car told her son to get away from the nigger and tried to run them both down. Her son was hit by the front of the car. They missed the colored boy and drove off.

He remembered she came into the bar the day of the boy's funeral and drank until she couldn't remember anything. Hell he remembered, he told her to clean herself up in the ladies bathroom and when she had finished she could wait on the customers to pay for her drinks. Floyd remembered, she never took another drink since that day, and that was over ten years ago. He walked back into the bar.

Chapter 95

Brooklyn, New York, the shoe drops...

"It's been more than a week. Have you heard anything from Myrtle?" Nurse Benton asked for the umpteenth time that morning. "No, only the message she left a few days ago with the night nurse. I expect her to be back soon. After all, she said there was an emergency in the family and she had a few things to take care of," answered Nurse Tate. "Oh, before I forget, the funeral attendant stopped by. He said to give you this package and this letter," said Nurse Benton as she carefully opened the cabinet door, reaching for the package and letter. Nurse Tate looked at Nurse Benton rather strangely. "Why would he give me a package and a letter?" "I'm not sure, but he said you left instructions about Ms. Jackson's body, and he mentioned something about you not wanting the body cremated," Nurse Benton finished. "Oh, okay thanks, Nurse Benton." She put the letter in the pocket of her sweater and placed the package under the nurses' counter. She had a lot on her mind this morning, and it did not entail the care and needs of the patients. She went over and over in her mind the last few words Rachel Jackson told her. She was sure the woman who died a week ago was Myrtle's mom. Should she tell Myrtle when she returns to work? Do I have that right, or should I just leave it alone? She wondered.

"Nurse Tate, we have another admission on the way up," Nurse Benton interrupted her thoughts. "Let me get a cup of coffee and I will be right with you okay," Nurse Tate answered as she walked into the little room where they often took their breaks and ate lunch. A few of the nurses made the room into a little eating area. It had a refrigerator, a table, few chairs and two coffee pots and a hot plate. It could use a new fresh coat of paint. The color of the walls resembled old sour milk. Streaks of gray like matter and a lumpy texture, evidence the walls needed painting over the past few years. A fresh coat of yellow paint would brighten the room, she was thinking.

She carefully touched the hot plate and the coffee pot to see if it was still warm. Good, she thought as she poured herself a cup of coffee, pulled out a chair and sat down at the table. One of the nurses had left a newspaper lying there from this morning. She flipped the pages of the paper, not really reading, just scanning a few articles. The headline hit her like a ton of bricks…

Two Half-White Colored Girls Left Huge Estate…in Tapasalle, North Carolina.

The residents in this large and prosperous county are wondering if Judge Patrick Dickerson is insane. Last week he ruled a will left by Mrs. Stella Louise Hayden in 1956 was indeed valid, and ordered the will to be executed in its entirety to the two young colored women, Myrtle and Sugar Pudding Jackson the only heirs of Mrs. Hayden's estate. The bulk of the will entitles the two women to a sizable portion of the Hayden Saw Mills and furniture business. Many of the Whites employed there, said they will quit before they work for a Negro. Reporters say Mrs. Hayden has two grandsons however; she did not include them in her will. We will have to see over time how this matter will turn out.

Nurse Tate stared at the article for a while. She felt the envelope in her pocket Nurse Benton had given her a few minutes ago. She knew, she was right…Rachel Jackson is Myrtle Jackson's mother. It's no coincident. My God…what do I do now!

She tore out the article, folded it quickly and put it in her pocket, pressing it close to her side as if she was afraid of losing it. Wait a minute… I can't go back to the ward. I have to get myself together. I don't want Nurse Benton asking me if I am alright. I might break down and tell her. No, I won't do that. I'm okay, she tried desperately to convince herself.

She got up from the table and walked over to the cracked mirror on the wall above the counter. She looked at herself, smoothed back her light brown shoulder length hair now streaked with gray, showing the ageing of her hair and not her body or her face. Admiring herself in the mirror, she thought she looked good for her thirty-seven years on earth, and quiet as it's kept, she and Dr. Adams have been seeing each other for the past five years. Hell, she was thinking to herself, I'm good at keeping secrets, and Dr. Adams knows that. After all, he's kept his secret of being half-white for years. Humming a little ditty, she went back to the ward.

Chapter 96

Giving it one last thought…

Myrtle wanted someone to pinch her. What happened last week? Is any of this for real? The papers in her hand looked real. I hope this is not a cruel joke she thought. She had read the contents repeatedly; looking for some clue as to why they were left the estate and what about their mama, the estate belonged to her as well. Well, she isn't here. Maybe this white lady knew her mama, and knew she abandoned us as small children, and this is her way of paying us back. No, that is too stupid for even me to realize. There is more to all this. I could see it in Mr. Baylor's face. He wasn't as happy as he pretended. He seems lost in thought, or wool gathering as grandma used to say when you weren't paying attention.

Sugar Pudding and I have gone from being the poorest of the poor, given a nice place to stay, and eventually getting our own apartment, to being two of the richest colored women alive. Yet, I do not feel nothing. It's not my money, land or houses. As long as we live, we will never own or enjoy any of it. It reminds me of the time we arrived in New York, It would be the first time I experienced exchanging names and gifts in school for Christmas. I remember drawing names out of the teacher's brown bag. As fate would have it, when it became time to exchange our gifts, the person who had drew my name never bought a gift to school. Everyone had something except me. I remember the teacher giving me a used pencil and a box of broken crayons to take home.

The houses are dangling in front of my sister and I like a freshly bake sweet potato pie. In our case, we will not get a piece, just the smell. However, she had made up in her mind over the past few days to go back to Tapasalle County and accept what is rightfully theirs. Everything good that has been thrown our way has been snatched away from us, and this sudden inheritance maybe no different. However, damn it! So much has happened. I don't want to make a horrible mistake. I have given it much thought. Yes, we are going back, she thought with exuberance. Oh, my goodness, I haven't called my job or Nurse Tate, she quickly remembered. All of us have just managed to exist since receiving the news of our white grandmother's estate.

Sugar spends most of her time making a list of what she needs. She never talks about moving or the estate that was left to us. It's probably her immaturity and youth that is controlling her thinking and decision making at this moment. I am relieved it has not stopped her from studying and doing her homework. The burden of making the right decision is left up to me, and only me to do what is best for us now. I will call Mr. Tyner in Jacksonville, Florida later today. I really want to resolve this matter as soon as possible.

Chapter 97

The beginning and end of revelations...

"Ilene, I really missed you. Was everything okay? Here, look what I picked up for you!" "You don't have to buy me anything Baylor, really," she commented, as she reached for the small slender black velvet box. She carefully untied the gold ribbon from around the box and removed the top. "Oh, my Lord, it's a diamond necklace!" "Let me help you with it Ilene." He fastened the necklace around her almond color neck, and kissed her on the lips. He held her for what seemed like an hour. He was happier then he had been in years. He vowed that when his first wife left him, he would not fall in love again. Well, he mused, too late now...!

Releasing her as if he would never see her again, he held on to her hand and seated her at the dinning table. "Ilene I...we may have to go back to North Carolina in a few days. I received a call this morning, and the client I represent wants to sell portions of the estate and resolve what she believes will undoubtedly be a serious problem if she makes any efforts to move or take over the estate, perhaps bring danger to her and her sister. You see they are half-white, and the estate was left to them by a well-known and respected white woman who owned half of the county of Tapsalle."

He rose from his seat, and walked over to the bay window in the massive living room. The sun felt warm on his face and somewhat comforting. "Baylor is anything wrong; you didn't finish telling me about the client's call?" Regaining his confidence and composure, he swallowed nervously. Damn, even Calvin couldn't fill in the words he was trying to find in his heart to tell her and what he thought. He closed and opened his eyes a few times, rubbed both hands down his face as if he was trying to wake up.

"Come on Baylor, it can't be that bad" she commented as she walked over to him. She reached up and gently turned his face toward her own. "Tell me what's on your mind. You have been a little distant since your return. I have a feeling there is something else wrong, that is laying heavy on your mind. Just tell me Baylor it won't kill you," she smiled at him and tugged at his tie.

"Ilene, that's not all…" He grabbed both of her hands. I am wrestling with the words to tell you. I don't want to lose you Ilene." his voice quivered. Worry and confusion appeared on her face and in her voice. "Lose me, what are you talking about Baylor? What has this got to do with me?"

"I just found out recently Ilene, as a matter of fact, just a few weeks ago….he paused searching his mind for the words. "Found out what?" She immediately interrupted. "Ilene I found some of your relatives," he answered quickly. The two clients I represented in Tapsalle County North Carolina are your granddaughters. I didn't say anything, because I had to be sure. You have to understand Ilene I didn't know who you were when I started seeing you!" I found out when we…well…through the detective I hired to find their mother Rachel Jackson.

The room suddenly took on a deep quietness. Baylor felt as if the quietness had engulfed and surrounded his whole body and mind. The quietness talked to him through the ticking of the clock that sat on the mantelpiece, the tiny scratching of steps the ant made as it walked across the window ledge.

"Don't just stand there staring at me…say something please," he pleaded. He looked at her face long and hard. It was void of emotions, eyes blank and her lips closed tightly. She walked slowly over to the chair where she was sitting earlier, and eased down with both hands straddling the edges of the seat. She lifted her right hand and began to finger slowly, the newly acquired diamond necklace around her neck. She finally spoke, her voice void of feeling, eyes staring into him like small sharp daggers.

"I am not sure what to say Baylor. It hardly matter's to me who they are, the grandchildren or who I am. I had abandoned my daughter and I have abandoned my only sister Emma, years ago. I wanted more out of life. I left Rachel when she was seventeen with a man we called Uncle Charlie. I believe Rachel knew deep down Uncle Charlie was not her real uncle but a friend of mind that was left over from a relationship that had grown distant. I had every intention of coming back for her. It took a lot longer than I thought to find a good job and a place to stay."

"All I could find was maid's work in hotels…cooking and cleaning for white people. As old as I was, I went back to school and got some training. I was tired of being ignorant and cleaning up after people Baylor," she said coldly and defensively. "After a few years had past, I honestly believed if I tried to find her, Rachel, well...she would have nothing to do with me. So, I disappeared. Now, you are standing here telling me, my only daughter is out there somewhere, and has two girls who now own part of the Hayden's estate! And they had lived with my sister Emma after they were abandoned!" Anger was mounting in her voice.

"What else have you got to tell me Baylor? She breathed in deeply." "I'm not sure how to say this Ilene, but your sister is dead. I was informed she died a while back." he rambled on and on. "Myrtle, your oldest granddaughter wanted to stop by their Aunt's home…you know to see it again before we left Tapasalle County. The telephone call this morning was Myrtle informing me she wanted me to sell everything… take care of it and bank the money. Ilene, there is so much I haven't told you. I really don't know where to begin." He sounded worried, tired and he looked exhausted. She got up from her chair. She did not want to hear anymore. As she turned quickly to walk away from him, he reached out his hand to her. She pushed it away, abruptly. "Baylor, can we talk later? I have a lot on my mind right now." She continued to walk away fingering the diamond necklace around her neck.

Chapter 98

Mirroring thoughts...

"Wouldn't it be nice to see the houses just once before you sell them?" asked Aunt Leola. "I was thinking the same thing this morning. However, I would not go there alone, you know without protection. I am pretty sure the white people in Tapasalle County don't want me no where near those houses or the land," Myrtle responded tiredly. "What are you thinking Myrtle? It's been almost two weeks since we got back, and you have said very little about your plans. You know you can talk to me. Do you really want to sell the houses? I was thinking Myrtle, maybe there are some things you may not want, and perhaps you could give them to Mr. Hayden.....and...I was thinking... that is... if you are afraid to live there...you and Sugar Pudding, well maybe Julia and I will come and stay with you until you decided on what you really want to do."

She watched the expression on Myrtle's face turn from worry to complete surprise. "Aunt Leola, would you do that for us? No, Really! Would you leave New York? What about Julia? Do you think she would want to leave?" Myrtle asked, firing questions to Aunt Leola with much excitement in her voice. "Well, we can find out later today," said Aunt Leola. "We have a problem Aunt Leola. Sugar Pudding may not want to go back, but if she knows you and Julia are moving with us, I am quite sure she would change her mind."

Myrtle heard footsteps and as if on cue, in walked Sugar. "I heard you all talking about me," she laughed. "Now, change my mind about what?" she asked playfully. "Hi Sugar Pudding! Aunt Leola and I were just talking about the houses and of course all that land that was left to us." She answered cheerfully trying to keep the harmony. Myrtle saw those familiar eyes cloud over, and in any minute they will filled with tears and outbursts of "I don't ever want to go back there declaration!" "Look, Sugar Pudding, Aunt Leola suggested that she and Julia would move to Tapasalle County to be with us, as a family. What do you think about that?" she asked, rather nonchalant as if she was leaving the decision up to Sugar Pudding. Just as Myrtle hoped, a smile of approval showed on Sugar's face quickly replacing that 'all-shit-not-again-look.'

"We will talk more about this when Julia gets home," Myrtle announced with more confidence and control in her voice than she had displayed earlier. "What about that old white man Mr. Haywood, Halen or something like that?" questioned Aunt Leola. "I know he is going to be a problem. You remember how he acted in court! He almost lost his mind!" Her eyes flashed a gentle but strong warning. "Maybe Mr. Baylor can come up with something," added Myrtle as she walked over to the telephone and picked up the receiver.

Chapter 99

Della's place, the wayward son goes home...

"When you gonna let me go home?" Willie questioned Della light heartily, all the while watching her massive wide hips swaying back and forth, as she walked. "You can leave anytime you want Willie. What's holding you up honey?" Della asked drinking the last of her coffee quickly and barely tasting it. She really had to leave for work or she would be late. She watched him finish his toast, drained his coffee cup and he stood up.

She liked Willie. He was like a stray cat that really needed a home she thought. The first few days all he talked about was how all of his family belongings was taken from him in court, that same evening she took him home to sober him up. She didn't have the nerve to tell Floyd he was still at her house.

Hell, she thought she wasn't desperate for a man, just someone to talk to every now and then. He was a gentleman, he slept in the room that used to be her son's, and the whole time he was there, he never made a pass or tried to get her in bed. Even though she thought, I left my bedroom door opened just incase. Her body didn't yearn for sex, just the closeness of a man every now and then would be all right. Just enough attention to let her know her body still could function. Her nipples began to hardened just thinking about it. Yes, she thought, as the old familiar feelings began to emerge from between her legs...it's still there.

Willie made use of the extra men clothes that were packed in the closet and dresser drawers in her son's room. She didn't even bother to lie when Willie asked about the clothes... telling him the clothes belong to a friend of hers and they had broken up a long time ago. Willie didn't seem to mind, he wore them anyway.

She really didn't want him to leave. Yet she felt there was something disturbing going on in that head of his. She watched his body language. He moved around a lot when he talked, especially when he talked about some houses or land or something he wanted back and he would do anything to get them back. She didn't understand much of what he was talking about and she usually responded with an understanding smile. She was a listener...not much of a talker.

Well, she thought I may as well get this over with. "Willie, are you riding with me this morning? Is there somewhere I can take you?" she asked cheerfully. "Yes, if you don't mind Della, I would like a ride home. I really appreciate what you did for me....I...I guess I was sort of out of it for a few days. I really have some important business to straiten out and I have to do it as soon as possible," he said with a touch of impatience. He rose from his chair, walked over to the counter and sat his coffee cup down. "I'm ready," he said walking quickly toward the door. Della watched as he walked hurriedly down the walk to her truck. A lot of thoughts ran through her mind. I wonder if this is the last time I see him. She locked the door to her house and joined him in the truck. He told her where he lived, and they rode in silence until she pulled the truck up to his front yard.

"Thanks Della...for everything. I'll call you okay," he said in a friendly but less than an enthusiastic tone of voice. "Willie, if you need anything or just someone to talk to...call me!" she called to him cheerfully. She smiled to herself, put the truck in gear and drove off.

Della noticed the morning sunrise over the horizon as it widens out in endless waves of colors and confusion, mirroring the very thoughts in her mind. Why do I want to be bothered with a man I hardly know, now that my life is perfectly calm, pure and free from stress, she asked herself?

Yet, she thought there was something about Willie. She couldn't quite put her finger on it, but he needs me. She walked in the front door of Triple Ace's Bar and Grill.

"Morning Della! You look awful pretty, today! New blouse?" Floyd greeted her almost the same way each morning as she walked through the door. It was as if he had to tell her something nice to make her day or perhaps because she wasn't as pretty as some of the ladies that come in the grill. I may not be the prettiest woman on earth, but I am surely not the ugliest! Somehow, his usual compliment this morning rubbed her the wrong way. "Morning Floyd," she called out to him, raising her chin with a cool stare. She walked slowly over to the counter, her massive hips moving up and down, brushing up against the counter knocking over the ketchup bottles. She carefully picked up the bottles from the counter floor, and started setting up for the morning customers. Floyd walked over to the front door and turned the sign around from "We Are Closed to We Are Open."

Chapter 100
The return...

"Myrtle what school will I go to if we leave New York?" Sugar Pudding looked at her with those large brown eyes moist but not on the verge of tears yet. "Sugar, Aunt Leola and I will work that out as best we can. If we move back to North Carolina, you will still have to face those classmates that do not like you because of the color of your skin." Her voice was full of concern.

"You see Sugar the schools in Tapsalle County are going through the same thing we are going through here in New York, only it's worse. The whites do not want their children going to school with coloreds or living in the same area as them. Remember how hard it was for you, when we arrived here in New York? The first couple of days you came home angry, sad and scared. You didn't want to go back. Look, you made friends and eventually some of the name-calling stopped. You got stronger because of it...I guess what I am trying to say Sugar Pudding...is...that you will have to be a lot stronger.

We are not the poor abandoned half-white girls that left years ago. Things will be different, harder, and maybe even a little dangerous when we go back," she said with a little apprehension in her voice. "Could we just sell everything...you know like you and Aunt Leola once talked about, and we can stay here, in New York?" Sugar asked pleadingly. "I don't know how to answer your question Sugar. I know we are going to be all right. We have a good family, and we are going to stick together and protect each other, okay. Don't worry about anything until it's time to worry." Myrtle walked over and gave her a hug. She stood back and looked at Sugar's face. There was calmness about her. Mmm, maybe she is ready to go back, thought Myrtle. I had better give Aunt Leola a call now. We need to start packing, she thought with sudden enthusiasm.

As she walked over to the table to use the telephone, it suddenly rang, startling her and Sugar Pudding. "Hello" she spoke into the mouthpiece. Yes, this is Ms. Myrtle Jackson! Hello Mr. Tyner! Yes, I have made up my mind. Sugar and I are going back to Tapsalle County and take over the houses, and what ever else, Mrs. Hayden left us in the will. Yes, that's right! Well, if you want to help us that will be fine! Thank you for calling, good-bye!"

"Okay, Sugar you heard the conversation…too late to back out now! Start packing we are going home."

Chapter 101
Moving on...

      Baylor placed the telephone back on it's receiver. He stared at the telephone for a moment. Did he really hear Myrtle say, they are going back to Tapasalle County to live? He was both shocked and moved. Relieved they would not give up and sell what is rightfully theirs. If they overcame the hatred, the unfairness and some unpleasant experiences in New York, they can indeed make it in Tapasalle County. I made a promise when Stella Louise Hayden was dying, that I would take care of everything. I intend to keep that promise. I owe them that much and more, he thought painfully to himself.

      He walked over toward the stairs, carrying himself neatly erect, he started up the stairs. He had to talk to Ilene, before he leaves for North Carolina. As he reached the top of the stairs, he looked toward their bedroom. He strode over to the door and knock softly, calling her name. "Ilene, could we talk, it's important?" Not hearing an answer, he slowly began to walk away.

      Hearing the sound of the door opening, he turned around quickly. He walked over to her, with haste and hugged her as tight as he could. He stood there holding her for a while before he spoke. "I am so sorry Ilene; I didn't mean to hurt you," his voice cracking with emotion. "Baylor, it all came as a shock. I wasn't ready for the memories I had purposely hidden away...never to be remembered again. I don't know where to start," her voice lower to a whisper and she held on to him as if he was going to disappear at any moment. As if she was reading his mind, she asked with seriousness in her voice, "Do you want me to go back to North Carolina with you?" Her eyes were misty with caring and emotion. "Yes, I do Ilene. You have to help me explain all this to our grandchildren. She gave him a smile that went straight to his heart.

Chapter 102

Entering into the lion's den...

"Whew! Damn! This place stinks!" Willie remarked loudly. How long was I gone he asked himself, walking back and forth from room to room trying to find where that damn awful smell was coming from. As he started for the back door, the smell became stronger. He quickly opened the door; his eyes fell upon a dead animal, lying beside the tall metal trashcan that somehow had fallen over on its side. Mold and some black ooze cover half of the dead animal's carcass lying on the floor of the back porch. Looking closer, holding his hand tightly over his mouth and nose, holding his breath, Willie recognized the animal as a large possum. Damn! I've got to get rid of this smell now!

He turned up the trash can with its rancid contents disturbed and half eaten, and grabbed the shovel from the corner of the back porch. He made several attempts, to pick up the dead animal, but it kept rolling away from the tip of the shovel, leaving a small trail of green and yellowish black ooze on the porch floor. I need more then this shovel, he said to himself. Looking around on the back porch, he found a pile of old newspapers. Covering up the foul animal and trying hard to mask the stench, he lit a cigarette. He took few puffs, threw it aside. Quickly without hesitation, he sucked in his breath, grabbed the mound in the middle of the paper and threw the newspaper-covered animal in the metal trashcan. "Hell! Enough of that stinking shit," he mumbled.

He dragged the trashcan to the middle of the yard, getting the stinking animal as far away from the house as possible. Willie rushed back in the house and washed his hands at the kitchen sink. Pushing away the thoughts of the smelly ass animal, he began to toy with the idea of moving into one of his grandmother's houses and staying there permanently.

He was still having second and third thoughts of forcibly taking the land as well, when a knock on the door interrupted his thinking.

Walking slowly, into the small living room, he grabbed the long piece of wood he kept by the door. He and his defense armor were ready for anyone. To his surprise, standing there was Mr. Reynolds. "What the hell does he want this early in the morning?" Willie thought to himself. "Yeah! Mr. Reynolds why are you here this early?" questioned Willie, eyeing Mr. Reynolds with a wish-you-would-go-back-home look. "Thought I would stop by Willie, I heard in town you lost your fight to get the houses and land. People are talking about it everywhere you go. They are saying them half-white colored girls got everything!" "Well," said Willie, his eyes narrowing furiously, "You got here just in time. Look I need a ride to the houses," he said coldly. "I have decided to move in…today! Let those damn guards or who the hell they think they are; try to make me get off my land!"

"Mr. Reynolds stood there waiting for Willie to open the screen door, all the while watching him for any signs of physical anger. Mr. Reynolds never took his eyes off Willie as he followed him inside. "What are you going to do Willie?" Mr. Reynolds asked, not really interested. "Whew! What the hell died in here? You need to open all your doors and windows! Now, what's this about a ride to your what? What house Willie? Now you know you can't go up there starting any shit with them guards. You just looking for trouble," Mr. Reynolds warned him with some irritation in his voice.

"I'm not going to be a part of it Willie!" "You don't have to be Mr. Reynolds, just give me the damn ride, and forget everything I told you," Willie said not hiding his impatience with the man. "Just give me a few minutes to pack a few things and lock up the house." He moved with quick steps to his bedroom, leaving Mr. Reynolds standing there.

Mr. Reynolds walked reluctantly out the door and got in his truck. He waited until Willie locked the front door. Willie eyed Mr. Reynolds sitting in the truck, and moved a little faster to get in, throwing his two bags on the back floor of the truck. Willie jumped up in the truck with an air of amusement on his face. "Okay, let's go Mr. Reynolds," he said impatiently. "How you gonna get in without being seen Willie? They got them guards all over the place," Mr. Reynolds questioned. "Don't worry about me; just drop me off a half a mile before we get to the houses. I know how to get in!" he said with confidence and eagerness in his voice. "Okay, Willie, we'll be there in another twenty minutes."

Mr. Reynolds pulled over to the side of the road to let Willie get out. "Look Willie, watch yourself!" he warned him again. Willie got out of the truck, grabbed his two bags and started walking up the hill toward his grandmother's houses. With a sharp "u" turn in the road, Mr. Reynolds never looked back. "That is one crazy ass fool," he muttered to himself.

Willie finally got through the back road to the large house. Shit he thought to himself, the guards didn't know about the old path that lead through the woods to the back of the house. Hell, he remembered when he and Clemmons were kids, they often use the path through the woods and around the creek as a short cut to their grandmother's property.

Willie was mentally congratulating himself for his splendid idea. He could see one of the houses up ahead. He stopped suddenly, he thought he heard footsteps. Willie felt a slight tap on his right shoulder. He never heard anything else.

Chapter 103

Humph, premonitions…

　　Della felt chills go all over her body and reached the bottom of her spine. Off in the distance she heard a dog howling, long and sorrowful. What did mama used to say about dogs howling? Oh, I remember, you will hear of a death of a friend or love one. Yes, she thought, and a dog dragging his stomach across the ground is measuring someone's grave.
　　Della gently rubbed the goose bumps on her arms and went about her normal duties, cleaning the booths before the lunch crowd rolls in.

Chapter 104

Sweet and bitter times of anticipation...

"Are you finishing packing your things Sugar? You know we have three hours to finish before the truck gets here. I don't want to keep the truck driver waiting." Myrtle called to her. "I'm almost through. What am I supposed to do with the plants?" Sugar asked. "We are going to give them to Kenny's mom downstairs. Just sit them in the hallway next to our apartment door, she is on her way up to get them okay," Myrtle answered distracted by old memories that were making every effort to change her mind about going back to Tapasalle County.

She stood in the middle of the living room, allowing herself to take in just one last long look before they leave for North Carolina. For a brief moment, she let herself go back in years to what it was like living in Tapasalle County when they were much younger. Unpleasant memories and faces flashed by like the blur of a fast train in the dark of night. One thought in particular crossed her mind, reminding her of the very first time she step foot in Mr. Tompkins house with grandma.

She wondered if all the rooms in the houses that were left to her and Sugar is painted yellow and white like Nancy Rose's room. Well, we'll see in few days, she was thinking. I am curious as to how the houses look in the inside. Most of all, I can't wait to celebrate Christmas. Myrtle let that last thought linger for a while. Picking up another box, she walked to the front door of their apartment and sat it on the outside of their door for the truck driver. "It was nice of Mr. Baylor to hire a truck to take our belongings a day ahead to Tapasalle County," she remarked to Sugar. All this choosing what to leave, what to take and the tedious process of packing was making her hungry.

Myrtle stopped immediately and strolled into the kitchen to make a snack for her and Sugar. Opening the refrigerator, she pulled out a bowl of cold fried chicken from the night before, and a few slices of bread.

"Come on Sugar! Let's eat a little something before the moving truck gets here!" she called to her, with a little excitement in her voice.

Chapter 105

The truth awakens...

"Mama, you sure we are making the right decision...you know—to leave New York to live in North Carolina?" asked Julia with a mountain of seriousness in her voice. "It's not that I don't want to go mama, but I feel like I want to stay here...in New York—with my friends. Why are we leaving anyway? Myrtle and Sugar is not family mama! You are not really their *Aunt Leola!*" Julia exclaimed with sarcasm in her voice. "Now, wait a minute Julia, why all of a sudden you are questioning a decision we both made together? Why the second thoughts? Come on! We can talk. What is bothering you about this move? Get it off your chest now Julia!" The tone of her voice was growing with frustration as she continued to throw things in the cardboard box sitting on the couch.

Leola Harvey knew her daughter all too well. She was not the type of mother to put words in her child's mouth. She knew exactly what was bothering Julia but she wanted her daughter to express it—out in the open. She watched the expression on her face and listened as Julia struggled to find the words. "Living with them, Myrtle and Sugar Pudding... people may think we are their maids! Mama look at the color of their skin; they can almost past for white! I don't want anybody thinking I am a Negro, Colored or a Black maid. I have experienced enough name-calling and insults about the color of my skin," She complained bitterly. Looking at her mother intently, shoulders slump, she eased down on the bed full of clothes waiting to be packed and placed on the truck that's going on ahead to North Carolina.

"Julia...she paused placing her arm around her daughter's shoulders, "I know this is hard for you to understand, but I made a promise to my brother that I would try to keep them safe. Julia you remember why they were sent here, and the horrible stories they told of how they lived and how they were treated? They asked us to go back with them out of love and support. Honey, they don't have to be our real family as you put it, but they need us and we need them. Myrtle has offered us one of the homes to us to live in…think about it Julia, there is no house payment, and the money I make working as a nurse can pay for the rest of your tuition. Does any of this make sense to you Julia?" she asked trying hard to suppress the worry that she held inside of her. Julia made a feeble attempt to smile. She pushed some of the clothes aside on the bed to make room for the box they were going in.

    Leola smiled at her only daughter, remembering how blessed they were. She thought about the many Negroes who were not as fortunate to live, work, and enjoy some freedom to come and go as they wish. She also knew living in North Carolina would be a test of their strength as well as their courage to face the unknown. She faced the unknown when she became pregnant with Julia, and shortly after she was born, her husband died suddenly. If she wanted to keep a roof over their heads, she had to find a job and quick. Her wonderful brother Earl and neighbors helped her through the hard times, she remembered with ease as she inhales deeply, to thank God for kind people.

    She had to show God and her brother she could survive. Yes, she thought to herself, I am worried but I am not afraid. This is what she wanted Julia to understand, and believe more than anything else in this world. They quietly pack the rest of the boxes in silence.

Chapter 106

Back to the beginning...

"Okay, Baylor that's all the packing! What time is the flight to North Carolina?" Ilene asked with excitement in her voice. They had talked all night preparing what to say to Myrtle and Sugar. She got goose pimples all over her body when she thought of how they would react to her telling them she is their grandmother. Well, she thought, this information maybe the final piece of the puzzle. She couldn't say exactly how she felt knowing she has two granddaughters she has never met, and they have grandfather who is White.

She was glad Baylor suggested a private ceremony. No one would believe they were married in this house, with Ms. Martinez the housekeeper as their only witness. Ilene took one last walk through the house. A house she never really got to know—because there was no bonding, no relationship, just a distant friend she was leaving with very few memories to take back to North Carolina. Ilene was thinking, even though she and Baylor were older, they still had plenty of time to make long lasting memories. Life for them was not going to be easy, and she didn't expect it would. However, she was not afraid of the unknown, just how people would treat them.

"Ilene, the flight leaves at six 'o' clock p.m. We have to arrive there a day ahead of time. I have to make sure everything is in order for the girls—oh, I mean our granddaughters," he smiled. A feeling of joyous anticipation flowed through his veins for a fleeting moment. He felt good inside. He was keeping a promise he made to Myrtle and Sugar Pudding's great-grandmother, Stella Louise Hayden before she died.

Baylor walked over to the massive bay window, and watched as his law clerk got out of the car and started up the steps. "Mmm," he was on time as usual. He wished for once he could be as organized as Calvin.

He slowly retraced through memory how he first met Calvin. He remembered walking down the long courthouse corridor on his way to the courtroom. Damn, he thought I am late again! That's when he walked right into the young clerk. The box in his hand felled to the floor and all the papers he had meticulously put in order for the trial was spread all over the corridor. He recalled Calvin, saying, "Excuse me sir! Let me give you a hand with that." In less than five minutes, he had the papers back in the box, the same way I had placed them. Without thinking, I asked him to come with me to court. During that trial, Calvin patiently and meticulously arranged my hard work in order so I would not have to waste the client's, or the court's time not being prepared. I hired him that day. Strange he thought, why he would remember that day in particular.

He brushed the memory aside and went to open the door for Calvin. They had a long flight ahead of them.

Chapter 107
Burning bridges...

"Have you heard anything from Ms. Jackson or Ms. Harvey?" Doctor Adams asked with an edge of irritability creeping into his voice. "No, I didn't speak with them personally, but last night Nurse Freeman left me a handwritten message that Nurse Harvey had called and said she needed more time off because of a family emergency. I have heard nothing from Ms. Jackson," Nurse Tate replied dragging herself up from the comfortable chair. "Is it time for rounds all ready?" she asked half distracted still by the article she had read a few weeks ago.

She carried that newspaper article around everyday in her purse, in hopes of hearing from Ms. Jackson. She had given it some serious thought, and made up her mind to call Ms. Jackson in few days if she didn't hear from her. This have got to be the same two people in the article, nurse Tate thought to herself everyday, over and over again. She still had a hard time trying to erase the last time she had talked with Myrtle's mother Rachel, before she died. No! she thought for the tenth time, I didn't see the birthmark Rachel described but I did notice Myrtle's strange colored eyes. "This is the same person in the newspaper article, I am sure of it," she said aloud. Startled by her own voice, she took a quick look around the room. Damn, she did not want anyone to hear her. What she doesn't need now is a lot questions. Absorbed in her thoughts, the sound of Dr. Adams calling her brought her back to the present.

"Yes, I will be right there Dr. Adams," she called out to him, trying very hard to appear and sound normal. She grabbed the cup of cold coffee on her way out the door, and raised the cup to her mouth with shaking hands.

Unaware of Dr. Adam's stare, she went through the motions half listening to Dr. Adams review of the patients condition before the next shift arrives. This is one afternoon, she wished she did not have to work overtime, but they were short of help. With Nurse Harvey, and the two assistant nurses, Ms. Jackson and Ms. Lee absent, all the work fell on her and nurse Benton. She was thinking, if I don't hear anything by the end of the evening shift, I will call Ms. Jackson and Nurse Harvey to find out when they are coming back. I have to tell Dr. Adams something so he can find us some more help.

Off in the distance, she heard Dr. Adam's voice, "this patient needs a new IV, Nurse Tate!"

Chapter 108

The far and stretching horizon…

They arrive to the airport on time. Myrtle looked at her watch, nine-ten a.m. She glance at their flight tickets; their plane is schedule for take off at ten 'o' clock a.m. "Aunt Leola we have a little while before we get on board. Let's get something to drink. I'm a little thirsty. Anyone else wants something?" Myrtle asked. "No, we are fine," Julia and Sugar, answered together.

The overhead speakers announced the flight to North Carolina boarding in fifteen minutes. This is it, Myrtle was thinking, no turning back if I wanted to. She glanced over at Sugar Pudding flipping through a magazine, and Aunt Leola talking quietly to Julia. Well at least they are smiling, and that's a good thing, she thought with enthusiasm.

Boarding the airplane, Myrtle placed her open hand to her chest. Her heart was beating rapidly. She sucked in her breath and stepped up to the plane's opening. Aunt Leola fingered a small cross in her hand, whispering a prayer. Julia took a lingering glance around as if it is for the last time. Sugar Pudding was staring at an old white man who suddenly jumped in front of Julia. "Step back so this pretty little lady can get on," he gestured at Julia waving the back of his hand. "You don't mind do you," the old white man said with a smirk on his face and a smile full of stained teeth, and a face full of hatred. Julia stood there, her fist clenched, and looking at the old white man as a cockroach needing to be stepped on.

Sugar stood there as the old white man beckoned her with his hand to walk toward him. She whispered to Julia nervously, "What do I do?" "Go ahead Sugar; we don't need any trouble okay." Julia stepped back so Sugar could get in front of her. Julia felt all eyes were on her. She remembers all to well how it feels to be slighted, and it hurt, real bad. Then it suddenly dawned on her, she understood what her mama was trying to say yesterday as they were packing.

Julia took her seat next to her mama. Myrtle and Sugar were seated in the front row, right directly in front of them. Fastenings and the sounds of clicking belts interrupted the low hum of the passenger's voices and their inner thoughts as they settled down. Slowly like the rising of the sun, their thoughts took flight the same time as the airplane's nose kissed the clouds.

Chapter 109

Time and events in measurable motion…

Off in the distance, sirens wailed. "Does anyone know what happened?" Do you know who lives in the houses?" asked the firefighter in disbelief. The guards shook their head from side to side. They all tried to speak at once. "Wait a minute! Calm down!

Get these gates down now!" the firefighter gestured emphatically.

Up in the clouds the familiar sound of an airplane as it soars through the blue of heaven's own tint. The constant ringing of a telephone, its sounds echoing about the empty rooms fell on silent ears.

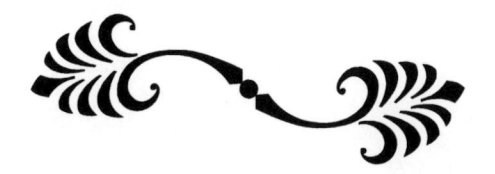

1362744

Made in the USA